SAVING THE WORLD
A GUIDE TO

D0179628

LYNNETTE PORTER, DAVID LAVERY, AND HILLARY ROBSON

ECW PRESS

Published by ECW PRESS
2120 Queen Street East, Suite 200, Toronto, Ontario, Canada M4E 1E2

LIBRARY AND ARCHIVES CANADA CATALOGUING IN PUBLICATION

Porter, Lynnette R., 1957-
Saving the world : a guide to Heroes / Lynnette Porter,
David Lavery and Hillary Robson.

ISBN 978-1-55022-805-2

1. Heroes (Television program)
I. Lavery, David, 1949- II. Robson, Hillary III. Title.

PN1992.77.H47P67 2007   791.45'72   C2007-904135-3

Developing Editor: Jennifer Hale
Cover Design: Erin Smith
Text Design: Melissa Kaita
Type: Mary Bowness
Production: Rachel Brooks
Printing: Thomson-Shore Inc.

This book is set in Scala.

DISTRIBUTION
CANADA: Jaguar Book Group, 100 Armstrong Avenue,
Georgetown, ON, L7G 5S4
UNITED STATES: Independent Publishers Group, 814 North Franklin Street,
Chicago, IL 60610

PRINTED AND BOUND IN THE UNITED STATES

ECW PRESS
ecwpress.com

Every hero is on a journey to find his place in the world. But it's a journey. You don't start at the end. Otherwise they can't make a movie about it later.

— Ando ("Better Halves")

CONTENTS

PART 2 ENHANCEMENTS

ACKNOWLEDGMENTS

THANKS TO JEN HALE, our wonderful editor, for such enthusiasm for *Heroes* and this book, and to ECW for understanding early on what a great series this is.

Special thanks to Supercollaborator, David, whose editing is faster than a speeding bullet, writing more powerful than a locomotive, well, you get the idea. As always, it's a joy to work with you.

Special thanks to Hillary, who continues to amaze me with her insights and knowledge, especially of fandom and all things Internet.

Finally, but never least, thanks to my personal heroes: Jimmie, Bart, Nancy, Elvis the Wonderdog, and Heather, who gives me hope for the future.

LYNNETTE PORTER

LIKE LYNNETTE AND HILLARY, my sincere thanks to Jen Hale, the only editor I know with a secret identity and powers to match. Thanks to our agent Uwe for finding Jen and making the deal happen. Thanks, of course, to Lynnette and Hillary, supercollaborators.

Thanks to Sarah, a former cheerleader morphing into a wonderful writer, who might just be as indestructible as Claire Bennet, and the amazing Rachel, who like Hiro loves New York and need not teleport there. They are the best daughters imaginable.

Special thanks, and endless love, to Joyce, who never lost faith in me during my year in fantasy camp. Even if I never do get her to watch *Heroes*, her superstrength holds me up. My contribution to this book is dedicated to her.

DAVID LAVERY

FIRST, I'D LIKE TO EXTEND my deepest appreciation to my amazing collaborators, David and Lynnette. You are both such a joy and pleasure to know personally and professionally. Thank you for letting me write alongside you — it's an honor.

To our editor — Jen Hale — your wit, wisdom, good humor, and love for *Heroes* has made the work of writing this book even more fun!

I'd like to express my gratitude for the authors who submitted their essays for inclusion in this volume — your inspired ideas and brilliant writing are so very appreciated.

And I mustn't forget a very special thanks to Don, whose good humor and patience has helped me see through even the darkest nights — you are my light.

HILLARY ROBSON

INTRODUCTION

HEROES WAS ONE OF THE FEW BREAKOUT hits of the 2006–07 U.S. television season, for NBC or any other network. By early March, when the series broke for a second too-long hiatus, it was the number-one new scripted television show of the year, winning more viewers than any other new show among adults 18–49, 25–54, 18–34, and total viewers. For still-troubled NBC, which would undergo a major leadership shakeup at season's end, *Heroes* has been its best performing series in five years.

In its Monday-night slot on American television, the series "stared down *24* in a hotly contested . . . ratings battle and proved that there are some adversaries Jack Bauer can't pistol-whip into submission." *Heroes'* finale became the number-eight show during a crowded final week of May ratings "sweeps" that included two instalments of *American Idol* and *Dancing with the Stars*, plus the *Lost* finale. On Monday night, *Heroes* clearly "bl[ew] away all competition in the timeslot." It was NBC's hero at the May 2007 upfronts, when networks unveil their television schedules for the coming year.

Sendhil Ramamurthy (Mohinder) seems mildly shocked at the

difference a year can make. On *Live with Regis and Kelly* a week after the upfronts, he explained that the previous year he carried a board identifying himself as a *Heroes* cast member because no one from the media knew who he or what the show was. "Now they're shouting all our names. It's nice," he said, acknowledging that the cast was highly sought for interviews now that the series is a hit.

WHY IS *HEROES* SO POPULAR?

Especially at the beginning of the 2006–07 season, *Heroes* was often compared to a surprise breakout from a previous season, *Lost* (a comparison analyzed in the next chapter). While both series depend on suspense, danger, an unfolding, complex mythology, large ensemble casts, and intense fan involvement, *Heroes* suggests a more hopeful future for a perilous world. Perhaps that's one reason for its growing popularity. *Heroes'* success, however, also depends on other factors: interesting characters and story, casting, scheduling, promotion, and critical acclaim.

Like other popular ensemble series, *Heroes* offers something to suit every viewer: troubled teens, shady politicians, young people at odds with parents (especially fathers), idealistic do-gooders, conspirators, serial killers, students and teachers, struggling working-class parents. Heroes also provides plenty of eye candy, with its cast of beautiful people. The cast represents different ethnicities, cultures, and ages; although predominately set in the United States (New York, Nevada, and Texas), the series at least tries to illustrate more global locations, such as Japan and India (filmed, of course, in an L.A. studio).

The actors themselves have proven to be personable and engaging while discussing the show in the media and are developing devoted fan bases. Cast members such as Adrian Pasdar also brought along fans to *Heroes*, especially an older female demographic, and the inclusion of *Star Trek*'s Sulu (George Takei), the Ninth Doctor (Christopher Eccleston) from the world's longest-running science fiction series, the BBC's *Doctor Who*, and even Shaft himself (Richard Roundtree) as (respectively) Kaito Nakamura, Claude, and Charles Deveaux, certainly didn't hurt.

The story follows the almost required "suspended enigma" structure of its popular ancestors *The X-Files*, *24*, and *Lost*. (Fittingly, NBC felt confident enough about *Heroes'* rising popularity to schedule it against Fox's *24* on Monday nights in spring 2007 — where it handily won the finale face-off; Global, *Heroes'* Canadian home network, broadcast *Heroes* an hour earlier than *24*, creating a powerhouse night of television.) Questions such as how the superpowers originate, who is behind the manipulation of not only the heroes but the larger population (and to what end), and how all the heroes are interconnected fed burgeoning viewer speculation, especially on the Internet, about the ongoing narrative.

Unlike its predecessors, however, *Heroes* at least provides some answers about the series' larger mythology and "chunks" segments of the story into chapters for a quicker pace. *Heroes* confronts issues and questions facing many in an increasingly chaotic world. Episodes refer to a wide range of problems across segments of the population, as well as global issues and fears, including the possibility of nuclear holocaust. Series' creator Tim Kring acknowledges that "with diminished resources and terrorism, 'there's a sort of a sense that people want a wish fulfillment, that somebody is going to rise up among us . . . and actually be able to do something about it. And so I was sort of trying to tap into that.'" While other series might paint the future as only bleak, *Heroes* provides hope.

The pilot episode indicates that the story to be told in the upcoming chapters/episodes will be only the beginning of an epic tale, a journey that clearly implies that humanity will survive the current threat and the narration is from some future point when the heroes' story can be told. Even if not all favorite heroes survive, humanity will. The future *is* a certainty, but just as certainly, humanity faces challenges and change. The May 2007 finale brings the first twenty-three chapters to a close; the "save the world" premise is realized and the "exploding man" revealed. In true cliff-hanger fashion, *Heroes* leaves the fate of several characters precariously balanced.

The series' success is, of course, partly due to the mechanics of television programming. *Heroes* was initially given a good Monday-night time slot, although only minimal promotion, for its initial episodes. However, when it easily won its time slot and continued to pick up viewers within the first month, NBC increased promotional efforts, making the actors available for a variety of talk and entertainment shows and special events such as Macy's Thanksgiving Day Parade. The added promotional push of *Heroes* trailers on the popular video Web site YouTube continued to draw in new viewers.

This publicity paid off, as did careful marketing of the now infamous "Save the cheerleader; save the world," which not only looks good on a T-shirt but is an easily repeatable catchphrase. After the first block of episodes ended in January 2007 with the cheerleader alive and well, a second catchphrase — "Are you on the list?" — led to more fan speculation on the Web and piqued viewer interest in the series' next direction. (For more on the marketing of *Heroes*, see Chapter 3.)

By early 2007, NBC treated *Heroes* as a bona fide hit, with the appropriate level of promotion and ad placement. Teaser trailers during primetime, repeats of previously aired episodes on the U.S. Sci Fi Channel, and the series' heavily promoted U.K. launch on the Sci Fi Channel in February 2007 brought in the channel's largest audience to date. When *Heroes* finished its second batch of first-run episodes in March and went on an almost two-month hiatus, its cast had graced the covers of (U.S.) *TV Guide* and *Entertainment Weekly* more than once, and the series had been nominated for a Golden Globe Award, receiving high praise (and good ratings) from critics and fans.[1]

It even received the "Future Classic" television series award from TV Land in late April 2007 — perhaps prophetically, Leonard Nimoy, best known to fans as *Star Trek*'s Spock, presented the award. *Heroes* often refers to *Star Trek* characters, including Spock, and Hiro in particular relishes his new power to bend space and time because it seems like a space-age superhero gift. It seems fitting that Nimoy handed the "Future Classic" trophy to Masi Oka (Hiro), a passing of the torch from one television generation to another.[2]

WHO ARE HEROES? ARE THEY "MADE" OR SELF-APPOINTED?

Heroes arise from every culture and in every generation. During this cynical time in world history, however, many people fear going out of their way to help others or think that helping others at one's own expense is not a pragmatic way to live. To many, the cost of acting heroically is too high. Even when heroes come forward, the media often seem to build them up only to tear them down; the public idolizes its heroes (such as politicians, celebrities) for a short time, only to create a backlash against them while moving on to the next big thing (the next new celebrity, next presidential candidate). It may not always be a good idea to be a hero in a world that often sets up unrealistic expectations and creates a multitude of problems for the individual. Although most viewers would agree someone or something should save us from myriad world problems, no one seems to want to volunteer to lead the way.

So . . . who should be our heroes, and where do they come from?

According to The Company, first represented by HRG (Horn Rimmed Glasses, Claire's adoptive father, Mr. Bennet), heroes are genetic anomalies who will be used for some purpose not yet disclosed. Those refusing to play by The Company's rules, such as defector Claude (an invisible man), are marked for death. Those in its employ are expected to do whatever is necessary to protect the organization and further its agenda. The paper company Primatech fronts HRG's tag-and-release program of identifying and testing the abilities of heroes before implanting them with some kind of tracking device. The whole operation is kept hush-hush with powerful, rich businesspeople (such as Mr. Linderman) and others (such as Nathan and Peter

Petrelli's parents, Hiro Nakamura's father, and Simone Deveaux's father) controlling more than one generation of heroes. As the series progresses, viewers learn that the emerging heroes from the beginning of season 1 aren't the only people to discover previously hidden fantastic talents: an earlier generation of heroes also had a turn at saving the world and presumably creating or evading The Company, a mythology to be developed and explored in season 2.

If heroes are defined only as people who have a superpower (not unlike the popular *X-Men* comic book and movie series), then heroes are indeed born, or made through evolution. Whether this evolution occurs over time (via natural selection, as Mohinder's geneticist father, Dr. Suresh, seems to have concluded before his death) or through medical engineering remains a secret in the series' mythology. However, if science alone is responsible for creating "heroes" and a hero is defined by superpower only, then heroic deeds have no moral basis. Heroes are simply a physical fact of life, whether they choose to use their superpower or not and, if they do, whether to use it for good or evil.

If heroes can be (or are, according to the series) genetically enhanced, then the rest of us regular mortals are off the hook as far as trying to save humanity collectively or one person at a time. Not everyone can be a hero. Heroism becomes a genetic imperative of the few, who can then wield their power as they see fit.

Not everyone agrees with this purely scientific assessment. Although Hiro Nakamura and Peter Petrelli might be genetically different from the general populace, they also desire to serve. These characters are more closely aligned with traditional literary heroes, such as those described by Joseph Campbell and other literary theorists. (For more on *Heroes* and Campbell's conception of the hero's journey, see Chapter 6: "The Making of a Hiro.") In fact, Hiro initially believes that once he wields the sword of a famous Japanese warrior (who starred in his childhood bedtime stories) he, too, will become a legendary hero. Peter goes out of his way, even risking his life, to help save the cheerleader; later, he truly fears his premonition that he may become a human nuclear reactor on overload, imperiling New York City. Hiro gives up his job to take on the challenge of saving Claire and continues to pursue not only his superability but the greater challenge of saving the world. (In "Distractions," he faces the question of whom he should save — his family or "the world" — in a confrontation with his father and chooses the latter.) These characters' desire to help others marks them as heroic in more general, popular definitions of hero, but it also distinguishes them from genetically enhanced humans such as Sylar, who seem bent on the destruction of others for personal gain, or political, media-savvy characters such as Nathan Petrelli, who often choose to use their powers only when it furthers their own agenda.

Heroes explores the question of who should (or even can) act heroically, even as it illustrates the reality that being a hero may be a risky proposition on many levels.

WHAT ROLE SHOULD HEROES PLAY IN SOCIETY?

The answer to this question varies among viewers, as it does in society itself. A popular fan site, HeroestheSeries.com, even hosted a poll asking, "If you had superpowers, what would you do with it [sic]?" The possible responses included "I will fight crime!" "Use it for my own gain!" and "Rule the world!" Of course, responding to such a poll on a fan site may not require the greatest sincerity in response, but the results are interesting. Of the 564 votes in early April 2007, 46 percent of respondents would use their superpowers to fight crime, but 31 percent would use them for their own gain and 12 percent would choose to rule the world. (A fourth response, "Moon pies are groovy," received another 12 percent, which may indicate how seriously fans take polls like this one.) Perhaps many fans want to believe in the innate goodness of superheroes as fantasy saviors who can solve our problems. The idea that these fans could act nobly if given a superpower is appealing; like Hiro, the character with whom most viewers identify, these fans want to help others with their special skills.

Hiro has no difficulty in determining what heroes should do, although his joy and naïveté in discovering his ability to bend space and time become progressively tempered with more time "on the job" and some not-so-pleasant experiences. Although Hiro helps "save the cheer-leader," he then discovers that the world is not automatically saved. Along the way, he finds he can't even prevent the death of the woman he loves by returning to the past and changing her personal history.

Nevertheless, from the first episodes, Hiro proclaims, in what seems like a *Heroes* 101 primer, all the characteristics of a classic hero. His personal heroes are based on popular culture from his childhood; *Star Trek* is a particular favorite. (It's especially fun for fans when George Takei, classic *Trek*'s Mr. Sulu himself, shows up as Hiro's father and a mastermind behind the mythology surrounding all heroes. The elder Nakamura's license plate — NCC 1701, the original *Enterprise*'s ID — evokes *Trek* trivia.) Hiro even follows Campbell's pattern of a classic literary hero.

Not all superheroes feel compelled to go on such a mission. Other heroes' responses reflect a range of modern perspectives on what it means to be identified as special in the public eye. Claire just wants to be a normal teenager, getting a spot on the cheerleading squad, being named homecoming queen, exploring friendships; she doesn't want to be labeled a freak. Like vampire slayer Buffy Summers before her, she grudgingly comes to realize that she does have a responsibility to others because she is, indeed, a special girl, even if she didn't ask to have special powers. (For more on Claire see Chapter 5: "Growing Pains: *Heroes* and the Quest for Identity.")

Nathan Petrelli knows how fickle the public can be. To gain votes, he wants to be perceived as one of the people, something an ability to fly would preclude. However, he also enjoys privilege and is far more easily wooed to the dark side than the audience or even he might have imagined. He first tries to rid the world of corruption represented by men such as Linderman and his own father, only later to turn the tables on a blackmail scheme to get Linderman's backing for his campaign. Like his mother, Nathan is also not above manipulating younger brother, Peter, by threatening to lock him away as mentally unstable and capable of suicide. Nathan doesn't care so much about truth as perception; he realizes just what the media could do with any indication that he could be a superhero.

Although Niki at first seems like a beleaguered mom having a hard time making ends meet and paying off debts, her alter-ego Jessica uses her superstrength to threaten or kill. Her estranged husband D.L. uses his ability to walk through walls to break out of prison or break into a padded cell where Jessica is imprisoned. Along with other characters such as the hedonistic (and soon dead) Eden and self-absorbed Sylar, they use their superpowers to help themselves, with little regard for the ramifications of their actions for others. The series' writers illustrate a wide range of typical superheroes whose choices about using their powers are as individualized as the powers themselves.

Even the *Heroes'* actors offer divergent views on what superheroes should be or do. Not every hero needs extraordinary power, although James Kyson Lee (Ando) says that being able to duplicate oneself would be a most interesting power, as would the ability to talk with animals. Of course, even a mundane power could come in handy sometimes; Lee jokes that maybe Ando could someday discover a power "that's unique but just random, like [to] make cheese out of thin air!"

The actors also take on some heroic characteristics themselves. Noah Gray-Cabey (Micah) has grown up with a philanthropic mindset; a concert pianist since age three, he frequently performed for fundraisers and early on felt that was the purpose for his music. After having a career in music and acting, he thinks toward a future in which he might serve the world. "I want to be a lawyer or I want to go into politics," he explains, although being a doctor isn't out of the question either. Upon hearing the suggestion that he might be able to change the world, he laughs but agrees: "Like *Heroes*, we want to change the world. Right. I'll save the world!" More seriously, he admits that "I don't know of any little kid who wouldn't want to save the world. Micah is the kind of kid who'd want to save the world, definitely." Perhaps one day Noah will look back on his *Heroes* experience as the starting point for a humanitarian career taking him beyond acting or music.

Greg Grunberg (Matt) has been able to blend music, acting, and philanthropy to raise money for a cause dear to his heart: the Epilepsy Foundation. His son's epilepsy prompted Grunberg to learn more about the condition. As a member of an actors' band featuring Hugh Laurie (*House*), James Denton (*Desperate Housewives*), singer Bonnie Somerville, and Bob Guiney (*The Bachelor*), Grunberg promises that they will play at any event that will pay their quarter-million-dollar fee, which goes to each band member's favorite charity. His efforts aren't limited to concerts and sales of the band's CD *Hoggin' the Covers*; celebrity auctions often feature items donated by actors with whom Grunberg has worked on previous series, including *Alias* and *Lost*. Whatever the role of heroes, in real life or television entertainment, *Heroes* encourages fans and the series' actors to consider how they might change the world.

Today's definition of a hero is debatable, although we might all agree that we could use one or more to help the world get back on track. *Heroes* shows the shades of gray (an area with which HRG says he's very comfortable) to which we're all exposed; never does one situation, or one character, have a black-and-white interpretation. These heroes can be fallible, but because they are, viewers are more likely to identify with them.

WHY THIS BOOK?

Heroes is a lot of fun, but it also provides some interesting responses to questions facing humanity today. It reflects a desire for someone or something to intervene in a world that seems increasingly mad and overwhelming; it illustrates our ambivalence about who should take a stand. As a television show, it takes its place among other critically respected, fan-popular series that reflect modern angst, especially *24* and *Lost*, but it "learned a lesson" from its predecessors by trying different ways to structure the story to avoid the pitfalls of earlier series.

In the following pages, we analyze just what makes *Heroes* so special, as a TV series, fan phenomenon, and reflection of popular culture. As HRG suggests, we should "go deep." To do so, we analyze both television and comics, as well as heroes and villains, and concepts of light and dark so prominent in the Heroesverse. Because the season 1 finale divided fans into camps who either liked or were disappointed by the finale, a "face-off" section takes a deeper look at "How to Stop an Exploding Man." Like the "heroes" themselves, our book offers special enhancements: a short encyclopedia, episode guide, title locator (to show where each chapter/episode title creatively appears on screen), list of superpowers, body count of unnatural deaths occurring throughout the season, and a list of occurrences of the Helix (or "godsend" symbol). The graphic novels published on the official NBC Web site are listed in a final section. Sources listed throughout chapters are gathered in the book's notes and bibliography, and each author's credits are provided in a biographical section before the index.

Through these chapters and enhancements we "dissect" *Heroes* and, far more benevolently than Sylar would, learn what makes it tick.

PART 1
GOING DEEP

ARE THESE HEROES LOST?

HEROES HAS FREQUENTLY BEEN compared to another highly successful television show, *Lost*. Although on the surface the two series seem worlds apart, *Lost*'s success undoubtedly played a large part in a series such as *Heroes* being broadcast. Like *Lost* two years before, *Heroes* became a breakout hit (albeit on a smaller scale) during the mainly dull 2006–07 television season. Its audience steadily grew from September through late November 2006, when it reached an impressive 16 million viewers. The midseason finale also was aired on the (U.S.) Sci Fi Channel and as an encore on NBC in the week following its much watched Monday-night regular broadcast. Multiple broadcasts of episodes, including a regular Friday-night time slot and occasional marathons on the Sci Fi Channel, helped increase the *Heroes* fanbase. Like *Lost* and other popular serials, the midseason hiatuses led to lower ratings when the series returned; however, *Heroes* remained in the top twenty U.S. programs.[1] It also received unofficial renewal long before the official notification came at the May upfronts in New York, where the cast was prominently featured.

Not only was *Heroes* renewed for a second season — with a full slate of twenty-four episodes — but a six-episode spin-off series,

Heroes: Origins, was unveiled. This spin-off encourages fans to vote for the hero they want most to be added to the regular series, and the combined thirty episodes ensure that *Heroes* avoids one of *Lost*'s problems in its first three years on air: the lack of a new episode each week during the regular TV season.

Although not yet the global phenomenon of *Lost*, *Heroes* appeals to a broader audience and has less of a cult image, which is surprising considering that it emerged as a hybrid of comic books and science fiction television, two genres that usually inspire cultdom. Its recent international release promises to make it a success around the world. Part of *Heroes'* popularity is its more hopeful look at the (super)human condition, whereas *Lost* often seems content to torture its characters as they seek redemption. Even when *Heroes* turns darker, it still offers as much character drama as ongoing mystery and makes use of humor in every episode. In spite of this important contrast, *Heroes* owes much to its famous predecessor. In fact, when NBC executives approached series creator Tim Kring in 2005, they were "desperate to match the success of serial dramas like *Lost* and *24*." *Heroes* learned from the best, but added its own creative twists to become an audience-friendly, intriguing new series. (For more on the making of the series, see chapter 2: "The Creation of *Heroes*.")

Table 1 illustrates some of the many similarities between *Heroes* and *Lost*, which clearly indicate that the latter is an important "ancestor text" to the former. Although some points of comparison (the Greg Grunberg factor) are minor, the two also share important examples of character or plot development.

TABLE 1. A *LOST-HEROES* COMPARISON

TYPE OF SIMILARITY	SIMILARITY	*LOST*	*HEROES*
Story Structure	Serialized storyline picked up for multiple seasons	In 2007, ABC picked up *Lost* for three more seasons, setting an ending date years in advance.	In early 2007, *Heroes* was unofficially picked up by NBC, which announced at the May 2007 upfronts a spin-off series to supplement regular episodes. The spin-off allows viewers to pick a new hero for the next season, a strong indicator that NBC plans to keep *Heroes* on the air for two more seasons.
	More questions than answers, although some answers are provided	*Lost* struggled with this issue through season 3, when the success of *Heroes* prompted the series' creators to offer more information within a shorter time period.	*Heroes* learned from *Lost* and created mini-arcs of stories within the first season to provide closure to some parts of the ongoing mystery.

TYPE OF SIMILARITY	SIMILARITY	*LOST*	*HEROES*
	Main characters' backstories	During the first three seasons, a *Lost* trademark was a character's backstory in each episode.	*Heroes* limited the use of backstories, but during season I included important background during a few episodes. Often the backstories were limited to scenes, sometimes in another country, and several characters' mini-backstories could be featured within one episode.
	Similar scenes	A teenage girl, Charlotte Malkin, presumed dead, wakes up during her autopsy. Desmond visits the future and knows he must change the past in order to have the future he wants.	A teenage girl, Claire Bennet, presumed dead, wakes up during her autopsy. Hiro visits the future and knows he must change the past in order to have the future he wants.

TYPE OF SIMILARITY	SIMILARITY	*LOST*	*HEROES*
	Episode titles	"Collision," "Homecoming"	"Collision," "Homecoming"
	Lines repeated by different characters	Locke, Eko, Charlie, and Jack all repeat variations of "Don't tell me what I can't do" throughout the series, for example.	Hiro tells Ando what a hero should do, and Ando repeats these lines several episodes later, for example.
	English subtitles for non-English dialogue	Korean to English	Japanese to English
	Scene locations outside the U.S.	During seasons 1 through 3, backstories included scenes in Iraq, England, Scotland, Australia, South Korea, Brazil, and Thailand.	During season 1, backstories included scenes in India and Japan.
	Seemingly prophetic (plot-driving) dreams or visions	Locke, Charlie, Eko, and Desmond have had dreams or visions of the future that guide their on-island actions.	Mohinder and Hiro have dreams (or even "visions" of the future through time travel) that portent the future.

TYPE OF SIMILARITY	SIMILARITY	*LOST*	*HEROES*
	Catchphrases	"Where are we?" "Live together; die alone." Plus, ABC's promotional phrases: "Find yourself *Lost*." Fan catchphrase based on *Heroes'* phrase: "Save the junkie; save the world."	"Save the cheerleader; save the world." Plus NBC's promotional phrases: "Are you on the list?" and "It's time to save the world."
	Writers who write for TV and comic books	Several current and former *Lost* scriptwriters, including Javier Grillo-Marxuach, create their own comics.	Several *Heroes* scriptwriters, including Jeph Loeb, create their own comics.
	Characters and cast	A large, racially and ethnically diverse cast. The original fourteen castaways represented the U.S., UK, Iraq, South Korea, and Australia.	The number of original heroes, their friends, and enemies changed throughout season 1; the main characters came from the U.S., India, and Japan.

TYPE OF SIMILARITY	SIMILARITY	LOST	HEROES
	An international cast	During the first three seasons, cast members included Naveen Andrews and Dominic Monaghan (England), Henry Ian Cusick (Peru, Scotland), Yunjin Kim (South Korea), Emilie de Ravin (Australia), and Rodrigo Santoro (Brazil).	During the first season, cast members included Santiago Cabrera (Chile, England) and Masi Oka (Japan, U.S.); Sendhil Ramamurthy's parents are Indian, and he's the first generation born in the U.S.
	Characters' inter-connectedness	Each character has at least one important and possibly several mundane connections with other main characters. Everyone has something or someone in common.	The growing number of connections ballooned during season 1's final episodes, as the heroes and their mentors and nemeses converged on New York City.

TYPE OF SIMILARITY	SIMILARITY	*LOST*	*HEROES*
	Main characters' deaths	Although not the first TV drama to kill off important characters (especially when the actors didn't want to leave and were fan favorites), *Lost* has become known for its high body count. During the first three seasons, castaways Shannon, Boone, Libby, Ana Lucia, and Charlie died, and Michael and Walt disappeared.	Following recent trends in TV programming, *Heroes* lost Isaac, Eden, Simone, Ted, and Linderman, while leaving D.L., Matt, and apparently Sylar wounded in the final episode.
	"Special" characters	Locke, Walt, and Charlie are deemed "special" by their mothers and others. The term usually denotes an unusual ability, such as psychic or spiritual power, even musical ability.	Micah, Claire, and Hiro think of themselves as "special" or have someone tell them that. Their super-powers make them special.

TYPE OF SIMILARITY	SIMILARITY	LOST	HEROES
	Character names	*Lost*'s Claire is a young blonde woman whose father is another series' character (Jack's father, Christian Shephard); Charlie, Isaac, and Nikki are other featured characters.	*Heroes*' Claire is a young blonde woman who discovers that her father is another series' character (Nathan Petrelli); Charlie, Isaac, and Niki are other featured characters.
	Similar characters	Hurley provides comic relief; Jack is a doctor who has to make tough decisions and face his father issues; Kate is a criminal who killed her father.	Hiro provides comic relief; Nathan is a politician who has to make tough decisions and face his father issues; Jessica is a criminal with serious father issues.
	A love triangle	The Jack-Kate-Sawyer triangle seems to be resolved in season 3, although the finale indicates elements of the triangle will continue to shift in the future.	The Isaac-Simone-Peter triangle is "resolved" when Simone dies.

TYPE OF SIMILARITY	SIMILARITY	*LOST*	*HEROES*
	A prescient child	Walt is "special," so much so that his seemingly psychic abilities frighten his step-father and win him attention from the Others. Walt seems to know a lot about the adults in his life.	Micah is "special," so much so that his ability to make computers "talk" to him involves him with Linderman's scheme to rig Nathan's election. Micah seems to know a lot about the adults in his life.
	An interracial marriage	Rose and Bernard	Niki and D.L.
	A recovering heroin addict/artist dies trying to help or save his friends	Charlie	Issac
	A person in a wheelchair is miraculously healed	Locke	Heidi Petrelli
	Greg Grunberg	Oceanic 815 pilot	Matt Parkman

TYPE OF SIMILARITY	SIMILARITY	*LOST*	*HEROES*
Scheduling and Programming Decisions	Experiments in scheduling, including widely hyped midseason breaks between story arcs	*Lost* experimented with a six-episode arc in fall 2006 and a sixteen-episode arc in spring 2007, before moving to a February 2008 start in season 4 with a full slate of episodes.	*Heroes* experimented with a half-season of episodes in fall 2006 and two shorter story arcs, one beginning in January and the other in March 2007, before changing to a full season interspersed with a spin-off series for thirty combined episodes in season 2.
Themes	Possible conspiracies	*Lost* thrives on speculation, and the continually twisting plot includes (so far) unexplained and possibly nefarious organizations such as the Dharma Initiative, Hanso Foundation, Widmore Industries, and Mittelos Bioscience, as well as intrigue and deceit among the many island dwellers.	*Heroes* makes it difficult to know who is a "hero" and who is a "bad guy/gal," as the characters redefine pragmatic ethics with shifts in the plot. HRG, Mr. Nakamura, and Mr. Linderman at times seem villainous but can show surprising empathy, too. The Company invites the most speculation about its purpose and direction.

TYPE OF SIMILARITY	SIMILARITY	LOST	HEROES
	Experimentation	The Dharma Initiative ran experiments on the island, as perhaps the Others or others do too.	The Company captures and tags the heroes and seems to manipulate their lives.
	Conflict between good and evil	Questions about the nature of humankind abound, as characters' motivations and actions make knowing who's good and who's not a changing, challenging game.	Even the best "heroes" have flaws, and the "bad guys/gals" sometimes show redeeming qualities. Like *Lost*, these characters live in a complex world with ambiguous morality.
	Destiny, Fate, and Hope	These philosophic ideas are often discussed and illustrated throughout *Lost*.	*Heroes*, too, drops these words into conversations and illustrates how these concepts are important in characters' lives.

TYPE OF SIMILARITY	SIMILARITY	LOST	HEROES
	Conflict between science and faith	Locke believes in faith as the guiding principle in life and feels he's directed by the island; Jack is a man of science who looks for logical explanations.	Mohinder and his father believe evolution controls humankind's actions (survival of the fittest); Hiro perceives a more spiritual calling; Mohinder's voiceovers frequently question the primary operating force in life: science or God.
	Biblical themes and names	Biblical names, including Jacob, Benjamin, Isaac, Naomi, and John, are prominent, and specific stories, such as Abraham and Isaac or the Garden of Eden, become part of the series' mythology.	Biblical names, including Micah, Isaac, Peter, Gabriel, Eden, and Noah, as well as season 1 chapter titles (e.g. "Genesis"), give an epic or biblical "feel" to the story.

TYPE OF SIMILARITY	SIMILARITY	LOST	HEROES
	"Daddy issues"	Everyone seems to have them, but the more intriguing dynamics involve sons Locke, Jack, and Ben and daughters Kate, Sun, and Claire.	Everyone seems to have them, but the more intriguing dynamics involve sons Hiro and Nathan and daughters Niki/Jessica and Claire.
	Wizard of Oz connection	A hot-air balloon, the name Henry Gale, and an episode entitled "The Man Behind the Curtain" are some allusions to *Oz*.	The online graphic novels include comments about the man behind the curtain.
Items	Comic book	Hurley's comic book is later found by Walt, and the images seem to provide clues about the mysterious island.	Micah, D.L., and Hiro read comic books; Hiro finds his future life story in issues of *9th Wonders*; Isaac creates the comic book series.
	Recurring items	Keys and maps are important items to many characters and become the focal point of several scenes.	Keys and maps are important items to many characters and become the focal point of several scenes.

TYPE OF SIMILARITY	SIMILARITY	LOST	HEROES
	Recurring symbols	The Dharma Initiative's logo variations	The Company's apparent use of the "Godsend" characters
	An important list of names	Jacob's list of "good people"	The Company's list of people with special powers
	Significant murals or drawings	The Hatch's mural and map on the blast door	Isaac's paintings, Sylar's drawings in a hidden room in his apartment

As indicated above, *Heroes* directly parallels *Lost* in two important areas: similar characters and themes of fate, destiny, faith, and hope.

FAMILIAR CHARACTERS: CLAIRE BENNET/CLAIRE LITTLETON, ISAAC/CHARLIE, HIRO/HURLEY, NATHAN/JACK, JESSICA/KATE

Common names often are repeated among popular series, but characters with similar traits or backgrounds may be more than coincidence. In both series, Claire is an important part of the ensemble, although *Heroes'* Claire Bennet has a much larger role in season 1 than *Lost's* Claire Littleton has had in recent seasons. During *Lost's* first season, pregnant Claire becomes involved with the Others' Ethan, a plot development that leads to many other arcs and subplots in seasons 2 and 3; however, she usually is relegated to the role of baby Aaron's mother. Claire Bennet gradually changes from a stereotypical high school cheerleader to a young woman who doesn't want the responsibility of her superpower to an increasingly mature and potentially powerful member of the Petrelli clan.

Both young, blonde characters are born out of wedlock and eventually meet their biological fathers, who have interesting connections with other characters. Claire Bennet's adoptive father, HRG (Horn Rimmed Glasses), develops into a complex character. He fiercely loves and protects his daughter but also spends the majority of his life as a loyal employee of The Company that hunts people with special powers. Claire is at first horrified by her father's real job but later is able to reconcile with him as he repeatedly offers to sacrifice himself to protect her. Nevertheless, she also is intrigued to learn that her biological father is secret superhero and newsworthy politico Nathan Petrelli. Claire Littleton meets her biological father but doesn't want to know his name; thus she doesn't realize she and castaway Jack are half-siblings. Claire Bennet becomes aware of her half-brothers and may someday become a recognized member of the Petrelli family.

Other characters share first names, although their real connection is with a different character. *Lost*'s Charlie Pace shares a first name with Hiro's now-deceased girlfriend, and *Heroes*' Isaac Mendez shares a given name with *Lost*'s guest-healer-from-Australia Isaac; however, the important connection is between Charlie Pace and Isaac Mendez. Charlie is a washed-up rocker and heroin addict when *Lost* begins; Isaac Mendez is a struggling painter and comic book artist who initially believes he can only "paint the future" while high on heroin.

Both characters come clean and want to stay that way, although they're tempted by drugs several times. Both become separated from the women they love because of their addiction: Claire banishes Charlie from her life when she thinks he's using heroin again; Simone leaves Isaac when he refuses to go into rehab. Charlie has limited success — about a year of international fame — with his band; similarly, although Simone sells some of Isaac's paintings (often to Linderman) and comic book fans know his work, he hasn't made it big. For both Charlie and Isaac, their talent drives them, even when they aren't commercially successful.

By the end of season 1, recovered addict Isaac provides Hiro with enough knowledge about Sylar to help stop him; Hiro confides to Isaac that he has seen the artist's future death. During the same TV season, Charlie hears Desmond's prophesy of his impending demise. Both characters accomplish heroic acts before their self-sacrificial deaths. Isaac smiles as Sylar approaches, content in the knowledge that he has become a true hero through his artwork, which provides key information for other heroes to save the world. Charlie makes the sign of the cross as he drowns, and makes communication with the outside world possible, in *Lost*'s season 3 finale.

Although *Lost* is usually the darker of the two series (see, however, Steven Peacock's essay on page 141), it provides comic relief through more serious characters' interactions with Hugo "Hurley" Reyes, who reacts to the weirdness of island life like most viewers would. Hurley and his late pal Charlie have normal conversations about comic book heroes, music, and women; they're more likely to have fun adventures. Hurley's one-liners and droll comments break up the serious nature of island life; his geeky references to popular culture imply how much time he's spent watching television and reading comics. *Heroes* injects even more character-driven humor into its series with the bantering Hiro Nakamura and pal Ando. They also debate everyday concerns and often enjoy the "coolness" of Hiro's ability to bend space and time. Admittedly nerdy Hiro reads comic books and loves to compare his abilities to those of his favorite television or movie heroes. Hiro's enthusiasm for life matches Hurley's, although both also understand how dire life can sometimes become. Hiro keeps looking at the bright side and refuses to give up or give in to pessimism, which is one reason why he has become a *Heroes*' fan favorite.

Nathan Petrelli shares superficial characteristics with Jack Shephard. Both are professionals: Nathan, a politician and newly elected congressman; Jack, a talented spinal surgeon. Both have issues with their dead fathers and believe they haven't lived up to parental expectations. They are compelled to lead others, which often puts them into morally ambiguous areas. What they are asked to do for the greater good — which to Nathan includes allowing much of New York City to be demolished — tests their humanity and makes them seem like "good" bad characters, depending on the situation.

Heroes' Jessica, the bad-girl side of Niki Sanders, is harder-edged than freckle-faced tomboy Kate Austen of *Lost*, but their backgrounds include some striking similarities. Both have abusive, detestable fathers (Kate kills hers); both are fugitives who, so far, haven't served prison sentences for their crimes but have been incarcerated. Both are pragmatists who do whatever it takes to remain free, which often surprises those who think they know the women best.

Of course, many of these familiar characters are becoming television archetypes: geeky Everymen, strong women with shady pasts, troubled leaders who have to compromise their ideals, and so on. It's not surprising that two highly popular series with large ensemble casts share similar character development of these archetypes. What is most striking is the Isaac-Charlie connection, which doesn't reflect a common TV archetype: former druggie/artist as hero. Perhaps these series are forging a new "typical" character for an age in which celebrities, in and out of rehab, often are admired for the ways they overcome their addictions; building up celebrities (including musicians and artists) as role models is not new, but redeeming these characters as heroes on prominent TV series and turning them into another archetype brings celebrity worship to a new level in entertainment.

FATE, DESTINY, FAITH, AND HOPE

Just as *Lost* frequently has characters discuss their philosophical ideas about fate, destiny, faith, or hope or works these words into dialogue, *Heroes* finds way to emphasize these themes throughout its first season:

- When Sylar (pretending to be Zane Taylor) accompanies Mohinder Suresh as he seeks out people with superhero abilities, he explains that he believes in fate and karma ("Unexpected"). Later in that episode, Sylar/Zane explains that finding other heroes is "our destiny."

- Hiro's father reveals that their family's fate includes the "ascension" of one who learns to wield his power; the senior Nakamura is surprised when Hiro turns out to be the individual destined to save the world ("Landslide").
- Hiro explains that getting the last Nissan from the rental agency is another sign of his destiny; in the futuristic *9th Wonders*, Hiro and Ando travel by Nissan Versa to Las Vegas ("One Giant Leap").
- During "Landslide," several heroes, including Claire, Hiro, and Nathan, question their destiny. The word comes up several times in several scenes.
- With his mother's encouragement, Nathan agrees that he has faith in his destiny to become a political leader, even president; he can set the tone of the world after the destruction of New York City ("The Hard Part").
- Part of Hiro's personal code of what it means to be a hero includes the need for hope, a caveat he shares with Ando just when their mission seems destined to fail ("Run!").

Such heavy themes are on the minds of characters as they deal with their emerging superpowers in a world that might consider them special but might also demonize them for being different. How each character finds a purpose in life and what he or she does with a special talent become an integral part of the story. Just as *Lost* invites audiences to think about how they, as much as the characters they watch, may be lost within themselves or the greater world, so, too, does *Heroes* encourage viewers to think about what makes a modern hero and how each person might be called upon to do something extraordinary. Because *Heroes* deals with life-or-death events and presents so many characters facing crisis points in their lives, it quite naturally provides a more philosophical framework for thinking — at least sometimes — about life's larger themes.

WHAT *LOST* TAUGHT

Heroes may not have been green-lighted a few years ago. According to Tim Kring, "a lot of these battles that [*Heroes'* creators and writers] would be fighting with the network or the studio — *Lost* made those battles go away." He openly admits that the creative team "certainly learned from *Lost*," although he also wanted to create a very different show. "They started with a central mystery. We didn't." Kring also noticed *Lost* was slow to pay off viewer patience with answers, so to avoid that problem with *Heroes*, he promised that "the apocalyptic event in *Heroes* will be resolved in season 1, and we'll move on to something else in season 2." The series' actors also acknowledge predecessors' success but emphasize the uniqueness of their own show. On *Larry King Live*, Adrian Pasdar (Nathan Petrelli) explained the series' unique appeal: by blending reality and fantasy, *Heroes* combines "the best of what television has to offer and it redefine[s] the landscape of what commercial and successful television can be."

Although fans may be well aware of what they like or dislike, not all network executives think like fans. Kring, unlike many a series creator, learns from the competition and pays attention to fans. He seems to have gleaned the following key points from *Lost's* groundbreaking success:

1. Serials, if done well and not dragged out *ad infinitum,* can be wildly popular.

Kring vows that *Heroes'* storylines will be self-contained, such as the "Save the cheerleader; save the world," "Are you on the list?" and "It's time to save the world" mini-arcs within season 1. By the season 1 finale, the New York City bomb dilemma is resolved. During season 2, a whole new set of adventures will be introduced, and they, too, will conclude quickly (in terms of serialized storytelling). Fans' questions should be answered within a season, if not a few episodes; the pace of the storytelling is accelerated, so that fans don't become frustrated waiting for plots to be resolved.

2. World turmoil is an excellent source for modern storytelling, as long as people, not just problems, carry the
story.

During the 2006–07 television season, many series, including *24*,
Jericho, and *Traveler*, dealt with terrorism, especially the possibility of
nuclear bombs. Few new series, however, did as well as expected;
many once-faithful viewers seemed reluctant to stick with Jack Bauer
during his latest twenty-four hours of destruction and death. Ratings
for the highly touted *Jericho* declined, and the series was canceled.
Perhaps because its end-of-season episodes once again provided some
heart-wrenching family moments, fans fought for the series and
finally succeeded in getting CBS to belatedly renew it for a few more
episodes.[2] Most series involving an apocalyptic event, however, failed
to win fans' loyalty; the exception to this trend is ratings-winner
Heroes.

Although the future nuclear demolition of New York City is the
backdrop for season 1, it isn't the only story being told. The lives of
interesting, intersecting characters who discover superpowers are the
series' real emphasis; a calamity to avert provides the setting where
these characters can come together.

Adrian Pasdar finds that "the reluctant hero who has to make a
decision to trade in his own personal life" to make the world a better
place is a perfect storyline for modern times. He adds, "In the times
we're faced with, it's great to be a part of something that endeavors to
explore that arena." The current geopolitical climate provides *Heroes'*
writers with many topical possibilities, including political issues.
Nathan Petrelli can't win election to Congress without the monetary
support and vote tampering provided by shady character Linderman.
Even Nathan's mother emphasizes that do-gooders can't save the
world; only shrewd politicians, with the courage to make tough decisions (such as sacrificing a few million people to unite the world via a
campaign of fear), are suitable leaders for the modern world.

The power of money plays a prominent role too. Niki Sanders finds it difficult to raise her son on her own, despite working more than one job and cutting corners as much as possible. The costs of private schools for her gifted son and computers to help him achieve his potential are out of her reach; the need for cash to pay the rent leads her to work for Linderman (through alter-ego Jessica) and (as Niki) to strip for online customers. Claire's biological mother, living in a trailer park, seems grateful to former lover Nathan when he gives her money after receiving information about their daughter. Even financially well-off Nathan lacks the kind of money needed to finance a winning political campaign; selling his soul to Linderman becomes a requirement for his future success.

Issues such as these often find their way into popular television, but *Heroes* uses these problems primarily as plot points — the real story is how characters, heroes and villains alike, deal with modern challenges, not that they exist. *Heroes* doesn't just bemoan the state of the world; it illustrates how people can change it. By focusing on people, rather than only issues or events, *Heroes* succeeds where other series tackling similar topics often fail. The quality of the storytelling and the depth of characterization help *Heroes* stand out from the crowd of competitors.

> 3. Character-driven series engage the audience and help attract new viewers.

Fans latch onto characters they like — or like to despise — and they return week after week to watch their favorites. To date, *Heroes* has done a good job of introducing new characters one or two at a time, developing their storylines without sacrificing the overall plot: to get everyone to New York to stop the bomb. Instead of focusing on one character's backstory at a time, as *Lost* does, each *Heroes* episode may include snippets of several characters' past as well as current lives, but the action keeps moving forward. Characters' pasts are incidental to their current and future actions.

Careful casting (perhaps even a bit of stunt casting) also keeps audiences watching, especially those familiar with science fiction. The inclusion of George (*Star Trek*) Takei and Christopher (*Doctor Who*) Eccleston in recurring roles, for example, potentially attracted more science fiction fans to *Heroes*. Comic creator Stan Lee even makes a brief appearance as a bus driver.

Even if *Heroes'* cast changes with the advancement of new characters and diminishment of older ones, as long as the writers continue to develop interesting characters and give each their key moments to shine, fans will likely remain satisfied. The possibility that old favorites may resurface should also help placate fans. The world of science fiction and comics provides more leeway for the dead to return to the living or the once-lost to be found.

4. "Hybrid" programs that blend several genres, including elements of science fiction, attract a wide range of ages, not just the coveted young demographic.

During 2005–07, science fiction became a hot topic for mainstream programming, but several shows billed that way disappeared quickly from the TV schedule. *Heroes* is honest about its comic book and science fiction roots, but again, these elements are only part of the whole story. The emphasis is on intriguing characters doing interesting things. Even people who normally don't watch science fiction can enjoy *Heroes* because they like the characters and can suspend disbelief about the "reality" of superpowers.

In the U.S., the Sci Fi Channel broadcasts a repeat performance of episodes after they have been shown on NBC. Hardcore science fiction fans are likely to tune in a second time each week to the Sci Fi Channel, or science fiction fans who haven't yet watched the series become aware of it because of its Sci Fi Channel connection. Once they begin watching, however, they discover that there's more to *Heroes* than mystical or futuristic plot devices to solve problems; potential superheroes face the same human dilemmas that occur in ordinary people's lives. *Heroes* has comedic elements as well and at times looks like a buddy road trip, parent-child relationship drama, or love story. *Heroes* surpasses a one-genre niche and, in so doing, attracts a much wider audience.

> 5. Fans expect to be more than passive viewers of innovative television series.

Heroes is even more interactive online than predecessor *Lost*, which early on courted Internet fandom. Although the series also relies on other media and sites, the "main digital extension of the show [became] an online comic book that [runs] concurrently and allow[s] a deeper appreciation of the stories" being told in weekly television episodes; one character, Hana Gittelman, first joined the cast of the comic book before being seen on camera. (See Chapter 3: "Empowering *Heroes*: Marketing the Series" for further discussion of its online presence.)

TO BE, OR NOT TO BE, THAT IS THE QUESTION
Lost is famous for killing major characters in surprising ways, seemingly for shock value. During season 1, the much-rumored killing of a castaway resulted in fan frenzy as viewers wondered who would die and when; Boone turned out to be the unlucky victim. During season 2, three characters die, two shot during the same episode. Only a few episodes into season 3, another major character (Mr. Eko) dies. Whereas *Lost* first began the practice to illustrate the fragility of life, especially on such a remote, sinister island, the creators later continued killing important characters so that new ones can join the large cast and the story be facilitated.

Many character deaths coincide with ratings sweeps or high-powered finales, to shock viewers just before a hiatus beginning in late November or May. At the end of season 3, for example, Charlie's long-prophesied death occurs in the action-packed finale, driving many fangirls to declare they'll never watch the series again. An unprecedented number of people die during May 2007 episodes: Charlie,

Locke's father, and a dozen Others, including the enigmatic Mr. Friendly. Locke looks like a goner after being shot (but reappears in the finale). *Lost* sometimes seems in danger of alienating its core fan base by killing favorite major characters, a fact that Tim Kring seems to have noticed.

Heroes' creators accepted the new television expectation that characters will die within a season. Other popular series, such as *Buffy the Vampire Slayer*, *24*, and *Desperate Housewives*, have also followed their killer instinct, and now audiences (and actors) expect that someone will die during the course of a story arc. Even primarily comedic new hit *Ugly Betty* concluded its first season with a shooting death of a recurring character close to the family.

Heroes soon followed *Lost*'s season 3 strategy for telling fans to anticipate a death in a certain episode, as Damon Lindelof and Carlton Cuse did with Mr. Eko's death in the fifth episode of the season (a rumor circulated by TV critics Kristin Veitch of *E!* and Michael Ausiello of *TV Guide*). "A hero will die!" the announcer dramatically intoned during each teaser for *Heroes'* midseason finale. On the early December 2006 day of the broadcast, the series' actors visited several entertainment news and talk shows, including *The Megan Mullally Show*, *Ellen*, and *Entertainment Tonight*; they talked about the impending death but, of course, wouldn't tell which character dies. When minor character Eden lost her head during a confrontation with Sylar, some fans were relieved that a more important character hadn't died, but others felt cheated after all the hype.

Although technically Eden is a superhero, she isn't a prominent character in these early episodes. Her role changes from trusted, normal girl next door who befriends Mohinder, as she did his now-deceased father, to a spy working for the bad guy. Her role again shifts when the bad guy HRG turns out to be running some type of scientific monitoring of the superheroes and she, his assistant, stands up for the captured Isaac. By overestimating her superpower, however, Eden is outmatched by the evil Sylar, who forces her to kill herself

("Fallout"). Although this death thickens the plot and provides something of a cliffhanger by making Sylar once again a formidable villain, fans didn't care as much about Eden as more important and well-developed characters. *Heroes* made good on the promise that "a hero will die," but the most important heroes survive the midseason break.

Early in season 1, Kring suggested that many heroes would die and the cast change dramatically from season to season. In one interview, Kring stated that "this show needs to be able to kill off characters once in awhile. I think I talked to every single one of [the actors] very early on that, that was going to be the nature of the show . . . Sometimes, the greater good would be served by thinning the herd or killing off a character that people loved. It has to be a world where no one is safe." Although character deaths are sprinkled throughout the season's episodes, Kring decided against a killing spree, despite his need to open the door to new characters: "I'm easing up on the slaughter — not everyone's going out in a casket. Some will simply go away; others are still around but we just won't see them." Before the season finale, he reiterated this position: "[N]ot all those who are killed are making their last appearance on the show."

Kring supposedly changed his mind in part because of the fans, who want to believe their time spent getting to know and care about characters will pay off. Kring has seen how hardcore fans may turn against a series if they tire of certain plotlines or become disgruntled with a series' direction. "[T]hese kinds of fans are very fickle, I mean the real hardcore fans. So, yes, you do worry about that." He vows that he's learned cautionary tales from previous television series, as well as fan response.[3]

Of course, some heroes are introduced and die within only one or two scenes; Sylar, for example, methodically hunts and kills those with powers he wants. Fans, however, have little time to get to know these characters before they are killed, and the emotional loss is minimal. Character deaths such as these can "thin the herd" without alienating viewers.

Fan favoritism may play a bigger role in *Heroes'* future development of characters. The spin-off series, *Heroes: Origins*, will encourage fans to vote for their favorite new hero, who then will join the cast of the regular series; this level of audience participation smacks of *American Idol* or even *Survivor*. Voting someone on, or off, the cast could take *Heroes'* story in dramatically different directions than the series' creators originally anticipated and give writers less control over some aspects of their characters' viability. How much fans may actually influence Kring's future story development is uncertain, but at least on the surface, he and NBC have passed even *Lost*'s creators' well-known commitment to paying attention to fans.

SOME INTERESTING DIFFERENCES

Lost's creative team prides itself on keeping storylines secret, and even with a looming hiatus of eight months (before season 4 begins in February 2008), creators/writers Damon Lindelof and Carlton Cuse only hinted that the season 3 finale would show fans the series' direction for its final three seasons, or forty-eight episodes. The full story will be told within six seasons; although some story arcs will rise and fall during the telling of this epic, audiences who want to know all the answers must wait until the story ends in 2010.

Heroes' creator Tim Kring seems much more open about the direction of season 2, which he wants to be very different from season 1. According to *Entertainment Weekly*, "Generations," the second volume in the heroes' saga, "will focus on putting the *Heroes* mythology in a grand historical context of superpowered family dynasties." Masi Oka (Hiro) reiterated that the second season will be about "heritage, the family line, and the source of the powers," which probably will feature the older generation of cast members, including Cristine Rose (Nathan's and Peter's mother) and George Takei (Hiro's father), with references likely made to the now-departed Linderman and his compatriots. Unlike *Lost*, which often has been teased about its cast of mostly young, beautiful people, *Heroes* seems to be moving its mythology in the direction of wisdom and age before (youthful) beauty.

Heroes is "a little more the 24 model than the *Lost* model" in that it may introduce many new characters with emerging superpowers. Although 24 keeps some characters year to year, new villains arrive each January, and even the cTU employee roster changes drastically. *Lost* also introduces new characters, such as the Others discovered on the other side of the island or people prominent in backstories and flashforwards, but many major cast members survive year to year. *Heroes* "could have new people and new storylines and new ideas and new threats and new bad guys and new heroes . . . it's not just a continuing serialized storyline about only these [original] people."

Lost's Cuse and Lindelof wanted to establish an end date so they knew how much story they needed to tell per episode and per season. Kring, however, has a different plan in mind for *Heroes*. "I just don't feel like doing that," he explained near the end of season 1, although he acknowledged that he wouldn't want the series to become an "albatross." For now, *Heroes* offers "unlimited possibilities."

Heroes seems destined for multiple TV seasons (after all, it opens with Chapter 1 of an epic story, thus promising many future adventures). Kring's story has an indeterminate number of books and chapters; unlike *Lost*'s story, which had a planned beginning, middle, and end from day one of production, Kring's story lines may expand or contract, depending on *Heroes*' continuing popularity. Each season brings a new set of chapters from what could be a virtually unlimited well of stories, with the possibility of many new characters taking the epic in unexpected directions. *Heroes* presents writers with more storytelling possibilities within the series' framework, which could make it more responsive to TV trends and viewers' preferences than *Lost* could ever be.

THE IMPORTANCE OF THE *LOST* CONNECTION

Lost signaled a new direction for television storytelling and began a great experiment of multimedia game playing and marketing (e.g., Internet, television broadcasts, online downloads, print, CD, DVD, games, and products) that influenced later programs. *Heroes* is the obvious benefactor of *Lost*'s trailblazing, but it also reaps the benefits of avoiding its predecessor's missteps. *Heroes* may never be such an innovator; however, it is a popular successor that takes elements from *Lost* (and other series) and turns them into television with a broader appeal to a mass audience. Through a carefully crafted Web presence, effective episode scheduling (a lesson likely learned from ABC's programming experiments), and multiple broadcasts online as well as on several networks, NBC has shown its support for *Heroes* and pushed it front and center as a favored program on its roster. Kring's commitment to fans, the appeal of the ensemble cast of heroes, and easy-to-follow story arcs leading to an end point each season indicate that *Heroes* may be saving the world (and network television) well past season 2.

The Creation
of Heroes

[Comic-Con] was mind-blowing. People had sort of warned me that it was going to be a real crazy experience. I had no idea it was going to be that wild. . . . When I walked out onto the stage and I looked out onto this sea of people and the first thing I saw, my eye went right to a guy with a horn coming out the middle of his head. The second thing I saw was, sitting in the front row, I kid you not, a four hundred pound Harry Potter. With a wand. And I was like, these are my people. It was a really amazing experience.

— Tim Kring

WHERE WOULD THE MOVIES BE these days without the superhero film? A quick check of the Internet Movie Database shows that thirty-two of the top 250 grossing films of all time worldwide are (broadly defined) superhero movies. The eleven superhero films in the top fifty have earned their studios an amazing $8,449,875,670 around the globe. With numbers that impressive, it seems hard to fathom (apart, that is, from the high cost of special effects budgets) why it took contemporary television so long to capitalize on the superhero — as NBC has now done with Heroes.

All it took was a network with a reverse Midas touch, seemingly incapable, post–*Seinfeld* and *Friends*, of generating a new hit, a network in trouble and willing to take risks on a radical departure series (such as ABC and *Lost* before it) — a gamble that has paid dividends; and a science fiction aficionado/comic book geek ready to persuade NBC to make such a program.

Without knowing the particulars, a knowledgeable, evolved human television viewer teleporting back to the present from some future/interplanetary adventure would immediately assume *Heroes* to be the work of, say, a Joss Whedon — fanboy, father of *Buffy the Vampire Slayer*, comic book author (*Fray, Astonishing X-Men, Buffy Season 8*), someone *Entertainment Weekly*'s Jeff Jensen would portray as "itching to make one of those newfangled serialized saga things[,] . . . [s]truck by the number of superheroes popping up on the movie screens during these catastrophe-shaken times" and ready to ask, "Why not on TV?" Whedon, however, had absolutely nothing to do with the creation of *Heroes*.

The mastermind behind *Heroes* (the individual Jensen was actually describing) was, in fact, Tim Kring — that name we first saw superimposed on the eclipse in the *Heroes* pilot "Genesis." Kring earned an MFA from the University of Southern California's vaunted film school prior to a more than twenty-five-year career as a television writer. Beginning with such fantasy exercises as *Knight Rider* and *Misfits of Science*, he contributed as well to mainstream fare such as *Providence* and *Chicago Hope* before his first opportunity to create and run his own show: the set-in-Boston police procedural/medical-examiner-as-detective *Crossing Jordan*, the *CSI* franchise's less sexy stepsister, recently canceled after six seasons and 122 episodes.

At *Heroes* night at the William S. Paley Television Festival in spring 2007, as his new show was coming to the end of its first season and well on its way to becoming "a lucrative worldwide brand for NBC,"

Kring was given his first opportunity to answer a question that had become a bit tiresome for his ensemble cast: What super power would you want to have? His answer — "the power to break an entire season of stories very quickly and painlessly" — was not exactly the response one might expect from the man behind television's most fully realized superhero series. The reply, however, was precisely the sort of insider joke a veteran of American network TV like Kring might give.

Perhaps the idea of morphing into something radically new had a unique appeal to Kring, who acknowledges having "gotten used to trying to reinvent myself over and over again. The strange thing is that I find myself coming full circle sometimes. When I first started writing TV movies, I was known as the 'horror' guy, then the 'thriller' guy, then the 'teen comedy' guy, etc." Kring, of course, has also offered a more skeptical explanation: "I think it just comes from a short attention span. I do something for a while and I start to feel like I used that muscle too much and I wanna try something new."

When American entertainment's newspaper of record *Variety* reviewed Kring's *Heroes* upon its premiere in September 2006, it smugly and erroneously predicted it was "destined to leave a small but outspoken fan contingent grumbling next summer at Comic-Con about its cancelation." If *Variety* had been able to see with Kring's own eyes at Comic-Con the summer before *Heroes'* debut (see the epigraph above) or commission as its critic *Heroes'* own Isaac Mendez, an evolved human who finds himself able to paint the future with unerring accuracy, it might have seen that the show would prove to be anything but a cult phenomenon with minimal appeal and a short run; instead, it has become a monster hit and now a worldwide phenomenon. At season's end, an *Entertainment Weekly* cover story would speak of its "marvelously madcap season" in which "the series [would] nudge aside *Lost* and *24* as the standard for serialized storytelling." At Comic-Con 2007, *Heroes* was one of the featured attractions.

How *Variety* got it so wrong and Kring got it so right is the subject of this chapter. *Heroes* may be born out of necessity, as Charles

Deveaux insists in Peter's "How to Stop an Exploding Man" dream/vision; *Heroes*, however, was definitely made: here's how.

ORIGIN MYTH

> The show's secret lay in finding that ever-elusive sweet spot
> between fanboy-friendly and widely accessible, while quickly
> answering mysteries and clarifying mythology before
> anyone got antsy enough to ask the dreaded question: Does
> this show really know what it's doing?
>
> — Jeff Jensen, *Entertainment Weekly*

All cultures have origin myths, complex stories of the beginning, the genesis, of a way of life, a mindset, a mythology. So it shouldn't surprise us that the unique life form of a television series would generate and sustain one as well. In interviews, Kring and his collaborators had already laid down a baseline account of how *Heroes* came into being even before the series aired. "It's always hard to go back and think about how you came up with something," Kring has cautioned, "especially when it took several months to come up with it." We do not, it is true, have a "string theory" as meticulous as the timeline Future Hiro creates in Isaac's studio ("Five Years Gone"), but we can pinpoint some key developments.

On *Crossing Jordan*, Kring's other show, there had been a moment in which a "very mild-mannered woman character . . . kicks the sh*t out of" an intruder "in this kind of kung fu way." In the sudden revelation that someone ordinary "had these abilities that nobody knew about," Kring pinpoints "the first spark" of *Heroes*' inspiration.

The serendipitous watching of two movies over two nights, *Eternal Sunshine of the Spotless Mind* (2004), written by Kring friend Charlie Kaufman, and the Pixar film *The Incredibles* (2004), marks another pivotal moment in *Heroes*' genesis. "I was really blown away by both movies," Kring recalls.

In a weird way, they started to kind of meld in my mind, taking the kind of Kaufmanesque hyper-real characters, very anonymous characters, people you would pass on the street and not think twice about, and I started blending them in my mind with the premise of *The Incredibles*, people trying to live ordinary lives while having these superpowers.

For being anything-but-a-comic-book-geek, Kring had clearly given the latter theme a great deal of thought: a superhero-in-training, he had concluded, would need to take baby steps at first, experience hard-to-reconcile conflicts between normal and extraordinary, and find it immensely difficult to find the proper path toward fulfillment of a destiny.

Kring also had a long-standing ambition to be "present at the creation" of the characters of a television show: "Whereas with most television shows you pick up with a cop and he's already a cop. You pick up with a doctor and he's working in the ER and that's where you start your series. I wanted to start it from the very inception." *Heroes*, Kring came to understand, could be his chance to realize that imaginative objective as well.

Another key kernel of the *Heroes'* origin myth was "The Walk," a stroll taken by Kring with his longtime friend and former collaborator Jeph Loeb (for more on Loeb, see Chapter 4: "Comic Book Heroes"). According to Loeb, he and Kring

spent some time on the phone together [talking about the idea of *Heroes*] and then decided we needed a much longer session. We met over at the Empath Magic Tree House [in Los Angeles] where I'm lucky enough to have a writing studio. . . . We started talking and walking together at like three in the afternoon and when it got to be about eight at night, we had walked so far into the next town that it was HOURS before we got back. But, during that time, Tim got to

just let it all out of him . . . he had the story completely
worked out and he really just needed a sounding board.

Under the sway of what Loeb calls, in another account of their peram-
bulation, the "Powers of Walk,"[1] Kring mapped out the entire story for
Loeb. "He hadn't written a word," Loeb recalled, impressed, "but he
knew exactly what was going to happen in every scene." When *Heroes*
later become a reality, Loeb was impressed. "What amazed me at first
was how faithful Kring had been to his pitch to me. So many of the
tiny details he had talked about in the abstract were now part of this
woven tapestry of madness. That, and it was smart. Really smart." It
was on this walk, too, where Loeb grasped for the first time just how
little his friend really knew about comic books and superheroes. (See
Chapter 4.)

As Aristotle taught, in order for something to come to being it
must have what he called an "efficient cause" — that which, practi-
cally speaking, makes it a reality. Of course *Heroes*, being an
expensive-to-produce-and-distribute television series and not just, say,
a comic book generated in a New York artist's loft, had that too. "I had
a development deal at the network," Kring tells us, "and I had to come
up with something. I seemed to only have this one idea and, as much
as I tried to deny it, it kept sort of showing up."

CHARACTER IS CHARACTER, WRITING IS WRITING

You'd think that Kring is a total geek, when he's not a comic
book guy at all. Which shows to go ya what we've always
known about comics — that it's CHARACTER that drives the
narrative mixed with the cool of the visuals. Kring just got it.
BAM.

— Jeph Loeb

Again and again in interviews Kring returns to the basic tenets of his
writing philosophy that give this section its title.

Certain, as he tells interviewer Edward Douglas, that anyone watching *Heroes* for the special effects is bound to be "wildly disappointed" (though the FX have turned out to be as good as anything seen on TV to date), Kring has declared himself wary of becoming too "invested in the 'powers'" of his heroes. Convinced the story he is telling is in reality "a character-based saga," he has committed himself to capitalizing on the unprecedented opportunities of serial television and a large ensemble cast for exploring their development.

His faith that character is character has spread to his staff and shaped his showrunning. Though he stocked his writing pool with "people who have more of a genre background," they were quickly infected by Kring's particular propensity: "It's interesting because I have to keep reminding them that they're genre writers, because so many of them were attracted to the show because of the character stuff. That was what attracted everybody to the script of the pilot."

Kring's second tenet emerges in response to a query concerning whether writing *Heroes* seems like a whole new kind of authorship, and his answer is telling: "The muscles used in facing a blank page are remarkably similar no matter what genre you're in. I still struggle over crafting a scene one line at a time. And I still look for truth and reality in every emotion." Only in the writers' room — where episodic concerns and the breaking of stories quickly become paramount — does writing seem like "a different animal."

COLLABORATION

So much struggle for meaning and purpose, and in the end we find it only in each other, our shared experience of the fantastic and the mundane.

> — from Mohinder's final voiceover in "How to Stop an
> Exploding Man," written by Tim Kring

The writers' room is a very mysterious, organic kind of place. You come in with a set idea, and very quickly watch it

morph and change and bend into something new. Almost
always something better.

— Tim Kring

As Jeffrey Stepakoff confirms in a recent book, *Billion-Dollar Kiss: The
Story of a Television Writer in the Hollywood Gold Rush*, perhaps the
most in-depth, behind-the-scenes account available on how television
shows get written, the writers' room — a.k.a. "story room," a.k.a. "The
Room" — is indeed a mysterious place: "off limits to everyone except
a show's writing staff. Outsiders of any kind, even actors and executives, no matter how powerful they may be, are never allowed in The
Room while legitimate work is in session." The individual culture of
a writers' room, Stepakoff observes, is "usually set by the showrunner," and so it is especially revealing that Tim Kring, *Heroes*
showrunner, has offered in interviews fairly detailed accounts of the
Heroes room.

The serial nature of *Heroes* has required a different "dynamic,"
according to Kring:[2]

> you have to be much more diligent in your storytelling
> because everything's connected, and one thread pulls part of
> the tapestry, one domino hits another domino. You have to
> be very careful in the storytelling to not unravel things.
> Sometimes a very small decision to go left instead of right
> changes the entire nature of the story. . . .

Rather than the customary path — in which individual writers (or
writing partners) complete assigned episodes by themselves and then
share the draft with the entire group — *Heroes* scripts are collabora-
tive efforts from the get-go. This different model was in part born of
necessity: "Because we had to hit the ground running so fast and so
hard, we had what I consider to be a very short amount of lead time,"[3]
Kring observes, "a kind of all hands on deck quality" was called for.

This anything but business-as-usual paradigm produced positive effects, according to Kring: "Everybody feels attached emotionally to the episode, and feels committed to it. Whereas in a normal drama, you feel very attached to your episode, and you hope that everybody else around you doesn't screw it up. On this, everybody has ownership and feels connected to it." As Jeph Loeb confirms in a different interview, "We are ALL involved in every bit of the script. We have a stake in each of the characters and work very hard to make sure that no one has a cooler story than the other."[4]

A writer of record for each episode does exist, of course — thus Michael Green is credited as the author of "Hiros"; Bryan Fuller goes into the IMDB as the writer of "Company Man." But what this really means is that this individual had the "responsibility to then go through [the semi-final draft] and make the scenes work with each other" — an absolutely essential step, as Loeb explains: "You need someone who is taking a single brush and going through the entire script. Oftentimes, that means rewriting an entire plot or character line simply because you didn't know whether or not it was going to work until you lined it all up. Eventually, the script becomes very much the writer whose name is on it." As showrunner, of course, Kring does a final review, making "sure that his signature is there."[5]

So communal is the imagination that generates television that Kring's collaborators even include a fellow showrunner from a rival — on another network — show and crucial ancestor. In an interview on the NBC Web site with close friend *Lost*'s (and ABC's) Damon Lindelof, we learn that he suggested an idea — a good one at that — used in "Genesis." "[T]hat moment at the end of the pilot, that everyone loves (and I always take credit for)," Kring reminds Lindelof, "was *your idea!*" (What idea he's referring to is unclear — the reveal that HRG is in fact Claire's father? Hiro's "Hello New York" teleportation to Times Square? Nathan's "Flying Man" catch of his brother?)

Last of all, it would be remiss not to mention Kring's oldest collaborator, the Victorian novelist Charles Dickens:

The storytelling is really a lot of fun and there are some very wild twists and turns. One of the things that we talked about early on when doing a big saga was Charles Dickens. Most of his novels were written in one-chapter segments from the newspaper, so that's why they have that big serialized feel to them. He never knew quite where they were going. He was just writing them one chapter at a time. We're doing obviously a very similar thing here, so the art of the coincidence becomes a big part of the show, how people cross, how people's lives come together, and it's a very fun way to tell stories.

BORROWING/STEALING

Immature poets imitate; mature poets steal; bad poets deface what they take, and good poets make it into something better, or at least something different.
— T.S. Eliot, *The Sacred Wood*

Did I miss something I should have stolen? Did I steal something and don't know I did?
— Tim Kring (responding to Damon Lindelof's question if he has read J. Michael Straczynski's *Rising Stars*)

One of the subjects discussed on "The Walk" was the issue of plagiarism. "Very early on in the process," Kring recalls, he "told [Jeph Loeb] I was not well versed in this world and wanted him to steer me away from anything that was derivative or just out and out stealing." To his dismay, he learned that all his ideas for *Heroes* "had not only been done once, but many times in many ways" and was forced to conclude that he "couldn't touch this subject without reinventing the wheel at best, and outright plagiarism at worst." Seeking to avoid the charge of what is sometimes now called "kleptonesia" — unconscious borrowing/pinching, especially of creative products, Kring believed that the only way to a clear conscience was to avoid all reading, all exposure to possible influences, or, as Jeph Loeb put it, "It was better for [Kring] to be able to get out the story that he had locked up inside of him than to have somebody preempt that by saying that it's just like this or just like that."

Such precautions have not, of course, prevented charges of thievery being leveled against *Heroes*. As we discuss in Chapter 3: "Empowering *Heroes*," *X-Men* fans seem especially unhappy with what they take to be theft of some of their favorite characters, motifs, themes, and superpowers. Prior to the airing of "Five Years Gone," David Kushner would predict "the real fanboy money shot will be the episode's extended allusion to the 'Days of Future Past' story line from *X-Men* issues 141 and 142," but, in fact, that was the episode that would raise the loudest cries of plagiarism from the offended.

Such charges are not unique to *Heroes*, of course. Quentin Tarantino, to cite but one example, has been accused of ripping off virtually everything from substance to style in movies such as *Reservoir Dogs*, said, with some justification, to be a clone of/graft from Ringo Lam's *Ring of Fire*. In the postmodern era, described by the critic Umberto Eco as the age of the "already said," it's not at all easy to identify where homage ends and pilfering begins.

In a scene in *Saturday Night Fever* — a film directed by John Badham, who also did two episodes of *Heroes* ("Fallout," "The Hard Part") — Tony Manero (John Travolta) demonstrates a disco move for his dance partner in the upcoming big contest. In admiration, she asks, "Did you make that up?" and Tony replies, "Yeah. Well, I saw it on TV, and then I made it up." Is Tony's response pure BS or genius?

Or, to quote considerably further up the cultural food chain, recall the remark/rationalization of Russian composer Igor Stravinsky, or was it Spanish/French painter Pablo Picasso, or American/British poet T.S. Eliot (ironic, isn't it, that we are not certain which certifiable genius should be credited with the insight?): bad artists borrow; great artists steal.

As we saw earlier, Kring's viewing of *The Incredibles*, in part a story of superheroes trying (not very successfully) to be ordinary human beings, was a significant moment in *Heroes'* creation myth. But Kring's indebtedness doesn't end there. Remember Syndrome, *The Incredibles'* bad guy, a geeky kid who desperately wants to be a hero, even going so far as stealing the powers of other supes and creating elaborately orchestrated scenarios in which he can pretend to be heroic? Though he slices open no skulls, eats no brains, and does not count cockroaches as his familiars, could not Syndrome be considered a kind of prototype for Sylar? Why is Pixar not lining up to sue Kring, *Heroes*, and NBC or at least complain? Why is the *X-Men*'s maker, the legendary Stan Lee, apparently not offended or ready to litigate, happy to do a cameo as Hiro's Greyhound Bus driver in "Unexpected"? Is it not because they recognize that, though *Heroes* may well have been "seen on TV" (and at the movies, and in the comic pages), it was also "made up," that is to say, fully imagined/re-imagined/born-again? It's really a question of "generations."

LESSONS LEARNED

If I have seen further it is by standing on the shoulders of Giants.

— Sir Isaac Newton

I'm sort of a student of television.

— Tim Kring

When the great British astronomer penned the words above in a letter to Robert Hooke only five years after Hiro Nakamura found himself in the middle of clashing samurai in a field outside Kyoto, Japan, he certainly did not have the creation of television in mind. The metaphor is relevant nonetheless. Successful television creators learn from the giant successes (and great failures) that came before. For example, virtually everyone now working in series TV cites that splendid aberration

Twin Peaks as both a model of breaking the mold and an abject lesson in how to turn success into failure.

The X-Files was yet another giant. Although Chris Carter's series had itself learned from *Twin Peaks* not to put all its eggs in one basket, dividing its episodic attention between monster-of-the-week tales and exploration of a dizzyingly complex overarching "mythology" concerning an alien invasion of Earth, its commitment to the latter proved to be constraining. "[T]he people that I know who wrote on *The X-Files*," Kring would tell Josh Weiland, "talked about how decisions were made based on committing to mythology that they probably shouldn't have." The downside of such an obligation is as much practical as metaphysical. Ever mindful from long experience that "twenty-two hours of television a year is a very, very large monster that needs to be fed," Kring admits that even on his own *Crossing Jordan,* a series with only a limited mythology (concerning Jordan Cavanaugh's search for her mother's killer), "knowing where it went, we ate through too much story too quickly" and is anxious to avoid such possible burnout on *Heroes.*

For Kring (as we show in the previous chapter, "Are These *Heroes Lost?*"), the most important giant on whose shoulders he sought to climb is *Lost.* In a revealing interview with its co-creator and co-showrunner, Kring acknowledges that "I have gotten this question [about the similarities between *Lost* and *Heroes*] many times already and the simple answer is that I fully embrace the comparisons and look at it only as a positive." But he does recognize that "a big complaint for *Lost* . . . was that you had to wade through too many shows before something happened." Lesson learned: don't get too "wrapped up in" or "[sink] too deeply into" a "meandering" mythology. In wrapping up its first chapter/arc in one self-contained season, while nevertheless introducing its next installment, Kring declared his allegiance (consciously or not) to another television giant: *Buffy the Vampire Slayer,* a series that devoted each and every one of its seven seasons to a different "Big Bad" and basically disavowed cliffhangers.[6]

"We have a general idea of where the story is going for a few years,"

Kring acknowledges, but he has designed his show to be "the kind of thing that can keep spinning and spinning. There is not an island to get off of or a time frame where the world ends." As he put it at the Paley Festival: "There is a sense that you can jump on or jump off if you want after you've seen one of these closed-ended stories. There are obviously continuing characters and continuing ideas and continuing stories, but a central theme and a central idea and a central storyline will be wrapped up within the course of each one of these."

A second lesson learned involved the role of the Internet in fostering fan interest and augmenting the narrative. Fox's attempt to shut down *X-Files* Web sites[7] now seems so last century. *Lost's* approach — developing Web sites (like The Fuselage) allowing fans access to the show's creators, offering a Web-based ARG (alternate reality game) such as *The Lost Experience* that supplies beyond-broadcast knowledge of *Lost's* characters and mythology, podcasting — has been an inspiration for "student of television" Kring and *Heroes*. "It doesn't take a genius to figure out that things are changing quickly," Kring told David Kushner. "Production costs are going up. We're losing eyeballs. We have to reach people in other ways. . . . When I pitched *Heroes*, I knew an important element to getting on air was how it can incorporate the Internet," he says. (See Chapter 3: "Empowering *Heroes*" for more on the series' use of the Web.)

GOOD MOVES

Successful television series almost always make fortunate choices and good moves in casting, story arcs, and long-term strategies. Rather than kill off the vampire Spike in season 2, *Buffy the Vampire Slayer* allowed him to grow and develop over five seasons in which he would become one of the series' (and television's) great creations. Although Kring and the *Heroes* team do admit to a false step or two[8] and received more than a few harsh reviews for the season finale (see Chapter 10: "Finale Face-off"), they consistently made good moves before and during season 1.

For example, the character of Hiro was a last-minute addition to the game plan, a response to feedback that the story needed lightening a bit. Good move! Kring had initially conceived of the telepathic cop Matt Parkman as a kind of Matt Dillon–type (no doubt having Oscar-winning *Crash* [2004] in mind), but Greg Grunberg's audition prompted a reconceptualization, as Kring tells Edward Douglas: "Suddenly, I saw him as an Everyman, and realized that his home life was going to be way more important to a guy like Greg." Instead of being a drug addict, Isaac Mendez was to have been a (literally) wounded artist who had cut off his hands! And father and son Suresh were one and the same: the idea of a son inheriting his murdered father's quest had not yet been hatched. All good moves. Mr. Bennet, a.k.a. HRG, was to be a second-tier figure, not the major redemptive character he would become. His expanded role and his metamorphosis are both "a testament to Jack [Coleman]," Kring recalls.

In an end-of-the-season wrap interview with Comic Book Resources, Kring calls special attention to a redirection that, in hindsight, might well have saved the series. As originally conceived, season 1 was to have had terrorism at its core.

> The bomb that ultimately goes off or is prevented from going off in New York was actually attached to a terrorist story and at the heart of that terrorist story was a very sympathetic character, a Middle Eastern engineer. A young, very brilliant engineer who had become disillusioned and disenfranchised and finds himself involved with a terrorist cell and is basically the architect of the bomb. That character could actually generate and emit a tremendous amount of radioactivity through his hands. That character became Ted on our show once we moved away from the terrorist story. The terrorist story was actually shot and beautifully finished, but it never saw the light of day. It didn't make it past the screening at the network.

Kring admits to being "relieved" the arc "went away." If *Heroes* had gone down this road, fans might well have been fantasizing a crossover with Monday-night competitor *24* and a visit from Jack Bauer with his own methods for stopping an exploding man.

FUTURE CHOICES

As we have seen, Kring and company learned a great deal from the history of prior serial television, and they made consistently sound choices in casting and narrative development. Will their choices concerning the series' future development be equally beneficial? On the set during the filming of the final episodes of season 1, Jeff Jensen would report that "Lessons have been learned, adjustments are being made." Spurred by a desire to "mix it up" and offer a narrative less like a runaway "freight train," Kring would speak of a desire in the future to "tell different kinds of stories." "Company Man's" HRG-centric episode was mentioned as a model.

The pressure, however, will no doubt be on, greatly compounded because of *Heroes*' status as one of NBC's few cash cows. Looking back, Kring recalls having nothing to lose during *Heroes*' birth process — didn't he already have a successful show, *Crossing Jordan*, on air? He found the position liberating. Now, however, he has become much more than just a writer-creator: "A modern TV creator like Kring," David Kushner notes, "can't think about just the next episode. He has to think about a world audience and plan several seasons out," as he becomes someone "managing a brand." Jensen reports that Kring — "both very practical and very ambitious" — is up for the challenge: "He's jazzed by the prospect that *Heroes* can be not just a TV show, but a boundless, viral form of entertainment."

EMPOWERING HEROES: MARKETING THE SERIES

NBC'S 2006 ABBREVIATED SUMMER season became more "Must Miss TV" than its touted "Must See" promotions. It was comprised of less-than-titillating reality game shows featuring contestants attempting to lose weight, becoming comic stand-up stars, or making or breaking deals with Howie Mandel. After a less-than-ideal 2005–06 regular prime-time season marred by failed freshman series and a slump in viewership, NBC had reached a point where a complete metamorphosis was necessary in order to survive.

The first step in revamping and revitalizing the once number-one Peacock Network's struggling line of programming was to enhance viewer interactivity, primarily through integrated, enhanced Web content. The network revised the Web content for existing shows, creating a flashier, more user-friendly network presence on the Internet. The largely successful half-hour comedy series *The Office* first received the interactive treatment with a series of summer "Webisodes" — Internet-only mini-episodes that featured secondary characters investigating a missing $3,000. The Webisodes were a major hit that helped make the third season launch of *The Office* even more popular.

For the freshman series of 2006–07, the call to interactivity meant providing audiences with a wealth of amusing, innovative Web content to inspire sustained viewership once the fall prime-time season launched. NBC's shining example of what could become possible with the right marketing strategy became clear when *Heroes* was unveiled at the 2006–07 network upfronts.

THE UPFRONTS AND INITIAL ADVERTISING

Every season, the prime-time major network players — ABC, NBC, CBS, FOX, and the CW — present their renewed series and the pilots picked up for prime-time launch at a press-filled event known as the "upfronts." After renewing tried-and-true rating winners (*ER*, the *Law and Order* franchise, *My Name Is Earl*, and *Medium*) and offering another chance to some not-so-stellar performers (*Scrubs*, *The Apprentice*, Tim Kring's *Crossing Jordan*), the Peacock Network announced eleven new series. One of those was *Heroes*.

Following the upfronts, networks begin a hectic schedule of fall promotions intended to hook a prospective viewing audience before the season even starts. Starting in May 2006, advertisements for new series flooded NBC, and one of the most highly promoted was *Heroes*. The long (by modern standards) forty-five to sixty-second television ads piqued audience interest with the first of a season filled with taglines: "They thought they were like everyone else . . . until they woke with incredible powers."

Initial promotional advertisements for *Heroes* were unique: they presented a cinematic approach as opposed to traditional television promos. They shied away from offering standard pilot-episode advertisements that present the basic premise, main characters, and plot in an easy-to-digest, thirty-second spot. *Heroes* characters were not introduced by name but by extraordinary power. Hiro was a Japanese office worker who could "teleport at will"; Isaac, an artist capable of painting the future; Matt Parkman, a "discontented [telepathic] beat cop." The preseason promotional materials' tone, lighting, and dramatic effect situated *Heroes* as a dark thriller with a mysterious interconnectivity between characters, a series asking a larger question of what could make a person a "hero" . . . and why.

At the same time, NBC launched *Heroes'* official Web site (www.nbc.com/heroes). The basic black background incorporates the trademark image of a total solar eclipse complemented by a subdued color scheme that gives a modern, yet mildly creepy, feeling to the site. In addition to serving as one of the first advertisements for the series, the Web site, in its early incarnation, also announced important news of the *Heroes'* presence at Comic-Con.

COMIC-CON 2006

Comic-Con International is an annual July meeting held at the San Diego Convention Center. The convention started during the 1970s as a showcase for American comic books, their creators, and fans but later expanded to other areas of attendee interest, including Japanese manga and anime. Today's Comic-Con is the ultimate fan experience, with exhibitions from a variety of genres, including future film and television releases. Comic-Con International is the largest event of its kind in North America, and the 2006 meeting featured more than six hundred hours of programming "on all aspects of comic books and pop culture, including breaking into the comic book business, film-making seminars, movies, interactive multimedia, and Japanese Animation."

NBC embraced the branding and marketing potential of *Heroes'* debut at the annual convention, wisely supposing that the right type of audience would attend. After all, competing networks had witnessed amazing successes after introducing new series such as *Lost* there, which became a major ABC hit. NBC made a wise decision in debuting *Heroes* at Comic-Con: the 2006 convention brought in 123,000 attendees and positioned *Heroes* amidst such stellar company as author Ray Bradbury, graphic novel genius Frank Miller, and *The Simpsons'* Matt Groening.

Comic-Con may have been a risk for NBC, but it proved a wildly successful gamble. From the opening day of the convention, NBC advertised the *Heroes* exposition with an issue of the *9th Wonders* graphic novel. On the day of the exposition, more than two thousand attendees waited in line as network reps passed out buttons advertising the *9th Wonders* Web site or featuring the likenesses of cast members.

An "official/unofficial" fan site run by the series' creative team, *9th Wonders* (www.9thwonders.com) features a comic book design with news, interviews, and discussion about the series. (*9th Wonders* is discussed in greater detail later in this chapter.) Staff members revealed to the eager prospective fans that the site had not only a wealth of insider information about the series but also officially sponsored flash videos, issues of the graphic novel, and a complex series of hidden information — Easter Eggs — that would enhance their viewing experience.

Kring never expected to fill the ballroom scheduled for the *Heroes* presentation and was surprised by the two thousand lucky viewers who crammed inside the room. Kring later noted: "We had no idea that there would be the kind of reception awaiting us when we walked in. It was pretty startling to see the reaction." The audience watched an advance screening of the seventy-two-minute pilot, then entitled "In His Own Image," without commercial interruption and were treated to a question-and-answer session with the creative team, cast, and producers. During the session, the team stressed they expected attendees would help to promote the series by telling their friends, family, colleagues — anyone who would listen — about *Heroes*.

Word of mouth, or viral, marketing has become a mainstay for the success of contemporary television series largely due to the Internet. The capacity for global communication at superfast speeds means that promising news of a forthcoming series can help to launch a relative unknown into the spotlight, and NBC's combined promotional efforts worked: ten million viewers would tune in to the pilot's on-air debut.

Almost overnight, *Heroes* was being touted as a success. The ratings were impressive, the viewers avid, and the official sites witnessed a jump in Internet traffic. But holding on to that success would require quite a bit of continued effort from the creative staff, the network, and the cast of *Heroes* that relied on keeping an increasingly fickle modern audience entertained through interaction and engagement with the show.

KRING'S THEORY OF "SECRETS"

Today's prime-time audience is not the same as it was even a decade ago. The modern audience has come to *expect* glossy, high-quality print advertisements, catchy marketing themes, and state-of-the-art audio and visual presentation of each new episode. Viewers don't tolerate sub-par acting or storytelling, and they demand characters they can engage with, believe in, root for, empathize with. Today's audience desires a film-quality hour of television week after week, and if they're disappointed in the end product, their loyalty wanes.

Tim Kring knows about nurturing an audience by meeting — and exceeding — expectations. It's not about rewarding the audience with little "reveals" each week; it's about keeping them entertained by generating many secrets that build and are answered within an acceptable time frame. The key is not giving the audience the opportunity to be disappointed. During an interview after the first season was three-fourths of the way complete, Kring revealed a primary goal: "One of the things that became important for us is this idea of revealing secrets. One of the main differences between *Heroes* and other shows is there's no one secret that is precious enough not to reveal."

As we have noted, one of Kring's closest friends and collaborators on *Crossing Jordan* was rival network ABC's Damon Lindelof of *Lost*, a series that has suffered drops in viewership and complaints from fans and critics alike about the slow pace of the narrative and the tease-and-tell nature of the island's secrets. While Lindelof and Kring share a healthy respect for each other, Kring is careful not to fall into the same

Bermuda Triangle of viewer dissatisfaction by baiting his audience with the promise of secrets that prove disappointing when finally exposed.

CONCEPTUALIZING *HEROES*

Heroes rivals its competition with an innovative narrative that other series lack, beginning with visual composition. The bold blend of vibrant primary colors and the ominous use of blue-gray shadows helps to create and sustain a feel of anxiety. The in-frame use of episode titles and the chapter story format allow viewers to get on the same page as the characters. Even English subtitles of Hiro's and Ando's Japanese conversations reflect true characterization, complete with italics for emphasis. These elements challenge the audience's traditional expectations of what television is supposed to be. But innovation alone cannot keep a series franchise afloat. It takes the dedication of the creative staff and network to keep the audience entertained.

Keeping an audience entertained means constant reinvention, which Kring and his team navigate by the introduction of new characters. The ten core characters grew in depth and complexity during the first season, and the second season promises the introduction of new heroes — good and bad — that guarantee to keep the audience's attention. The release of the season 1 DVD also promises to fuel viewer excitement by providing high definition DVD content, integrating missing scenes, and recutting the story into individual character arcs to give fans a new way of looking at the story.

ACCESSIBILITY AND ENGAGEMENT

The official NBC *Heroes* site (www.nbc.com/heroes) allows viewers the chance to do what few other television shows do — truly access the series and feel connected. While new episodes air, fans can take polls and participate in content-based quizzes. When the episode is complete, post-episode rundowns by the creative team and cast are offered in online chat forums. The *9th Wonders* Web site promises a "direct connection" to the show, most of which is conducted through message board forums regularly updated and visited by key cast members and the creative team. During the summer hiatus following the season 1 finale, fans were treated to "Inside Heroes": a "series [that] will take fans through visual effects, music, wardrobe, stunts, make-up effects, artwork, and even the catering and create the feeling of being there with the people who make it all happen."

This sense of connectedness is assisted by the efforts of creator Kring, who invests in the series' success by maintaining a sense of approachability. Through live blogs, a presence on the *9th Wonders* message boards, and a genuine warmth reflected in his interviews, fans feel as if they know Kring. At the close of season 1, following a live blogging session with actress Hayden Panettiere, Kring demonstrated the humble nature fans had grown to love: "The fans have been *so* amazing this year, and we owe everything to all of you out there. We hope you'll stay with us for many years here, as we take these characters on incredible adventures."

Fan engagement has been a huge part of the success of *Heroes*, falling in line with NBC's broad goal of creating an interactive space for the audience. The primary avenue for audience engagement has been, by far, the Internet. Throughout season 1, the official site enhanced and built upon its content and currently offers viewers the opportunity to watch each episode with limited commercial interruption and cast commentary, a comprehensive character guide, episode recaps, interviews with cast and crew, message boards, and photo galleries. This content, while extensive, is standard fare — the *Heroes* official site shines with enhanced content: *Heroes 360*, the graphic novels, and games.

HEROES 360

Beginning in January 2007, *Heroes 360*, an integrated mobile phone and Web promotional platform, was launched to enhance viewer access and engagement with the *Heroes* text. It offered information unavailable through other media and enticed hardcore fans to participate. NBC's pitch (on the official Web site) was this: "Each week, immerse yourself in the *Heroes 360* Experience where you become part of this season's biggest hit. Through original content created specifically for TV, online, and mobile, the *Heroes 360* Experience lets you explore, interact, and discover exciting new characters, sneak peaks, new and expanded storylines and much more." The *Heroes 360* experience offers both supplemental materials that enhance viewer enjoyment (Hiro's blog, the interactive "Hero" map, the Yamagato Fellowship Web site, the abilities quiz) and the *Heroes 360* alternate reality game (ARG), a real-time supplement that provides intriguing Easter eggs that ultimately don't impact the overall televisual story. ARGS enhance viewer enjoyment and increase fan interactivity and engagement with the show. The *Heroes 360* ARG creates three levels of players based on their responses to the Primatech Paper hiring game that interviewed text-messaging or call-in respondents about their eligibility to be managers.

SO YOU WANT TO WORK FOR PRIMATECH?
Introduced in "Godsend" when Mohinder receives a business card from Mr. Bennet, the Primatech Paper Web site (www.primatechpaper.com) encourages its visitors to subscribe to text-message feeds, apply for a job in management, or call the toll free 1-800-PRIMAI6 for more information. The main function of the Primatech Paper site was to separate the ARG players into three categories: Type One (similar to those in "management," such as Mr. Bennet), Type Two (investigative, similar to Suresh), and Type Three (a conformist type). The categories create a system to disseminate information to distinct groups, thus making the game far more complex and interactive. Different levels of players brought the game to life, without redundancies in the material. The process also formed a social hierarchy of game players based on the type of information being received.

Following "Godsend" and the opportunity to fill out an employment application, game players received an e-mail informing them of their hiring status at the end of January 2007. Type One and Two applicants were informed that the company was interested in hiring them. Type Three applicants were told that they did not qualify at that time. All three were invited to continue to receive SMS (text) messages for updates about Primatech Paper but received a different text-back response based on their category.

The Primatech Paper campaign was an important test for the interactivity that had become such an important component of the 2006–07 programming schedule, and NBC passed with flying colors. Through the positive viewer response, the network was made aware of *Heroes* fans' commitment to, and interest in, the series as a whole.

HANA GITTELMAN

Though she makes few appearances in season 1, Hana Gittelman is the subject of several graphic novels and an important figure in the ARG, providing hack codes and secret information to the players, including how to access hidden files on the Primatech Paper Web site and find Web sites in the game. Hana's primary goal is to bring down The Company and expose its secrets.

Hana's involvement in the game coincided with the Primatech Paper Web site launch in January 2007, following *Heroes'* midseason hiatus. Through text messages, Hana provides players with access to her blog, hosted at www.samantha48616e61.com, and to other Web sites as well, including www.activatingevolution.org, which provides insider-track information about the Suresh family's research in genetics and evolved human abilities.

By the close of season 1, Hana had helped to reveal that the man we once knew as "HRG," Mr. Bennet, was not (as we were once led to believe) evil, hacked into Linderman's computer systems on multiple occasions, and concluded the season with news she would be shot into space . . . for the good of all humankind, of course.

Hana's role in the ARG is significant; she is not only a part of the *Heroes* narrative fabric, she also serves as the common person that players use as a means for making connections and inferences, thus influencing the overall continuity of the gameplay.

VOTE PETRELLI

In April 2007, during the airing of "0.7%," NBC prompted viewers to "Text Nathan" at "466-22," which accessed the Petrelli campaign and provided a link to the mobile access site at mobi.votepetrelli.com. In May, players received an inspirational phone call from Nathan Petrelli, encouraging them to support his run for office: "Hi. This is Nathan Petrelli, and I'm running for Congress. You know, I believe our children deserve a better future. A future where they can look into the darkness and find hope. Help me build this brighter future. Let's do it together. Let's show them all exactly what we're capable of. For more information about my campaign, please visit votepetrelli.com. And again, thank you for your time."

This campaign served a role similar to Primatech, inciting viewer interest and adding a depth to the ARG gameplay by allowing true interactivity between the fans and a character from the series, thus giving the sense that what was happening onscreen was all the more real. This blurring of realities helped to deepen the intensity of viewer engagement and kept the audience invested for the closing episodes of the first season.

THE GRAPHIC NOVELS

Comic books have always played an important part in *Heroes*, beginning with the May 2006 upfronts when Kring commissioned comic artist Tim Sale to create two comic book narratives based on Claire and Hiro. These comics were combined in a flash animation known as "Claire and the Cat" and marked the first edition of comic book storytelling for *Heroes*. The comic was available online through Tim Sale's Web site (www.TimSale1.com) and the official NBC site (but has since been removed). It showcases Claire's regenerative power and Hiro's ability to manipulate time; the raw images were later incorporated into the 9th *Wonders* comic distributed at Comic-Con. The 9th *Wonders* comic, drawn in the series by Isaac, performed a crucial function in augmenting *Heroes'* diegetic narrative. The red/green colorblind Sale created all of Isaac's paintings in black and white, after which they were digitally colored. He also contributed twenty "Isaac" panel prints and thirty comic book panels and created the brush font for *Heroes* (the "Tim Sale Brush Font") for season 1.

The extradiegetic comics — the graphic novels released weekly on the official Web site — continue to provide a means by which fans engage with the series even during hiatuses. They are often used to introduce new heroes or expand on the pasts of others we know, including Hana Gittelman, the Haitian, and Hiro. NBC provides the comic in online form as PDF downloads or through online viewers, and many novels have multiple volumes.

HEROIC FRUITS OF LABOR: THE *HEROES* FANDOM

Following the season 1 finale, *Heroes the Series* fansite owner, Sam, and Dave Deas, owner of the fansite *The Organization Without Initials*, or *OWI*, agreed to an interview about their involvement with the show's fandom. The owners also graciously provided their visitors with a link to an online survey about *Heroes*. Thanks to their help, 447 total respondents took the fan survey, and from those respondents, a total of 403 were used to reflect the innermost thoughts, passions, and interests of the average *Heroes* fan. Respondents were limited to individuals aged thirteen and older that had seen the entire first season.

Sam launched the *Heroes the Series* site in May 2006, six months before the first episode aired. The site is the earliest fansite and the most visited by fans — Sam receives hundreds of thousands of unique visitors after a new episode airs, and averages in the upper thousands during the breaks in between episodes and seasons. When asked about the motivations for the hard work and personal costs associated with running a fansite, Sam explains, "HeroesTheSeries. com is never a chore for me, because I love the show and I love talking, writing, and reporting on it. Basically, that's why I started the site in the first place. The premise sounded so cool to me, and I knew I'd instantly love it. And I was right."

Similarly, Dave Deas of the fansite *The Organization Without Initials*, which launched during the winter hiatus of season 1 in December 2006, is a fan who regularly posted to the official NBC message boards for *Heroes* and penned one of the most popular theories about the show — the "Unified Theory," viewed nearly a million times at the time of writing this chapter. When the message boards became too crowded with discussion about relationship pairings and other idle chatter, Deas created his own site for fans to visit and discuss their favorite show. Deas says, "From the start, I wanted my site to be different than the other 'news/fan' sites. I wanted my viewers to get much more of an 'experience' and to have a chance to contribute in either artwork or writing. Almost all of my content is fan submitted. I am constantly trying new contests and e-mails with that viral and authentic feel."

Deas explains that the fans constitute a special family — like his unified theory of interconnectedness among the fictional heroes, there's an interconnectedness among fans. When Deas suffered financial hardships, visitors of his site reached out and offered their support with such overwhelming generosity that Deas is still awed by "the help that came to me. People kept telling me that myself [sic] and the site had given them something to latch on to . . . to give them a place to be themselves."

So, who are the members of this family? The average fan of *Heroes*, during the first season, was under age thirty-four and enrolled in college or high school. There are more males (58 percent) than females, and most fans (91 percent) learned of *Heroes* from an official sanctioned promotion — such as a television, radio, or print advertisement. Nearly three-fourths watched the show whenever it aired on television. Fans also said they often watched the show online at the official Web site or that they record the episode to watch later. About half of the fans read the graphic novels posted online, either by reading them on the screen or downloading and printing them.

A favored pastime of *Heroes* fans is telling other fans about the show: 95 percent of our survey participants said they had told another person about the series and enjoyed activities that supported talking about the show, such as visiting message boards and blogs and leaving comments. These activities help to support an already thriving *Heroes* community and help to further the community's success as a whole. Our survey participants were also very Internet savvy: on top of visiting the official site (which a whopping 96 percent had done), searching the Net for news and information about the show, creating their own blogs, fansites, or other online presence, and communicating with others online was a huge component of fan activity. Fans also liked to listen to official podcasts and even made their own podcasts, wrote their own episode reviews, or blogged about the series.

While scouring the Web for news about the series, 80 percent of fans participating in the survey admitted to reading spoilers online. All this searching took time — a lot of time: fans averaged around 10 hours a week searching for *Heroes* content online, discussing the show, or rewatching episodes. Other fans admitted to spending as many as eighty hours a week on their favorite series, and 25 percent spent between fifteen and thirty hours a week on the show!

Heroes' fans are devoted — a clear majority (79 percent) indicated that they plan to purchase the season 1 DVDs, and 100 percent affirmed that they would be glued to the television set for season 2. But why are these fans so invested? Most said it was the characters: the diverse array of individuals helped them to find someone to identify with. Others claimed the ingenious marketing, from the catchy slogans to the innovative viral techniques, kept them interested. When offered the opportunity to give free-response answers to why they liked *Heroes* so much, most said that the series characters and storylines are what keeps them wanting more.

Some fans were critical of the season 1 finale, only 48 percent claimed to love the episode, the others fell somewhere in the middle, and a clear 10 percent simply did not like it at all. The main problem? Fans argued that the finale was too simplistic and anticlimactic. Many fans cited the showdown between Peter and Sylar as disappointing — they wanted more. Yet most of the fans were forgiving: while they may have wanted a bit more action, one fan explains that "the finale accomplished its purpose: it convincingly brought all the heroes together, wrapped up all the loose ends of the first season story, and still left plenty of open possibilities for next season."

With season 2 ripe with possibilities, NBC is charged with keeping the fanbase happy — a goal it will attempt to achieve by fueling interest through the introduction of new characters in the spin-off *Heroes: Origins*, a longer schedule of thirty episodes, and the continuation of weekly installments of the graphic novels. As *Heroes* embarks on its journey of season 2, a sea of eager fans wait and expect excellence. If season 1 is any indication, they need not be worried.

COMIC BOOK HEROES

CO-AUTHORED BY SEAN HOCKETT

Comic books have become reference points in the most popular and the most esoteric fiction and art. Everyone understands a Superman allusion or a Batman joke. . . . The critics,
teachers, philanthropists, and religious leaders who once
denounced comic books as a national disgrace have embraced
them. . . . Nothing has tested or proven or forced the fluidity
of contemporary arts like comic book superheroes.
    — Gerard Jones, *Men of Tomorrow: Geeks, Gangsters,*
                    and the Birth of the Comic Book

THE "GONIFFS, SHMENDRICKS, AND SHLEMIELS" who gave birth
to the comic book,[1] that "cultural form," in the words of Gerard Jones,
"that came like a revelation to kids of every class and ethnicity, that
would evolve to become part of adolescent and adult fantasy," certainly could not have anticipated that their creation "would outlast its
initial fad of sixty years and set an entertainment norm in an era vastly
different from the one that spawned it." *Heroes* — the most indebted-
to-the-comic-book-aesthetic American television program ever — is,
of course, the latest manifestation of that form.

COMIC COLLABORATORS

As we discussed in "The Creation of *Heroes*," Tim Kring may well be an unlikely comic book television mastermind. Jeph Loeb recalls, for example, a revealing moment on their walk when he first realized his friend's ignorance about the form in which he wanted to work:

> Tim had absolutely no knowledge of comic books. My favorite moment was when he talked about how one of the characters would have the powers of a magnet and could lift up a car with a wave of his hand and throw it. I said, "That's Magneto," and Tim's reaction was that he didn't know whether "Magneto" was a person or a power.

Consequently, as *Wired*'s profile of Kring suggests, *Heroes* had to be "reverse engineered."[2] Its comic-book-ishness had to be layered on top of a character-based foundation, and Kring's ignorance was actually essential to this process, as Masi Oka (Hiro) observed:

> [Tim Kring's] a great barometer for people who are not into comics. . . . If Tim understands it, the whole world will. The writers might geek out and come up with some time-travel-ing, mind-bending fifth-dimensional thing. Tim says, "Whoa, what does that *mean*?"

The people with whom Kring surrounded himself, however, and Loeb in particular, definitely have their comic credentials in order.

In an interview with www.9thwonders.com, *Heroes*' own "official unofficial" Web site, we nevertheless find Loeb discounting his own qualifications and commending his collaborators' comic chops:

> . . . between Jesse Alexander, Aron Coleite, Joe Pokaski, Michael Green — and guys like Harrison Wilcox and Oliver Grigsby working in the writing office, I'm just another geek

with a lame excuse on Wednesdays to sneak out of the office
to buy new comics!

Fans of television series such as *Alias* (Alexander), *Lost* (Alexander),
Crossing Jordan (Coleite, Pokaski), or *Smallville* (Green, Loeb) may recognize some of these names. Scratch below the surface and we find
that Coleite, Loeb, and Chuck Kim (not yet working for *Heroes* at the
time of the interview quoted above) are likewise involved in comic
books at more than just a fan level.

Coleite, for example, wrote the 2006 graphic novel *The Covenant*,
prequel to the film of the same name released in the same year: the
story of young men coming to terms with newfound powers that
passed from father to son through the generations. Sound familiar?
Kim (".07%" was his first television script), who joined the team
through his friendship with artist Tim Sale (see below), came to the
show with extensive experience as a comic book writer for both
Marvel and DC, contributing to *Justice League Showcase Giant*,
Superman, *Dexter's Lab*, and *Powerpuff Girls*. Not surprisingly, Coleite
(author/co-author of twelve to date) and Kim (author of two) have both
contributed to *Heroes*' online graphic novels, but other staff writers
like Alexander (four) and Joe Pokaski (ten), with no prior experience
as comic scribes, have also written/co-written *Heroes* graphics. (For
more on the graphic novels, see Chapter 3: "Empowering *Heroes*" and
Chapter 9: "The *Heroes* Kaleidoscope.")

And Loeb, of course, has authored a wide variety of popular
comics over the past ten years. From *Batman: The Long Halloween* (a
thirteen-issue stand-alone series published monthly by DC Comics in
1996 and 1997), to *Superman/Batman Public Enemies* (a six-issue
mini-series published in 2003) to *Spider-Man: Blue* (another six-issue,
self-contained story, published by Marvel Comics in 2002 and 2003)
Loeb has plied his trade with the two biggest comic book publishers
in the world and written for not only these superheroes but
Challengers of the Unknown, Daredevil, and Hulk as well. As if this

were not confirmation enough, Loeb served for a time as supervising producer for *Smallville*, the "no tights/no flights" series about the early years of one Clark Kent. Like the DNA of many of its protagonists, *Heroes'* own is thus suffused with comic book heritage and inflection.

Even Masi Oka, the former Industrial Light and Magic software engineer, who admits to trying to smuggle "geeky references" into his performance, might be considered a comic collaborator. He told *Wired* his portrayal of the full of wonder and exuberance teleporter is based on a *Dragonball* anime role model, and hopes the writers will include more references to manga.

If Tim Kring, the comic book novice, remains the primary instigator of *Heroes'* comic book aesthetic and ethos, and Loeb, the comic book veteran, his chief informant, the impact of another Tim (Tim Sale) can scarcely be overestimated. A "Marvel zombie" as a boy who has grown up to become a prolific comic artist and frequent Loeb collaborator (it was Loeb, in fact, who served as matchmaker between his old friend Kring and the artist), Sale has worked on *Heroes* since the pilot. Sale has compared his work to that of the real cops brought in to coach the character of Detective Sipowicz (Dennis Franz) on *NYPD Blue*, and admits that his involvement as a full-time comic book artist has been limited primarily to working with the props department.

But Sale's contribution is much more tangible than that. Isaac's artwork is his — originally created by Sale as washes on comic book paper, then computer-colored by Dave Stewart and transferred (enlarged as necessary) to canvas. The *9th Wonders* comic books that figure so prominently in the season I narrative are likewise Sale's work (see the discussion below).

Sale acknowledges noirish tendencies, a penchant that has no doubt contributed to the series' tendency to "go dark" (see Steven Peacock's essay on page 141) and which may have more than a little to do with his already mentioned color blindness. Sale's monochrome vision is far from the only influence on Isaac's ominous art: in talking with actor Santiago Cabrera, Sale learned of his love for the Spanish

master Francisco Goya (1746–1828), an artist known for his gruesome, grotesque visions of human depravity, and has tried to
incorporate Goyan touches into his *Heroes* work.

Color blindness is not Sale's only limitation as an artist: by his
own admission, he isn't terribly good at likenesses and can't render
recognizable faces unless working from a photograph. As he tells
Robert Taylor, however, he compensates for this failing by
"Eisnering" — trying to capture mood and theme in the style of the
great comic book artist Will Eisner (1917–2005).

With Isaac now dead, it remains to be seen how much of a hands-
on role Sale will play in subsequent seasons, but his foundational
influence on the basic look of *Heroes* will certainly endure.

FRAMES WITHIN FRAMES: *HEROES* AND COMIC BOOKS AESTHETICS

Not surprisingly, *Heroes* translates some of the distinctive appearance
of the comic book from the page to the small screen. In an interview
with Comic Book Resources before *Heroes'* first episode had aired,
Kring explained his intent to provide shout-outs to comic book fans in
the very look of the series, including graphic novels: "There are certain very wide shots and the 16:9 format we shoot in allows us to have
a frame that sort of pays homage to a lot of comic book angles and
graphic design."

This tendency announces itself in the pilot (directed by David
Semel) and continues throughout season 1. When Mohinder and
Nirand visit his late father's apartment in Madras, the pillar of the stair-
case they climb in the right half of the frame separates them from the
teeming street scene below and to the left, thus creating in effect two
frames. Moments later, an internal shot of the apartment shows
Mohinder approaching Chandra Suresh's wall map from the left and a
mysterious man (Mr. Bennet) on the other side of the wall. Separated
by the wall, and at that point unaware of each other, the two characters exist within the same space but are completely isolated, as if
drawn separately on a page.

We can also see how some character shots approximate the arrangement of the comic book page. Whether it's Mohinder standing in front of a framed atlas of the world, its extremities forming the frame within a frame in which he stands, or Hiro encased within the verticality of the metal tubing of a subway train, the parallels are obvious. We see examples of single character framing when we are introduced to Niki/Jessica Sanders as she lies on her bed, "entertaining" a client, the position of the laptop in the foreground not only creating a frame for her but also showing the character in digital form in a frame on its screen. We are also introduced to Nathan Petrelli as Peter sits in a taxi and his brother's picture on the side of a passing bus is not only within a frame but framed by the window of the taxi.

In another much-remarked-upon deviation from standard television conventions, *Heroes* not only shows us, in-frame, always inventively, and in a font type with definite leanings toward the comic book world, the title of every episode (see the "Episode Title Locator" among the Enhancements at the end of this book), but reminds us — again in-frame at the end of each episode (even the season finale) — that the story is "To Be Continued."

The use of subtitles for the Japanese dialogue of Hiro and Ando likewise affirms *Heroes'* heritage. While many of the subtitles are positioned more conventionally at the bottom of the frame, in some cases the position relative to the character is reminiscent of the comic book speech bubble. In the case of Hiro exclaiming in "Genesis" that he has managed to stop time, if only for one second, we see the words "I did it!" following him as he runs through the cubicles at Yamagato Industries.

When, later in the same episode, he and Ando have been thrown out of the karaoke club after Hiro teleports himself into the ladies restroom, they are shown together, once again in two-shot framing, giving us the opportunity to visualize the position of any relevant speech bubbles through the use of the subtitles.

Even the actors' expressions, a sigh or growl of frustration, sometimes end up in the subtitled dialogue, reminding us of *Batman*'s fight effect of "oofs" and "arghs" in the 1960s' television series, itself a direct link to typical comic book conventions.[3]

COMIC BOOKS IN THE HEROESVERSE

Throughout season 1 of *Heroes*, comic books put in regular and significant appearances. In one sense, these are analogous to creator cameos, akin to Alfred Hitchcock's famous, ingenious stepping-out-from-behind-the-curtain in his films, inspiring a game of "Find the Hitch," or Marvelous Stan Lee's appearances in adaptations of his comic books. Though similarly playful, the role of comic books in *Heroes*' story world is actually of central importance.

When Peter Petrelli tells Isaac Mendez, *9th Wonders*' diegetic creator, that his paintings are "just like a comic book," we smile at the meta-comment, a knowing nod to the behind-the-scenes work of comic artist Tim Sale, their real, extra-diegetic creator.[4] We also chuckle at Hiro's self-referential insistence to Simone ("Godsend") that he is not so round-faced as his comic book likeness.

For some characters, comics are an obsession, while for others they are essential to their destinies. In his first appearance ("Genesis"), technopath Micah Sanders shows himself to be not only a computer whiz but a comic book geek: reading *9th Wonders #13*. Later in the season he will talk comics with his dad ("Better Halves"), agree with D.L. to be Batman and Robin together ("Homecoming"), listen, perplexed as Hiro explains how he actually performed the amazing feats in *9th Wonders #14* (which he has brought back from the future), and be temporarily placated with a stack of comics (including *Silver Surfer #1*) during his kidnapping by Linderman ("Landslide").

In "Don't Look Back," Hiro's discovery of #14 at a Times Square newsstand convinces him he is acting out his fate and, in "One Giant Step," enables him (after he performs the rescue of a young girl from an oncoming truck — just like in the comic) to persuade Ando too.

For Isaac Mendez, *9th Wonders* is not only a means to share his visionary art with a wider world but the very reason he has lived. Having delivered the final issue of his comic to a courier (".07%"), he is able to face his brutal, painful, self-prophesied death at the hands of Sylar with courage, steeled by the knowledge he has "at least . . . done one good thing before I died. I stopped the bomb. I finally get to be a hero."

In a moment very near the end of "Unexpected," Hiro prepares to part company with trusty sidekick Ando, who seeks to dissuade him from his course by reminding him of the destiny laid out for them together in *9th Wonders*. Hiro's response seems heretical to the *Heroes* universe, particularly considering that the episode was written by the series' resident comic genius Jeph Loeb: "Life is not a comic book," Hiro insists. But for Hiro, it is a momentary conviction only, the product of a stage in the hero's quest (described in "The Making of a Hiro" elsewhere in these pages): a customary moment of doubt and regret, but not the last word. As if to remind us that, though indeed life is not a comic book, *Heroes* might well be — an epic version of one, now brought to TV — the door of the Greyhound Bus Hiro is about to board opens to reveal none other than Stan Lee, creator of Spider-Man, the Incredible Hulk, the X-Men, the Fantastic Four . . . in the driver's seat.

HEROES AT GROUND ZERO

The final chapter of Bradford W. Wright's superb *Comic Book Nation: The Transformation of Youth Culture in America* is entitled "Spider-Man at Ground Zero: a 9/11 Postscript." In it, he wrestles with the question of the future of the comic book hero in the aftermath of the destruction of the World Trade Center in New York in 2001 (and in particular the Big Apple's most indigenous superhero). Comic books, Wright observes,

> long ago anticipated the multi-billion dollar fantasy industry now dominated by video games, motion pictures, and television. And unfortunately, that is not all that they predicted.

Countless buildings have been bombed and destroyed in comic books, especially in New York. . . . The real world has once again caught up to that of the comic books. In the most horrible sense, the fantasy of comic book nightmares has become our reality.

Such a recognition still leaves us with very large questions, however:

Can comic books continue to balance escapism and relevance in this frightening post–9/11 world? Will superheroes still hold the power to stir our imaginations and inspire our dreams? I hope so. For we need them now more than ever.

Does not *Heroes* come close, with its first season saga of an exploding human nuke that devastates New York — a 9/11-ish calamity averted thanks to several acts of superheroism — achieve just the equilibrium Wright contemplates? How apropos, then, that its climatic scene transpires not at 9/11's ground zero but in Kirby Plaza, named, of course, for comic book king Jack Kirby (1917–94)?

GROWING PAINS:
HEROES AND THE
QUEST FOR IDENTITY

BEN STRICKLAND

MANY OF THE HEROES CHARACTERS discover their powers and themselves in a fashion reminiscent of Marvel Comics' characters of the 1960s such as Spider-Man and the X-Men. This discovery is primarily an existential process wherein these people, usually young and inexperienced, learn who they are by fumbling about with their abilities. They test their limits, make mistakes, and learn to make good choices that incorporate their humanity along with their metahuman powers. These heroes must learn to be super without losing sight of who they are as human beings.

Before the Marvel model, superheroes tended to belong to the DC Comics mold established in the 1930s. Their heroes, particularly Superman and Batman, tended to be men somewhere in their early thirties with stable jobs and satisfying alternate identities. In essence, they were mature, seasoned professionals, and everything they did worked out well in the end, both for them and law-abiding citizenry everywhere. They were always more than a match for their super-powered foes, and the nearest they came to a real-world worry came in the form of lightly comic romantic misunderstandings — Lois Lane pining away for Superman while a grinning Clark Kent winks just off to the side, for example. By the 1960s, DC had established a canon of virtually indistinguishable superheroes. True enough, this era's Superman, Batman, Hawkman, and the Flash all sported different costumes and boasted different abilities, but underneath all that they were handsome white men who fought crime, respected authority, saved the day, and had a distressing habit of speaking in unindividuated, even interchangeable, dialogue.

In the 1960s, Marvel Comics' Stan Lee confounded these staid, essentially identical archetypal figures with a note of realism. He set his stories in real places, such as New York, instead of a Metropolis, Gotham, or another stand-in for an actual city. Then, to better speak to Marvel's target audience of children and adolescents, Lee pulled his heroes' ages into the late teens and loaded them up with worries that kids could understand. Through Spider-Man/Peter Parker, Lee and artist Steve Ditko give us a superhero with the usual run of super-villains to battle, but with the added burden of mundane problems. Spider-Man not only has to battle the Scorpion and the Green Goblin but must also find time to finish his homework, make dinner, and balance his checkbook.

Similar real-world problems plague the young X-Men, who also have classes to attend; in addition, because their mutant status sets them apart from the rest of humanity, they must learn to cope with discrimination in between exhausting field trips to save the world. The *Heroes* characters are designed to discover themselves after a style that is most reminiscent of these X-Men. As opposed to iconic characters such as Superman, who in the 1930s was simply a visitor from another world ready and able to battle injustice on any front, or Batman, whose story is typically one of steady and methodical self-invention, the *Heroes'* characters owe more to Stan Lee's Marvel. They quit jobs, reassess relationships, and make typically human mistakes on their way toward finding a new purpose as individuals. The old-school Superman somehow always knew how and when to draw upon a particular power from his extensive store of abilities, Batman always happened to have just the right device at hand to address a particular problem, but modern super-heroes labor for society's understanding and acceptance while they learn to cope with their extraordinary growing pains.

Lee made sure that power and virtue did not guarantee an easy life. Peter Parker actually gets tired, but Bruce Wayne never did. Parker's Spider-Man outfit gets dirty and torn, and he complains about the smell if he hasn't had time to do his laundry. Superman always looked pristine. Superman could count on the *Daily Planet* to sing his praises, whereas Spider-Man is forever battling bad press from the *Daily Bugle*. The environment affects Spider-Man and the *Heroes* characters in ways that early Superman's and Batman's never did, and so the modern hero has slipped down from what literary critic Northrop Frye would term the romantic mode into a mimetic mode, one based more on *imitation* of life rather than on *idealization* of life.

LITERARY MODES & THE EVOLUTION OF THE EXISTENTIAL SUPERHERO

Frye splits his hierarchy of literary modes into five parts. At the top there is *myth*, in which the hero is superior in *kind* to others and to the environment and so may be regarded as a divine being. Zeus and early era Superman belong here. Next comes the *romantic* mode (not to be confused with the stuff of love stories), in which the hero is of a kind with others and the environment but is superior in *degree*. This is the place for the bulk of mainstream superheroes who, through the benefit of a superpower, are all able to transcend natural laws such as gravity. Batman and others who have no metahuman abilities are still able to construct and use devices in ways that shape the environment according to their will. Later era Superman has lost much of his quasi-divine status now that he has to contend with kryptonite, which makes his death a possibility.[1]

The next step down brings us to the *high-mimetic* mode, where the hero is superior to others but not the environment and is therefore eminently well suited to leadership. Odysseus belongs here, as do charismatic villains such as Lex Luthor and Captain Ahab. A hero who is on equal standing with others and the environment is "one of us" and occupies the *low-mimetic* mode, that mode which most closely mimics our own experience. This is the realm of Charles Dickens and Art Spiegelman, whose graphic novel *Maus* tells the story of a Holocaust survivor.

The last mode is the *ironic*, in which the audience has a "sense of looking down on a scene of bondage, frustration, or absurdity," such as those scenes in which the characters in Samuel Beckett's *Waiting for Godot* suffer, or when a captured villain takes center stage, as in some of the darker Batman stories centered around the inmates of Arkham Asylum.

These modes tend to overlap: the hero is still superior in degree to other people, whether through quasi-divine or magical metahuman abilities or, as in the case of Batman, exaggerated intelligence and drive, but the environment presents a persistent set of commonplace problems to be overcome. These problems confound his or her ability to perform the primary superhero function: to save innocent people from supervillains and other disasters. Modern heroes are put in positions where they must make choices, often at the expense of their own desires, and so become existential beings whose character is revealed through an examination of why they act as they do.

POWER-FANTASY VERSUS SELF-DISCOVERY

When a superhero inhabits a fictional environment that mimics the audience's environment, the mimetic modes intertwine with the romantic to create a mode of wish-fulfillment through power-fantasy. Characters begin as drones in cubicles or as those with established careers who are certain that there is more that they can do. Once a superpower is manifested, the hero's first response is often one of relief and exaltation. But alas, the naive days of rushing in and saving the day are long gone.

Look at Matt Parkman of *Heroes*, the career cop who can't seem to get anything right. He repeatedly fails his exams for advancement and seems doomed to remain where he is professionally; his marriage barely bears the strain of his frustration. He has found his natural level, one of competent mediocrity. Anything above that is beyond his grasp, and he must struggle to remain where he is, when suddenly he begins to hear voices. A little investigation reveals that these voices are actually the thoughts of others registering in his mind. With this new tool at his disposal, Matt has a fresh opportunity to grow.

Unfortunately, though Matt is a telepath, he is not yet a very good one, and he discovers that this godlike talent does not solve his problems. He has the potential to know what everyone around him is thinking, but the actual execution is spotty and difficult. To make matters worse, Matt is something of a bumbler, physically and mentally, and does not have the finesse necessary to use his talent well. A cleverer man would be able to use the information he gathers surreptitiously to great effect, but not Matt. All he manages to do is alienate his colleagues, get himself fired, and disappoint Audrey Hanson, the FBI agent who is willing to take a chance on him. He has a bit more success using his talent to salve his marriage, but mainly because his unfaithful wife is willing to be generous and patient and give him the benefit of the doubt. Matt slips down into the ironic mode in which everything he does worsens his position, but this is part of the process by which he figures out how to incorporate his human and metahuman qualities into a functioning whole. Unlike the early presentations of Superman, Matt Parkman and this next generation of people with extraordinary powers must struggle and *learn* how to become heroes.

Part of the difficulty facing the new heroes is that however spectacular a superpower, it is not enough to form a coherent identity. The flat storylines of old comic books belonging to past generations still stigmatize the medium, particularly the superhero genre. Back then, a mindreader would be solving crimes left and right and going home after every adventure boasting a contented smile, secure in the knowledge that justice has been served. This naive approach to characterization is why superheroes are still dismissed as the fodder of kids' stories.

Writer Alan Moore and artist Dave Gibbons powerfully put the lie to this assumption with their comic book series *Watchmen* (1986–7). Their superhero story is set in a decidedly realistic world. With the exception of Jon Osterman, who through a scientific experiment gone awry becomes the supremely powerful Dr. Manhattan, the entire cast is devoid of superpowers. Moore and Gibbons deconstruct the super-hero genre by applying an existentialist's lens and discovering why a person might don a costume and venture outdoors to fight crime. How a character *chooses* to use a skill or talent determines whether he or she has depth or is merely a caricature.

In the beginning, Claire Bennet seems to be just such a cartoon character. *Heroes* cleverly maintains the initial impression that she is a stereotype. She is young, cute, blonde, and otherwise defined by the omnipresent cheerleader outfit that she wears in episode after episode. She can think of nothing to do with her ability to heal from seemingly any injury except document it time and again, almost as if she is unsure that it really exists. It is not until she takes revenge on the boy who tries to rape her that she finds an active use for her power ("Collision"). With that, she moves beyond the role of victim and becomes someone who tries to change her world. She is still referred to as "the cheerleader" for a time, but she has taken the steps toward growth by making choices and acting on them. By the end of the first season, she takes on more typical teenage concerns. Like any X-Man, she comes to feel that her abilities set her apart from her friends and naturally bar her from living a normal life. She feels like an outsider and the cause of all of her family's misfortunes, and as audiences watch her work through these difficult times, they see an extraordinary young woman evolve out of a stock character.

FAILURE AS A GUIDE

Matt and Claire fumble about discovering themselves in light of their odd capabilities, but Peter and Hiro have a tougher time. Poor Peter's talent is so confusing that it takes him (and the audience) quite some time to discover its nature. Hiro seems to improve at manipulating space and time with practice, only to lose his abilities for a while. Neither character has a solid grasp of what he can do or how to do it. Because of the complexity behind what they can do and the weight of what they are expected to do, both Peter and Hiro require models and guides in order to discover how they can face the destiny they feel pressing down.

Hiro pulls himself out of the drudgery of office life and dives into the task of self-discovery. His method is to define himself by reference to heroic archetypes; he decides what to do by following the models of heroes past. His journey naturally parallels classical motifs, including the many dangerous twists and turns in which his resolve is tested, he searches for a talisman that provides a physical link between himself and his heroes, and he serves a stint in an underworld of sorts in which he faces down the ultimate catastrophe. The potential future represented in "Five Years Gone" is a bleakly dystopic vision where metahumans are hunted and Hiro sees his future self fall in a desperate battle. Few heroes bear such direct witness to their own death. Even Achilles in Homer's *Iliad*, for all of his foreknowledge, is spared that level of immediacy. Hiro must overcome the shock and terror of his mortality and the specter of his possible, even probable failure, and continue. (For more on Hiro's journey, see Chapter 6: "The Making of a Hiro.")

The heroes of classical epic and romance regularly experience failure on their way to eventual success. Odysseus is plagued with setback after setback on his way home to Ithaca; Spenser's Redcrosse Knight begins his career as a headstrong youth who charges into situations well beyond his abilities in *The Faerie Queene* and needs the help of his friends to pull him out of trouble.

This order of failure is still a relatively new experience for superheroes. Before the 1960s, it was expected that superheroes would naturally save the day, and simplistic storylines led them straight to that point. But *Heroes* is set in a fictionalized world that mimics our own, whether in low- or high-mimetic terms, and so the good guys naturally have a tougher time of it. Christopher Nolan's *Batman Begins* (2005) makes a point of showing that failure and the acceptance of that failure are necessary parts of the learning process — Odysseus, Redcrosse, Batman, and Hiro all fall so they may learn to pick themselves up.

Another holdover from the classics is the mentor figure. A mentor is a teacher in the best sense of the word, a guide who helps the burgeoning hero along the path but who knows when to step away so that the hero may take over and face the crisis by putting theory into practice. (The role is named for the old man Odysseus asked to look after Ithaca while he was off in Troy in the *Odyssey*.)[2] The wise-old-man model persists in the forms of Gandalf, Obi-Wan Kenobi, and Professor Dumbledore, but *Heroes* for the most part avoids the standard in favor of a more adventurous twist. Matt finally finds his guide in Mr. Bennet, the reformed villain who possesses vast inside knowledge about many characters, including Matt himself. Mr. Bennet, a.k.a. HRG, has faith in Matt and patiently coaches him in the practical, meaningful use of his telepathy.

Peter learns how to access the abilities he absorbs and how to start thinking in active, not reactive, terms under the tutelage of Claude the invisible man ("Distractions"). Unfortunately, their relationship is cut short, before Peter is really ready to venture out on his own. He confronts Isaac in a jealous rage, and when he decides to use his powers to toy with him, Peter becomes indirectly responsible for Simone's death ("Unexpected"). His mistake matches Peter Parker's, whose inaction leads directly to the murder of his Uncle Ben and represents a potentially crushing failure. Both Peter Petrelli and Peter Parker fail because they used their abilities immaturely, and each heroically finds ways of harnessing their guilt to act for good.

Hiro can boast the widest and strangest array of guides, the most conventional being his father, even if the two are remote for the span of the first season. In a rather densely compacted scene, Hiro's father trains his son in swordplay, reassures him he is fulfilling his destiny, and, most importantly, tells him the sword he's been searching for doesn't matter: the journey itself has shaped Hiro into a worthy warrior ("Landslide"). Their lesson culminates in Hiro's renewed awareness of the virtues of self-sacrifice. The hero's relationship with his father is another old motif that returns again and again in forms as disparate as Telemachus/Odysseus to Luke Skywalker/Darth Vader. After a great deal of testing and frustration, it appears that Hiro has comfortably and honorably settled matters with his father.

Hiro is the only character with a sidekick, a companion who helps the hero through the many obstacles they encounter. Ando is a wise choice for many reasons, not the least of which is that in many ways he is Hiro's match. The two bounce ideas off each other and reason through possibilities together. When he believes Hiro has given up, Ando has courage enough to chase down Sylar on his own ("Landslide"). Ando will surely fail, but he is willing to try, which is enough for Hiro to tell him, "You have shown me what bravery is" ("How to Stop an Exploding Man"). Faithful, supportive Ando guides by example.

Most interestingly, Hiro acts as his *own* guide. First, he is given a prophecy in the comic book *9th Wonders*, in which he stars; the prophecy is transmitted by Isaac, the artist who can look into the future and paint or draw what he sees. In those pages, Hiro sees the challenges fate will set before him, all of which he consciously chooses to meet. More startlingly, Hiro meets a future version of himself, a stern, polished figure with only a passing resemblance to the Hiro audiences know. Hiro's future self is serious, world-weary, wise, and exceptionally skilled. What horrible events transpired in those five years to change Hiro from the sweetly endearing comic book fanboy of the beginning into the supremely confident warrior? What choices will he be forced to make that take him to that point? Without indulging in speculation as to what he suffers in the future, audiences are already confident that Hiro possesses the will and drive to carry on. Just as

Peter Parker, stripped of his Spider-Man abilities, still runs into a burning building to save a child in Sam Raimi's *Spider-Man 2* (2004), so Hiro, who for a long time cannot access his own superhuman skills, still tries to follow the heroic paradigm. This is reminiscent of another lesson from Nolan's *Batman Begins*: one of Bruce Wayne's mentors, Ra's Al Ghul, forcefully explains that mere "training is nothing, will is everything — the will to act." Hiro and the rest are heroes because they *act* like heroes, despite their mistakes and failures.

UNIFORMS, COSTUMES, AND OTHER IDENTITIES

In order to remind us that in many ways *Heroes* operates in a mimetic mode of fiction rather than a solidly romantic one, the writers finally allow some characters to wear clothing other than their uniforms. Early in the series, social roles (cheerleader, police officer, nurse) often determine clothing choices. When Peter links the (catch)phrase "Save the cheerleader; save the world" to Isaac's painting, he has enough information to further the plotline. (True, the cheerleader's name would have been nice but far too easy. Heroes cannot be given all information; otherwise they will never be given the opportunity to prove themselves. Characters do not grow if they have nothing to discover alone.) Peter knows that it is desperately important to find this cheerleader in time, and so he acts to make sure he does. Thankfully, once he has found her, the story allows Claire to grow beyond her cheerleader persona, and midway through the first season audiences at last see her dressed in something other than her cheerleader outfit. The same goes for Matt, who early on seems always to wear his police uniform. Peter also wears his scrubs an awful lot at the beginning of the series. As the story progresses, the personas built into these outfits have served their introductory purpose and, now that the audience is comfortable with them, may be safely discarded. In that way *Heroes* avoids the old superhero trope of costumed heroes and villains. A costume is a shorthand device that looks out of place in the mimetic mode where characters follow a more natural path of self-discovery.

The first run of *X-Men* in the late 1960s had each teammate wearing a uniform for a short while, though Iceman tended to stand out by virtue of his talent. That trend didn't last, and the X-Men started choosing outfits to match their personalities. The X-Men of recent films don uniforms only when they come together on business and it is essential that they are perceived as a united front. Of the superhero teams, only the Fantastic Four still cling to their standardized uniform, though the Human Torch's power and the Thing's physicality tend to supersede their clothes, and the Invisible Woman vanishes altogether.

Although the *Heroes'* characters don't wear costumes, they always dress for their part, and those viewers apt to dismiss costumes as silly comic book stuff should take note. A congressional candidate (Nathan Petrelli) is expected to dress a certain way, as is an office worker (Hiro or Ando), a manager of a paper distributor (HRG), and, strangely enough, a stripper (Niki). In watching an imitation of reality, or our perceptions of reality, audiences are given a chance to realize how much of an individual's identity is dictated by the role he or she has taken and, by extension, how much function dictates form.

A business suit is not as flashy or grand a symbol as a bat or spider suit, but in a way, when we put on uncomfortable shoes or a tie in preparation for the work day, we are sacrificing one persona for another. That sacrifice often carries the price of freedom in that the workday persona must kowtow to the rest of the similarly garbed workers' expectations. This suppression of individuality runs counter to the romantic mode, which is a genre of wish fulfillment. In a romantic story, the characters have the potential to become whatever they want, to follow their destiny to a richly rewarding, satisfying new identity.

In the romantic mode, once an alternate identity is established, it is given a costume as a symbol meant to establish who this new person is, what he or she can do, and what can be expected of him or her. A costume is not a uniform, a set of clothing marked by common features that signals that the wearer is a part of some larger force. A costume sets another identity free to do what it likes; it gives full rein to repressed drives and ambitions. Bruce Wayne, Clark Kent, and Peter Parker have all settled on the costume as the best way to allow them to go freely about their superhero chores, and they owe a great deal of thanks to the romantic undertone that infuses their respective settings. In the predominantly low-mimetic world of *Watchmen*, the costumed heroes begin to look ridiculous once their costumed foes decide to retire, go straight, or try their hands at more conventional criminal methods.

The *Heroes* characters have no need for costumes because they act as themselves. Their mission to save or destroy the world does not require that they hide, only that they discover who they are and what they can do. *Heroes* is about characters finding themselves without resorting to an alternate identity, though there is the unsettling case of the Misses Sanders. As an apparent schizophrenic, Niki/Jessica Sanders presents the true case of the alter ego, egos that are often in conflict, and she is the character most consistently defined by her roles. She is Jessica the powerful assassin, Niki the Internet stripper, or Micah's mother. Without those externals to guide her, audiences are not sure who she really is.

Sam Raimi forces Peter Parker into a similar existential dilemma in *Spider-Man 2*. Peter is having difficulty reconciling his life as a college student with that of a superhero; he finally understands that until he makes a decision as to what his identity should be and takes steps to successfully bring these identities together, he is no one. With his costume, Peter Parker has the advantage of a tangible symbol to represent an aspect of his personality, but as a pair of consciousnesses battling over a single body, Niki/Jessica's problem is far worse. Jessica simply cannot resolve some conflicts without Niki, and many times Niki must pretend to be Jessica. With all of these puzzles perplexing her, Niki/Jessica is never sure where or when one personality will displace the other, and it is fitting that she of all characters is having the hardest time adjusting to her superpower.

Sylar is faced with a similar inner conflict. He begins the series as a rather unremarkable fellow who repairs watches, a debut that matches Jon Osterman's in *Watchmen*. Both Sylar and Osterman likewise gain tremendous power. Audiences do not see Sylar rise to the godlike dimensions of Osterman/Dr. Manhattan, but his power is potentially limitless. He confronts a power greater than his own, that of fate. The vision he paints after he has stolen Isaac's power frightens him; one of the most potentially powerful beings on the planet is *afraid* of the fate he sees coming, and he makes an effort to return to his life repairing watches ("The Hard Part"). He takes on a mild-mannered, Clark Kent–style disguise complete with thick-rimmed black glasses and goes to visit his mother, but that persona and that life ultimately do not suit him. His is a reactive pathology that will not be restrained by a humble façade. He cannot maintain the illusion that he is an ordinary man for long, and after revealing a few of his powers to his mother, she demonizes him. She refuses to see her son in him and effectively casts him out of (her) society. Sylar then reacts the only way he knows how — violently.

Peter mirrors Sylar as another amalgam of other metahumans, but whereas Peter copies and replicates power, Sylar seizes and destroys. Peter is the virtuous citizen to Sylar's predator. By murdering those whose powers he takes, Sylar obliterates his competition, but Peter is not so insecure and is willing and able to coexist with the superhuman.

PROTAGONISTS AND OTHER VILLAINS

In these stories, the villain tends to have a vision that provides the impetus for other characters to act. Their machinations provide the plot and push the action of the story forward. The Green Goblin wants to destroy something, so Spider-Man must stop him. If Lex Luthor tries to take over the planet, Superman tries to stop him. In the overarching storyline of the first season of *Heroes*, Mr. Linderman drives the plot, and audiences watch as the others choose either to try to stop his plan to kill half of the citizens of New York City or to let it happen. Although everyone has heard the venerable adage "knowledge is power," only *applied* knowledge is power. Likewise, superpowered characters, no matter how powerful, have no purpose without a chance to apply their power. The villain provides everyone with an opportunity to act. Without a villain, there would be no story.

Linderman has tremendous knowledge and foresight, and in the Haitian and Candice Wilmer (and sometimes Jessica), he has gathered just the superhumans he needs to his side. He gives them the chance to use their abilities in his service, to fulfill a role and gain a purpose in a larger scheme. Even Sylar, the apparent wild card, is being led into place. The villains have their chief to tell them what to do. In order to stop Linderman's plans, the heroes must find out how their skills work, how they can apply them, and determine whether or not they should. It is the mark, and burden, of a hero to decide. Their villainous counterparts are led.

Even though the Haitian can alter memory and block metahuman abilities, he is ultimately quite weak. With his ability to render any superhero ordinary and to change the memories of anyone, no identity is secure when he is around. Despite this tremendous power, he only does what he is told by Mr. Bennet or, later, Angela Petrelli. He is a subject beneath more kingly personalities. So, too, Candice, who has the magnificent ability to manipulate perception, tends to act as an illusionist and uses her power, like Mystique in *The X-Men*, to pretend to be someone else at her boss's orders. Candice and the Haitian are both supremely skilled at what they do but have reached a point where they have no purpose outside of their abilities. Neither has any compelling identity beyond what he or she can do. They are merely tools. The true hero is able to find a suitable guide, not a leader, and if the guide makes demands that should not be met, the hero knows when to break free, as in the case of Bruce Wayne's split with Ra's Al Ghul in *Batman Begins*.

Moore and Gibbons explore this dynamic between power and the will to use it with Jon Osterman, the brilliant but submissive scientist who becomes Dr. Manhattan in *Watchmen*. Osterman's youth and young adulthood are typified by others making decisions for him, notably his father, and Dr. Manhattan's career as a superhero is marked by service to the government, even down to the detail of his absurd and meaningless name. Dr. Manhattan becomes America's greatest weapon against foreign powers even as he himself steadily withdraws from all but a passing interest in humanity. Great power without drive is dangerous or merely empty potential. The Haitian, Candice, and Dr. Manhattan are guided by forceful, unyielding personalities, and none has the will to act alone. Candice in particular puts a great deal of faith in Linderman, the man she believes will "heal the world." Audiences are given a glimpse into Candice's background, apparently characterized by intolerance and hate, but she allies herself with a false savior and, as long as she is kept comfortable and happy, will remain a devoted and submissive follower.

A PLATONIC LOOK AT SUPERHEROES

After the overt physical threat represented by Sylar, Mr. Linderman is the most fearsome character, the mastermind orchestrating all events who uses his tools, particularly the Haitian and Candice, to great effect. By quietly altering his opponents' perceptions, Linderman controls people while letting them believe they are acting as they want. He takes the equivocal role of the villainous humanitarian.

To gently push the irony, the show's creators give him the superhuman talent to heal others. He is the "clever craftsman" Glaucon describes in Plato's *Republic*. Dismayed with the condition of man, he is trying to create a utopia, because "people need hope" (".07%"). The troubling thing is that he is right. He has a point. People are not living as well as they could and so, like Plato's Socrates, Linderman wonders how to make it right. But whereas Socrates would control the citizens of his republic with subtle manipulation, Linderman is more forceful and direct and falls just short of the divine in scale. Instead of an apocalyptic event such as the floods in the Bible and Ovid's *Metamorphosis* that destroy virtually all human life, Linderman is planning the relatively restrained sacrifice of half the population of New York City.

Comics fans will surely notice the parallel with *Watchmen* and per-haps also *Watchmen*'s debt to an old *Outer Limits* episode. Beyond their well-mannered, gentlemanly exteriors and vast intelligences, *Heroes*' Linderman has little in common with *Watchmen*'s retired superhero Adrian Veidt/Ozymandias, but their motivations and methods are much the same. Each is prepared to sacrifice a relatively small number of people in order to shock or scare the rest into virtue.

Veidt has been at his plan for years, and his goal is to forestall the nuclear war he predicts. He kills half of the city's population so that, he reasons, billions will be saved from nuclear armageddon. His plan works, and war is averted. Countless innocents are spared, and the only risk is that the surviving masses will somehow discover and resent what he's done. Ozymandias has already killed everyone involved in his machinations because he believes that if people were to learn that it was all a ruse, that they averted war through a false pre-tense, they will regress back into vice. Similarly, as Glaucon's "clever craftsman," Linderman's "successful attempts at injustice must remain undetected [. . .] if he is to be believed to be just without being just." He is involved in politics, the Mafia, and genetic breeding. It seems that he, too, has also been about his plan for quite some time if he has bred young Micah for his own purposes. Even if he succeeds and his "tragedy will be a catalyst for good" (".07%"), it is crucial that the masses never know that someone planned to kill millions so that billions would be open to his guidance, however benevolent and right-eous that guidance may prove to be. So, too, must Socrates' Guardian class never let it be known that the citizens of Plato's utopia are being controlled from above. There is a good deal of manipulation underly-ing Socrates' utopic state, particularly genetic manipulation and censorship of the arts, and should these secrets come out, the citi-zenry will most likely rebel. The ruling class has an interest in keeping the masses comfortably right where they are.

It is distressing to realize that Socrates, Ozymandias, and

Linderman all make valid points. These three have little faith in the idea that people will choose to act virtuously on their own, and so they devise their plans to correct this problem based on careful, minute observations of how things are, not through a lens of romantic potential, but in terms of a mimetic impression of real life. Any effort at making society better must take into account the way its citizens actually act, not how they want to act. That is why secrecy is so important. Even if people say they want to be good, they hate to be tricked and will undo any good they have done if they believe it has been forced upon them.

The Platonic view is unabashedly cynical and seemingly outside the provenance of an uplifting TV show about superheroes, but *Heroes* provides a direct line to the *Republic* and the very breed of vice Socrates would curtail not only through Linderman, but with Claude the invisible man. In the course of their conversation on justice, Glaucon reminds Socrates and the rest of the story of the ring of Gyges, a magical device with the power to render its wearer invisible. The man who finds it rapes the queen, murders the king, and takes his place. True, Claude does not seem to be the sort to murder and rape, and when Peter discovers him he is nothing more than an opportunistic, petty thief. Audiences never see him do anyone any real harm, certainly nothing that hours lost on the phone to credit card customer service and in line at the Department of Motor Vehicles will not repair, and so he is not particularly dangerous at this point. But Glaucon would argue that because injustice is a slippery slope, Claude only needs more time to fall into full-bodied, rapacious vice. His pattern is not particularly promising. Claude works with HRG until he realizes that they are not ultimately protecting people, despite the company line, a realization that HRG himself comes to all too slowly. Claude escapes execution, barely, and goes into hiding ("Company Man"). Alas, rather than continue to work against Linderman and company, he stays in hiding and begins his petty life of crime. Even though Peter finds him and becomes his student, once Claude is threatened again, he vanishes. With opportunity, ability, and the freedom from repercussion, humanity's self-interest will always take over and run rampant, notable exceptions notwithstanding.

Peter and Hiro may well be virtuous enough not to abuse their abilities, but both Hiro and HRG have decided that murder can be legitimate — they would destroy Sylar, Linderman, and Linderman's metahuman tracking system in order to save a great(er) number of people. This is the same utilitarian reasoning that Linderman and Ozymandias follow. It does *not* matter that Linderman's "system" turns out to be an innocent and adorable little girl. Once HRG decides to kill, he has taken a terrible step, and he should be thankful that she takes the form she does so that he may justly falter in his resolve ("How to Stop an Exploding Man"). Only Sylar and Linderman are legitimate targets because they have chosen to use force against an unwary populace.

Linderman explains that "we all have our role to play in the events to come" (".07%"), and so he gives the heroes something to do and a chance to define themselves. It is comforting to have a purpose, to discover, like Hiro, that there is more to accomplish. Claire begins to look ahead in "Landslide" and tells Peter that once the present crisis is over, she might go on patrol and use her talents "to jump in front of bullets or something." Peter replies that that's all well and good, but he won't be putting on tights and wearing his underwear on the outside. With that, Peter reminds us of *Heroes'* message: a superpower is not to be confused with an identity. Look at Peter's brother, Nathan, the man who can fly but who rarely bothers to do so. His ability might just as well be playing the harmonica in a blues band on weekends. This is not to say that he derides his ability, but rather that he is smart enough and driven enough to do other things with his life and refuses to let a single attribute define him.

Recent movie and TV incarnations of the old heroes have departed from established characterizations and begun to look at them again in terms of where they come from, and so rework high epic and romantic characters in terms of the immediate and relevant mimetic modes. By focusing on Clark Kent, Bryan Singer's *Superman Returns* (2006) begins to answer the question *why* a supremely powerful being would even bother living with humans in a way that allows him to become emotionally accessible. Similarly, Christopher Nolan's *Batman Begins* (2005) looks at how, with a heavy emphasis on the influence of his various father figures, Bruce Wayne progresses from traumatized child and angry young man to the steely heroic Batman. The *Smallville* television show is a modern reconstruction of the Superman myth that begins where Stan Lee might have, with the origin story. The writers of *Smallville* (including for a time *Heroes'* Jeph Loeb), Bryan Singer, and other like-minded creators are no longer content to let Superman be the flat savior figure of the 1930s who appears on Earth essentially at random and is nice enough to help solve human problems. Instead, their young Clark Kent grows up, attends high school, makes mistakes, and otherwise discovers who he is in terms of what he *can* do and what he *should* do.

Heroes is just such a hybrid of modes with stories and characters that combine romantic elements with the low and high mimetic. Audiences can watch *Heroes* to see how ordinary people learn to use their extraordinary powers based on a model of self-discovery and increasing confidence in ability. This format speaks directly to viewers living in an uncertain, unsteady world by presenting individual, local, national, and global issues through a reassuring lens of romantic wish fulfillment.

HEROES AND VILLAINS

THE MAKING OF A HIRO

Your whole life you talked about your favorite stories . . .
Star Wars, *Star Trek*, Superman, Kensei . . . All the heroes
you wanted to be . . . one day people will tell the story of
Hiro Nakamura.
— Ando to Hiro in "How to Stop an Exploding Man"

ALTHOUGH ALL BUDDING HEROES face challenges as they discover
their new powers, decide what to do with them, and begin to understand how that decision will change their lives, Hiro Nakamura
accepts the call to become a hero with great exuberance. Even late in
season 1, after some sobering experiences that prove being a hero isn't
all trips to Las Vegas and sacred swords, Hiro still raises his arms in
triumph. "We'll save you, New York!" he enthusiastically promises as
he stands atop the Deveaux roof.

More than any other character, Hiro follows the path of a traditional
literary hero. His story may be told in comic books and on screen, but
he exemplifies Joseph Campbell's ideal hero and his journey, as discussed in Campbell's seminal work, *The Hero with a Thousand Faces*.
Heroes, however, doesn't stop with Campbell's analysis of mythology; it

systematically documents Hiro's heroes from Japanese literature and popular culture.

The Bushido Code, which Hiro frequently mentions to sidekick Ando, and stories of those who followed it underpin Hiro's understanding of just what a hero should be. Although the senior Nakamura seems stern in present time and flashbacks, even standing stiffly while Hiro hugs him good-bye, the pair must have shared some quality father-son time during Hiro's childhood. Hiro clearly remembers his father telling him stories of Takezo Kensei, a samurai who became a great leader. To his father's chagrin, Hiro absorbed these stories and now wants to emulate his samurai hero.

The online *Heroes* comic series provides even more background; Hiro is named in honor of his grandfather, a Hiroshima survivor who becomes his grandson's hero for surviving the blast as well as battling cancer. (He also gives Hiro his valuable *Action Comics* #1.)

This grandfather must know that Hiro is also a culture geek, who grew up with *Star Trek* and *Star Wars* and peppers conversations, in Japanese and English, with popular culture references. The mythology in space sagas emphasizes heroes' proper behavior, and in fact, these more modern stories pay homage to the types of heroes Campbell describes in literature and every culture reveres in its history and legends. As an article in *Wired* recently acknowledged, Hiro succeeds because of his interest in popular culture: "it's his geekiness that gives him an edge," creating the "cheeky conceit [of] the chubby nebbish Hiro [as] the central hero of *Heroes*." With this rich background in heroic myths, Hiro quite appropriately seems the most likely of all the newly emerging heroes to know immediately what to do with his power and to accept the call to action.

JOSEPH CAMPBELL AND A TWELVE-STEP HERO PROGRAM

Joseph Campbell's influence becomes apparent in *Heroes* within the first two episodes. The opening screen crawl presents the premise of the story, similarly to *Star Wars'* introduction of Luke Skywalker's epic tale in the very first movie. *Heroes* promises that the title characters "will not only save the world, but change it forever" and explains that this is only the beginning, "Volume 1 of their epic tale." Having a volume 1 implies at least a volume 2; the heroes' story that audiences began to watch in volume 1 has already occurred, and whatever mission they undertake or crisis they avert is in the (probably recent) past. Like a favorite bedtime story, these heroes' adventures might inspire viewers, as all good hero stories should. The voiceover narration says their "transformation [a term Campbell uses] from ordinary to extraordinary" is about to begin ("Genesis"). The audiovisual story is structured in volumes and chapters like a book, although individual shots, the use of subtitles and fonts, and color schemes also show the heavy influence of comic books. Paying tribute to "hero stories," including books and comic books, brings Campbell into the picture.

The second episode's voiceover discusses "man's"[1] role in societal evolution and the call to action in troubled times: "he can only choose how to stand when the call to destiny comes, hoping he'll have the courage to answer" ("Don't Look Back"). According to Campbell, the hero first has to answer such a call in order to begin an adventure. When the hero leaves home after accepting this call, as the episode title indicates, he can't look back; by leaving home and all that's familiar, he enters a new life.

More than perhaps any other published scholar, Campbell analyzed world mythology and determined exactly what heroes have in common. Although his focus is literature and folklore, including stories passed down through oral tradition, the qualities of a classical hero also pertain to movie and TV heroes who strictly adhere to a moral code as the basis of their actions. Not everyone audiences might call a "hero" fits Campbell's definition, but Hiro, more than the other characters on *Heroes*, matches the description most closely. A very rough paraphrase of Campbell's ideas about a hero's departure, initiation, and return can be divided into these twelve parts, with the hero moving from one event or stage to another in order[2]:

1. The hero lives in a world that, frankly, needs heroes. Problems need to be solved; something is left undone; a new crisis is about to be revealed.

2. Into this troubled time comes a call — to action, to change, to adventure, perhaps to heroism. The potential hero hears this call and decides to answer.

3. A life of adventure is difficult, however, and the one who follows the call may question his decision, become afraid when he is first challenged, and, in short, wonder if this is a very good idea at all.

4. The hero meets a mentor who acknowledges what he is going through and who he is. This mentor helps the hero on his journey, sometimes with knowledge, special tools, and training, or other types of support.

5. The hero crosses a First Threshold, which might be a test or major event (a first battle or proof of skill). The hero then realizes his life is truly changing; he may become even more scared about his destiny.

6. Just when the hero might decide that the call to adventure really isn't working out as he envisioned, he meets people who can help — and hurt. A period of tests or challenges is stressful, but the hero better understands just what his life might become and what heroes might be called upon to do.

7. The Inmost Cave is the hero's dark side, which he must visit to understand who he truly is. He confronts his fears and his past, often having to deal with aspects of

his personality he has previously chosen to ignore or
hide.

8. To become a fully realized hero, he must then take this
   understanding of his dark side and integrate it with the
   rest of himself; he must use both natures.

9. The hero often receives a weapon, or achieves a level of
   mastery over one, that helps him to become a fully integrated personality and realize his potential. A sword is
   the typical weapon of choice, but more importantly, the
   hero knows exactly who he is and becomes passionate
   about his quest or mission. He achieves what he set out
   to do; he has become a true hero.

10. With this newfound knowledge and experience, the hero
    must return to the "normal" world. Because the hero
    knows what he can do and often sees a way to save
    others, he becomes frustrated with those (often in
    power) who don't have the same understanding. The
    hero is separate from the majority of people, who don't
    view the world his way. (He might return home from a
    grand adventure, for example, and find that everyone
    back home thinks he's changed or may not appreciate
    his challenges and sacrifices. He might be hired into a
    corporation but not be allowed to make the sweeping
    changes he'd like. Once he's become a hero, he can't go
    back to being "normal.")

11. The hero faces his death and evaluates his life. He may
    narrowly avoid being killed and gain insights from this
    near-death experience. This resurrection phase may
    involve the hero's physical death and return to the world

(in the next step) to teach others what he has learned. (Think of Obi-Wan Kenobi sacrificing himself during a light-saber battle, only to guide Luke with his voice and, in the happy ending to the first trilogy, as a glowing apparition.)

12. The hero shares his knowledge with younger heroes in the everyday world, thus helping to ensure a new generation of heroes to succeed him.

Movies are more likely to illustrate this depth of character development because they can focus on one story in great detail. *Star Wars* is an effective (and frequently used) example of the development of a hero, Luke Skywalker.[3] Across three films, his character development follows Campbell's traditional path of a hero. The restless Luke leaves his home on Tatooine when he learns about his father's Jedi past. He receives a call to adventure ("Save the princess; save the universe"). He studies under a mentor, Obi-Wan Kenobi, and later learns from Yoda, but throughout his journey he makes new friends and allies who also teach him about the larger world and himself. He learns how to fight with a light saber and develops his battle skills, including his talent for flying. He discovers the Dark Side, not only of the Force but himself, and must deal with his father issues before he can become a true hero. He fights and wins battles, but he suffers too. By the end of the third film, he's helped to save the universe and is able to enjoy his place within it (while seeing his sister/princess live happily ever after). Someday he'll probably open his own little Jedi school on the fringes of the galaxy, taking Obi-Wan's place as a mentor/teacher to the next generation.

Some serial television shows, such as predecessor *Buffy the Vampire Slayer*[4] as well as *Heroes*, take the time to develop a character through this traditional plot structure, but these types of stories on TV are rare. More than any other *Heroes* character, Hiro's journey to become a hero follows the pattern Campbell documented, a conscious decision by creator Tim Kring. Hiro, according to Kring, has been "stripped down to . . . the essence of the classic Joseph Campbell hero myth . . . In many ways he does embody a lot of what the themes of the show are." Perhaps this familiar format is one reason why Hiro becomes an early fan favorite (although actor Masi Oka's infectious joy of discovery is another).

Early in season 1, Hiro discovers he can first freeze time and then teleport, or "bend space." During an unexpected first teleportation to New York, he finds a comic book about his future and, more significantly, sees the nuking of the city. This call to action leads him far from his home in Japan. Along the physical journey — from Tokyo to Los Angeles to Las Vegas (several times) to small Texas towns to New York City — and to the future and back, Hiro overcomes challenges to the way he thinks of himself and learns as well to fight physical battles. During a time of deepest doubt, when Hiro admits, "Maybe I'm not the hero I thought I was," Ando reminds him that every hero is on a journey "to find his place in the world . . . You don't start at the end" ("Better Halves"). Comforted by the idea that perhaps he only needs to develop his skills in order to be more effective, Hiro continues his journey.

Hiro is often scared, not only of failing but of succeeding, because even if he succeeds, those he loves may die. He loses his powers in the aftermath of girlfriend Charlie's death. Once again, however, he gains insight — this time in the form of a sword once wielded by one of his heroes, the samurai Takezo Kensei. By retrieving (i.e., stealing) the sword, Hiro develops even greater power as well as the self-confidence to use it.

Most television series ramp up the action at the expense of extensive character development. Quiet, introspective moments or a multi-episode quest don't take place as often as, for example, car chases or violent confrontations. Most dramas provide a plot that can be wrapped up in less than an hour; even the success of recent serialized series (such as 24 and Lost) doesn't buy much additional time in which to supply audiences with answers to long-running mysteries or to tie up story arcs. Despite audience impatience with sidestories that seem to have very little action, *Heroes* doesn't skip or scrimp on Hiro's quest for the sword.

Ironically, this crucial step in a classic hero's development concerned critics and fans, who thought the subplot slowed the story too much. *Entertainment Weekly*'s TV guru Jeff Jensen summed up the discontent: "The idea was to present a mettle-testing challenge for a near-omnipotent being and, sure, save some dough on special effects. But it also took the fun out of *Heroes'* most endearing hero." Masi Oka (Hiro) realized the problem of injecting comedy into a serious quest: "Hiro is a major source of comic relief, but a lot of that humor came from this enthusiasm he had for his powers. When you took that away, some of the comedy became more of the traditional sitcom variety." In other words, it often fell flat. With sword in hand, however, Hiro has passed this step in Campbell's myth-making process and can move on with his (fans hope more action-packed) journey.

Hiro matures as a man as well as a hero during his many tests on the road to New York. He meets other heroes who also accept but fear their call to adventure. He develops a closer relationship with pal Ando, who becomes his greatest source of support. Hiro even meets Future Hiro, a dark, scary version of himself. This Hiro kills frequently and easily, and his younger self fervently does not want to become that man. Even so, Hiro comes to understand the darker side of himself, and just how much his friendship with Ando may cost him.

This knowledge spurs him to accept what to Hiro is a great challenge — to kill another. He normally would never do such a thing, but if he is the only one who can kill Sylar and thus prevent the destruction of New York, he reluctantly accepts this part of his mission. He incorporates the part of himself that could become Future Hiro and knows that he can kill in order to save millions of lives. Table 2 lists some highlights of Hiro's journey within Campbell's framework.

TABLE 2. HIRO'S JOURNEY ALONG CAMPBELL'S TWELVE-STEP PATH TO BECOMING A HERO

THE HERO'S JOURNEY (STEPS)	HIRO'S ACTIONS	EPISODE
1–2 — Problems exist in the hero's world; the hero receives a call to action.	Bored with "cube" life, Hiro stops time and later teleports.	"Genesis"
3 — The hero wonders if he's up to the challenge.	Hiro finds Isaac's body, is arrested, and sees the destruction of New York City.	"Don't Look Back"
	Hiro doesn't attempt to help the gamblers, who are killed in a shootout.	"Collision"
	Hiro can't save Charlie from death.	"Seven Minutes to Midnight"
	Hiro wonders if he really can kill Sylar, even if that is his mission.	"The Hard Part"
4 — The hero finds a mentor or guide.	Hiro finds Isaac's *9th Wonders* comic book, which outlines Hiro's heroic saga. (Isaac's other painting and comic books further guide Hiro.)	"Genesis"

THE HERO'S JOURNEY (STEPS)	HIRO'S ACTIONS	EPISODE
	Hiro meets Nathan, who gives him a ride, and simply by flying in, lets Hiro know others also have special powers.	"Hiros"
	Peter gives Hiro a message from his future self. (In this way, Future Hiro is a mentor to his younger self, as he also is in "Five Years Gone.")	"Hiros"
	Nathan helps Hiro get through Linderman's security so that he can deliver a painting (and steal a sword).	"Parasite"
5 — The hero passes a first test, survives an important event, or shows proof of his skills.	Hiro saves a girl from being hit by a bus.	"One Giant Leap"
6 — The hero meets allies as well as enemies	Hiro meets "flying man" Nathan.	"Hiros"

THE HERO'S JOURNEY (STEPS)	HIRO'S ACTIONS	EPISODE
	Hiro meets D.L. and Micah. He helps D.L. rescue a person from a burning car and shows Micah the 9th Wonders comic book.	"Nothing to Hide"
	Sylar kills Charlie.	"Seven Minutes to Midnight"
	Hiro's messages to Peter allow him to save the cheerleader.	"Homecoming"
7 — The hero confronts his darker side.	Hiro meets Future Hiro and is afraid of him.	"Five Years Gone"
8 — The hero integrates this darker side into his personality.	Hiro learns to use his sword and comes to understand the meaning of sacrifice during a training session with his father.	"Landslide"
	Hiro stabs Sylar.	"How to Stop an Exploding Man"
9 — The hero receives a weapon or masters its use.	Hiro learns that his future self carries a sword.	"Hiros"

THE HERO'S JOURNEY (STEPS)	HIRO'S ACTIONS	EPISODE
	Hiro discovers the sword of a famous hero and steals it, only to discover that it's a fake.	"Godsend"
	Hiro steals the real sword.	"Parasite"
	Hiro masters swordplay.	"Landslide"
10 — The hero returns to the "normal" world and becomes frustrated when others don't believe in his power or don't want him to change anything.	Hiro confronts his displeased father, who wants him to return to the family business.	"The Fix"
11 — The hero faces his death and evaluates his life.	Hiro watches Future Hiro die, and seeing the man he may become convinces Present Hiro to change the future.	"Five Years Gone"
12 — The hero teaches others.	Hiro shows Micah the comic book outlining his adventures. On some level, Micah may understand that Hiro, like Micah's family, is special.	"Nothing to Hide"

Of course, viewers hope that Hiro's journey is far from over. By the end of season 1, he seems comfortable around Steps 9–11. He might even someday return home or share what he's learned with other young heroes, such as Molly or Micah, but his life as a hero will require him to respond to future calls to new adventures.

THE BUSHIDO CODE AND JAPANESE HISTORY

After Hiro learns that his future self carries a sword and then discovers that it's not any sword, but the sacred weapon of his childhood hero, Takezo Kensei, he begins to follow the Bushido Code more closely. (*Kensei* is an honorary title given to an expert swordsman, which makes this particular sword and level of skill so important to Hiro.) Like the ancient *bushi*, a Japanese warrior class, Hiro understands that he now must live by a strict moral code of behavior if he is to be a true hero. Between the ninth and twelfth centuries, the code was initially passed by word of mouth from one generation to the next; Confucius is credited with writing the code and thus becoming the father of these virtues. Justice, benevolence, love, sincerity, honesty, and self-control were prized values. The samurai disagreed with parts of Confucius' interpretation of the code, especially that which encouraged a scholarly, if isolated, life of reading and writing poetry. Samurai believed that man and the universe were to be alike in spirit and ethics, and they, as warriors, needed to interact with the world.

The code clearly guided their relationships: master-servant, father-son, husband-wife, older brother–younger brother, friend-friend. Samurai were loyal to the lord they served, but they also had responsibilities within their families. A samurai's word was his bond, an aspect of the Bushido Code that Hiro seems determined to follow. The samurai, however, were calm and composed, seemingly passionless and stoic.[5] Present Hiro is far from passionless, although Future Hiro seems to have gained a stoic demeanor. Present Hiro may have difficulty achieving this part of the code, preferring to maintain his childlike enthusiasm for life; he seems afraid that he might become as detached as his future self.

The Bushido Code has much in common with the philosophies of Zen Buddhism, Shintoism, and, of course, Confucianism. It became more than etiquette; it was a culture with profound influence. Hiro seems to understand this part of his heritage very well, but as a hero in training and living in a complex modern world, living strictly by the code is challenging.

Hiro wants to steal Takezo Kensei's sword from the powerful Mr. Linderman, an act that Ando reminds him is definitely not in the code. Hiro has to quickly rationalize his plan before he steals the sword. He first condones the theft because the sword is in New York, which will be destroyed if he doesn't save the city, and to do that, he needs the sword. When this sword turns out to be a fake, he returns it to the museum. Hiro then learns that the real sword is in Linderman's Las Vegas hotel, but again he rationalizes the theft because Linderman is a bad guy. Such a sword should be wielded by a modern samurai.

In "The Hard Part," Hiro finally has the sword and plans to kill Sylar with it to prevent him from becoming "the exploding man" who blasts New York. Future Hiro has told him to kill Sylar on the day after Nathan Petrelli's election ("Five Years Gone"), but Ando and Hiro track Sylar to his mother's home a few days early. They watch as Sylar has a rocky reunion with his mother; when she locks herself in a bedroom, Sylar slumps against the door and asks her forgiveness. Ando suggests that Hiro kill Sylar while he is distracted, but Hiro disagrees. The Bushido Code doesn't allow killing when a man is asking forgiveness; Hiro can't take advantage of a possibly redemptive moment for Sylar. His mother refuses to forgive him, however, denying that this monster is her sweet little boy; she even brandishes scissors to keep him away, an act that leads to her accidental death. Hiro then has nothing to prevent him from killing Sylar. After freezing time for a few moments, Hiro approaches Sylar, places the sword against his neck, and sincerely says he's sorry for what he's about to do. Sylar is able to "unfreeze" the moment, challenges Hiro to kill him, but then freezes and breaks the sword. Hiro flees and doesn't know how he will kill Sylar now that the sword is broken. By following the Bushido Code and trying to kill a man "honorably," Hiro misses what he and Ando believe is their best, perhaps only, opportunity to stop Sylar.

REACHING FOR THE STARS: CONNECTIONS WITH *STAR TREK* AND *STAR WARS*

Another strong but more recent cultural influence particularly on young men is science fiction. Audiences first meet Hiro in his office cubicle as he struggles to stop time. Upon succeeding, giddy with joy, he shares his discovery with good friend Ando. The skeptical Ando, however, doesn't believe Hiro, thinking him equally bored with the job. (Ando spends his time watching Niki Sanders, a "hero" he has yet to meet, on an Internet porn site.) Hiro attempts to describe what he's discovered he can do, a feat that Ando compares to a *Star Trek* phenomenon. Hiro is his Spock. When their supervisor drags Hiro back to his job, Ando laughingly suggests that Hiro/Spock use the Vulcan death grip to free himself ("Genesis"). Thus begins a series of *Star Trek* allusions that culminate with the revelation that Hiro's father looks suspiciously like *Trek*'s Mr. Sulu ("The Fix").

Although the manipulative thief Hope derisively calls Hiro "Sulu" when he acts like he doesn't understand English ("Run!"), Hiro seems more like the alien Spock to his family and Ando. They don't quite understand his hero complex. After Ando agrees to come along on Hiro's mission and begins to see firsthand the strange events that lead them toward their date with destiny, he becomes more of a partner and less of a tagalong, with fewer references to Hiro as Spock or suggestions to "Beam me up" to get out of a difficult situation.

Hiro admits that he wants to "boldly go where no man has gone before" instead of being average ("Genesis"). He frequently uses the

Vulcan "live long and prosper" hand greeting and, as any good alien should, says he comes in peace ("Don't Look Back"). His ideal hero understands a moral code of behavior and can protect others. He seems especially happy to learn from Peter Petrelli that his future self carries a sword. "I had a sword," he smiles smugly after the phone call. Swashbuckling heroes, from the samurai of history and legend to Luke Skywalker of film, all carry a form of sword, and Hiro is happy to be destined to join their ranks. He even makes the whirring sound of a light saber as he practices with an imaginary weapon in the car ("Better Halves").

Of course, using a sword adds more items to Hiro's ever-growing code for heroes. "A samurai's weapon must be used with honor. And respect," Hiro reminds Ando ("The Fix"). He tries to follow the Bushido Code once he carries Takezo Kensei's sword, marked with the characters for "godsend" or "great talent" ("Godsend").[6] Indeed, Hiro treats this sword as a sacred object. By liberating the sword and choosing to use it to help others, Hiro feels he is completing part of his mission. "With this sword, there is no limit to what I can accomplish," he vows before Ando. Of course, his next line indicates how he perceives himself as a hero: "Our life of legend begins" ("Godsend"). Without such a divine sword to help him perform great deeds, Hiro believes he can't truly become the same quality of hero as his idols from story and screen.

James Kyson Lee (Ando) sees a clear *Star Wars* parallel between his character and Han Solo. "I like to compare [the relationship between Ando and Hiro] to Han Solo and Luke Skywalker. Ando has become sort of a Han Solo, and he's very adventurous." Also like Solo, Ando has his eye on Hiro's/Luke's no-nonsense, highly capable sister. Kimiko even reacts to Ando similarly to Princess Leia's early wariness of Solo. Han Solo gradually shifted from sidekick to hero in his own right, something Lee can see happening with Ando. Changing from "a sidekick character who was a realist who thinks Hiro is like a child living in a fantasy land, he's become sort of this happy-go-lucky character which becomes the comedic element of the show, as now Hiro is . . . burdened with this mission and is becoming more and more serious." Perhaps by the end of the series, Ando, like Solo, will even get the girl.

Although Hiro's father doesn't seem quite as treacherous as Darth Vader, he may be a part of *Heroes'* Dark Side. Hiro, unlike Luke, knows that his father lives and wants his heir to succeed him some-day in the family business; however, Hiro apparently has no idea of his father's other business with Linderman. The implication not only in "Distractions" but in HRG's flashback in "Company Man" is that Hiro's father is a stern man with strong loyalties, which, as revealed in "Company Man," are given to The Company as well as his family. Audiences are led to believe that Hiro's father may be one of the bad guys; in any case, he is certainly powerful and knows a great deal about "heroes." Like Luke, Hiro discovers his father's involvement goes deep into a powerful, often subversive organization; Kaito Nakamura knows all about his son's potential superhero power but hasn't previously thought the geeky Hiro might step forward as a leader of his generation.

The long-awaited confrontation between Hiro and his father takes place — but in an unexpected way. Instead of the two fighting each other, à la Luke and Vader, the elder Nakamura teaches his son how to wield the sword and master his emotions in order to kill his oppo-nent when necessary. The full-out fight scene, swords flashing, becomes a highlight of "Landslide." Hiro, like Luke, may learn from his father's past mistakes in order to take his rightful place as a future "hero."

Almost everything Hiro knows about the nature of heroes and even his gift of bending space and time seem derived from science fic-tion. He compares teleportation to being beamed between locations, à la *Star Trek*. He freaks out when he calls Yamagato Industries from a very different time zone in the U.S. and finds himself taking his own call in Japan ("Six Months Ago"); he is afraid that if he meets himself in time, he will create a temporal anomaly (a typical TV theory). Hiro is convinced of the accuracy of these TV-based theories about the nature of space and time, but Ando thinks he just makes up the information. Hiro's understanding of time travel is more *Star Trek* than physics; he knows how to be a space-age hero, but translating that knowledge into practical action sometimes eludes him.

HIRO'S CODE FOR MODERN HEROES

Hiro may be an unlikely "Super Hiro," even to himself. He wonders aloud why he's been given this gift; after all, he was terrible in sports and last in his class ("Genesis"). His father thinks he's weird, and his sister laughingly calls him insane ("Distractions"). He is not the ideal candidate to succeed his father as CEO of Yamagato Industries. He watches television and reads comic books, and his young adult persona seems childlike and naive. Hiro may not be as smart or business savvy as his family would like, and neither he nor Ando seems overly excited about his job. Nevertheless, because Hiro is well versed in ancient samurai lore featuring codes of honor, the comic book world of superheroes, and science fiction films and television series that illustrate traditional heroes' development, he really is the ideal candidate to become a modern classic hero.

His belief that he must act in accordance with heroes' codes of behavior causes him to spout his own Heroes 101 guidelines. He sounds like he's memorized the list, which he repeats often enough that Ando eventually can quote him word for word, which Hiro finds annoying when he has doubts about the superhero business. Some of his favorite axioms about heroes include

> Rule 1. "Every hero must learn his purpose. Then he'll be tested and called to greatness" ("Genesis"). Taking this idea straight out of Joseph Campbell's description of a hero's journey, Hiro knows this stage very well and accepts it as his personal credo.

Rule 2. "A superhero doesn't use his power for personal gain" ("Genesis"). This one proves more difficult to remember, and Hiro has to learn the hard way not to use his power just to help himself (or Ando). His ability to teleport into the women's restroom gets him bounced out of a karaoke bar and into an alley ("Genesis"). During his road trip across the U.S., Hiro and Ando cheat at roulette and poker, but they lose their money, are roughed up by the high rollers they cheat, and barely escape being slaughtered ("Better Halves"). Hiro goes back in time to save Charlie — not part of his original mission — because he loves her; he fails, despite his good intentions ("Homecoming").

Rule 3. "A hero doesn't run away from his destiny" ("One Giant Leap"). When Ando suggests it's more logical to run from a bomb than toward it, Hiro smugly states this part of the hero's code. Once again, Hiro finds this a difficult concept to master as the stakes become higher and the odds that he'll lose loved ones increase. Even so, he stands up to his father and steadfastly maintains that his life path must differ from the comfortable if boring life his father has lined up for him. Time after time, Hiro returns to his mission, despite his fear or discomfort.

Rule 4. "You don't have to have superpowers to be a hero" ("Better Halves"). Said first to convince Ando he, too, can be heroic and has a place in Hiro's journey, Hiro later becomes annoyed when Ando reminds him, after he loses his power, that even though he can't teleport or stop time, he still has a mission to complete ("Run!").

Rule 5. "A hero doesn't hide" ("Six Months Ago"). "He does if he wants to live," Ando replies as he helps a shocked Hiro escape through a window. Hiro begins to question whether he's cut out to be a hero after he listens to the murder of the men with whom Ando has been playing poker; he does nothing to save them. This fact bothers Hiro, who questions whether he should save anyone in need or stick to his mission to save New York. When Hiro finds guns in the closet of the man from whom he and Ando plan to steal a bag, he wants to run away. "A hero doesn't run," Ando reminds him in a variation of Rule 5 ("Run!"). Of course, Ando has more to win in this situation; he plans to return the missing bag to a woman he believes likes him and needs his help. When Hiro does run away, Ando takes the bag on his own but gets into trouble when the woman turns out to be a criminal. Although Hiro has fled, he finds a way to rescue Ando, putting his own life in jeopardy in the process.

Rule 6. "A hero never gives up" ("The Fix"). Hiro refuses to surrender to men who chase him and Ando, even resorting to hiding under a car and jumping a fence to get away. He only gives himself up when Ando is captured; Hiro then tells Ando he won't betray him, but he doesn't plan on giving the man who wants to see them whatever it is he wants. (It turns out that the man is Hiro's stern father, and true to his word, Hiro refuses to return quietly to Tokyo.)

Rule 7. "You cannot bribe a hero. His heart is pure" ("The Fix"). The lure of first-class seats to Tokyo can't sway Hiro from his mission. Even his father's promise to make him a CEO in the family business doesn't change his mind. Hiro struggles with the choice of whether to save his family, by returning to Japan and accepting a more important role in the family business, or to save the world, but he doesn't allow himself to be deterred from his mission.

Rule 8. "More than anything, a hero must have hope" ("Run!"). Ando should've paid attention to the lower-case h in hope; he immediately falls into the clutches of buxom, blonde Hope, who leads him and Hiro into danger.[7] Audiences, however, have the feeling by the end of season 1 that Hiro may need to repeat Rule 8 to reassure himself during future daring missions.

Rule 9. "A hero's journey takes him down many dark paths before returning to the light" ("The Hard Part"). Again straight from Campbell's phases of a hero's development, this rule is probably the most difficult for Hiro to accept, although his cross-country journey parallels his mental, emotional, and spiritual journeys to become an effective hero. Seeing the man he will become if the current timeline isn't changed motivates Hiro to do what to him is a morally wrong act: take Sylar's life. Nevertheless, Hiro accepts this dark path, because sidestepping it now would lead only to an even darker, longer road in the future. (Whether Hiro has succeeded in killing Sylar, which seems unlikely in the season 1 finale, may be revealed in season 2.)

Part comic book, part science fiction, part Japanese history, Hiro's Code for Heroes lists the most important rules for his life. As the epic story unfolds, Hiro may add new rules to his list, but he more likely will find the code is hard to live by as he tries to rationalize his and others' pragmatic behavior in (as HRG puts it) a "morally gray" world.

HIRO'S ROLE IN THE *HEROES* EPIC

Initially, Hiro seemed consigned to comic relief, but as the first season's story arcs expanded, so did his character. Although he still makes witty remarks and glows with childlike exuberance, his increasing sorrow, regret, and responsibility for others deepen his character.

Hiro realizes that he can't save the world by himself; he is only one of a network of people who, by working together and adding their special power to the mix, can change the future. Most important, Hiro acts as a catalyst for other heroes. He convinces Peter to save the cheerleader. He provides Isaac with foreknowledge of the artist's death but also the importance of his comic books. He encourages Ando (although not a superhero, quite possibly a hero) to take their mission seriously and to act more nobly. His belief in Nathan's inner goodness and his gentle conviction that they both have important jobs to complete persuade Nathan to get him past Linderman's security so that he can retrieve the sword. (Although Hiro later concludes that Nathan is a villain, his initial faith in "flying man" seems justified by Nathan's actions in the final moments of "How to Stop an Exploding Man.") Even in small ways, such as telling Micah that heroes exist and showing him the *9th Wonders* comic book of his life, Hiro encourages each hero to play a part in saving the world and to accept being special.

Hiro is the Everyhero, the character with whom audiences can identify. He and Ando, a modern Odd Couple or Skywalker/Solo dynamic duo, say and think what most people would in a situation; they're not always fearless, but they have good intentions. Hiro is a lovable loser who makes good, a son who disappoints his father, a friend who's weird and geeky, a lover who loses the girl — but he still keeps trying and mostly remains positive in spite of setbacks. He worries when he fails and then doubts himself. He has a conscience;

when Hiro contemplates doing something illegal or immoral, the act carries more weight, because he is a normally law-abiding citizen. He doesn't want to hurt anyone, and the idea of killing Sylar pains him, even if he wants to work for the greater good. Hiro is the ideal hero for this age: he's far from perfect, but he tries to do his best and he thinks about the consequences of his actions.

THE AMBIGUITY OF
EVIL IN HEROES

IN A HUMOROUS SCENE FROM "Godsend," Nathan doesn't understand Hiro's pronunciation of *villain* and works with him to pronounce the *v* sound. Ironically, Hiro gets it right on election day, when he attempts to convince Nathan to help him stop Sylar. Nathan whispers that no one can stop New York's destruction, leaving behind a distraught Hiro to call after him, "Villain! Villain!" ("Landslide"). Even Sylar, the character most viewers might identify as the season 1 villain, smugly tells Peter, the soon-to-be-exploding man, "You're the villain, Peter. I'm the hero" ("How to Stop an Exploding Man"). "Bad guy" Sylar won't annihilate millions; "good guy" Peter will.

The terms *villain* and *hero* come up often enough throughout the series to confuse viewers about a character's "true" nature. Ambiguous characters who gain depth by acting nobly and lovingly in one episode become callous killers in another. Mr. Bennet/HRG is a prime example; he is a shadowy figure in early episodes who redeems himself by becoming Claire's protective dad but returns to his darker side when he attempts to destroy The Company for which he's long worked.

Nathan embodies traits people often detest in politicians: manipulation of power for personal gain; misinformation skillfully delivered to the public; a handsome, philanthropic veneer covering deeper roots in corruption. In early season 1 episodes, Nathan resents Peter's desire to be something special and discover what he believes are superpowers; he nevertheless reveals his own ability to fly when he feels compelled to save his brother from a fall ("Genesis"). He both loves Peter and threatens to confine him in a mental institution. In "Landslide," when Nathan seems to embrace his destiny as a future leader uniting the world after a nuclear holocaust, audiences can believe that he really will fly away in a helicopter instead of using his power to save New York. When Nathan does the latter in the season finale, he gives a noble speech, almost like previous public speeches and media sound bites. He chokes up when he admits his love for his brother, but there's still the question whether, should Nathan survive, he'll always act altruistically in the future.

Many viewers don't expect politicians to remain altruistic all the time; the sheer monetary cost of becoming an elected official means that deals are likely made along the way. Although audiences may feel that Nathan isn't a "good guy" for taking Linderman's money (and looking the other way while his election is rigged), he still does nothing worse than what many viewers expect happens frequently in real-world politics.

Part of the problem may be that these "heroes" are not perfect role models; the "good guys" potentially pattern their behavior on some less-than-stellar examples. Young Molly Walker tearfully reiterates that police officer Matt Parkman is her hero ("How to Stop an Exploding Man") because he once saved her from Sylar, and yet along the journey to New York, Matt steals diamonds, helps hold a family hostage, and breaks into Primatech to look for answers. He even plans to help HRG destroy the Walker System, which turns out to be Molly and a murder that Matt can't condone. But no matter what else he does, Matt remains Molly's hero.

Nathan seems to feel the same way about his father, a man Linderman and Nathan's mother describe as weak. He initially vows to expose his father's corruption and shady business deals with Linderman, at first portrayed as more of a mob boss than a suave CEO. Nathan dislikes Linderman once he, too, begins working with him, but he still needs his support and financial backing for his campaign; however, he won't tolerate his mentor berating Mr. Petrelli. He stubbornly insists that his father was his hero ("Landslide"), and the son does seem to be following in his father's footsteps.

Ambiguous behavior is typical among the major players in season 1. Each potential hero seems just as capable of acts ranging from theft to murder as do any of the series' more readily labeled villains. Although at first *Heroes* seems like a positive, easy-to-understand title, episodes quickly illustrate that the definition of *hero* may be an ever-shifting identity that forces audiences to evaluate not only the types of people they want to save them but also the sociopolitical environment that encourages such ambiguous illustrations of good or bad characters.

"BAD GUYS": THE COMPANY, JESSICA, AND SYLAR

The Company suggests business leaders run amok, who, like Linderman in his kitchen, have their fingers in many business pies (Primatech Paper, The Corinthian, Yamagato Industries, and who knows what else). The existence of a large, socioeconomically invasive Company is a looming threat to people with much less economic or political power (which is to say most characters and viewers). Even if it doesn't directly threaten the lives of civilians (those without superpowers), it determines tomorrow's political leaders and invites globalization of big business. The Company represents one form of potential villainy, but individuals, as well as faceless corporations, may be perceived as primarily bad. Jessica and Sylar are two examples.

An apparently loose association of rich international businesspeople forms The Company, which abducts, marks, and tracks genetically enhanced people with a superpower. It masks its identity through other businesses, such as Primatech Paper, and requires loyal manager HRG (later known as Noah Bennet) to make frequent business trips to locate potential "heroes," bring them in for testing, or solve problems and clean up messes (such as hide Simone Deveaux's death). The Corinthian, an exclusive Las Vegas hotel, becomes an enclave of deception and death as well as beauty and elegance. On the surface, hotel owner and Company mastermind Linderman benevolently oversees his empire; he even cooks in the Corinthian kitchen and masquerades as a kindly grandfather to Micah after his abduction. Beneath the surface, Linderman manipulates lives. He coerces Jessica to have sex (captured on hidden camera) with married soon-to-be-congressman Petrelli so the politician will be more easily controlled; he later offers her millions to kill D.L. In one room, he keeps files on every aspect of the lives of "heroes" he manipulates; in another, he collects and catalogues cultural treasures.

As the series progresses, other wealthy, manipulative parents are revealed to be members of The Company, although viewers aren't sure just how they're involved or what they control. Mama Petrelli identifies elder son Nathan as the go-to man for future political machinations. She primes her son to be strong and faithful to The Company's cause, which includes wiping out a mere .07% of the earth's population (New York City residents) in order to unify the globe under one Company-backed leader (".07%"). If younger, gentler son Peter needs to be sacrificed along the way (after all, his ability to self-heal may help him survive being a nuclear explosion), then so be it. Sacrifices must be made to achieve the greater plan ("Landslide").

Hiro's father, Kaito Nakamura, turns up in HRG's flashback; after an incident, Nakamura gives baby Claire to him for safe keeping. Although the lower-level employee clearly isn't all that interested in becoming a father, Nakamura insists that Bennet rear Claire and be prepared to return her to The Company if she should manifest special powers.

Even Charles Deveaux, who at first seems like a nice old man dying of a terminal disease, later reveals his true identity as part of this global regulatory group of rich parents. Whether in a dream or through time travel, an invisible Peter overhears Deveaux talking with Angela Petrelli. Whereas she insists that Peter is weak and Nathan is the one to accomplish their goals, Deveaux explains that Peter has a pure heart and can love unconditionally; he represents the hope needed to change the world ("How to Stop an Exploding Man"). All these parents seem aware of, if not directly involved with, The Company's plans for New York and the aftermath of its destruction.

Of all the characters bent on controlling the world and remaking it in their image, only Linderman's henchman Thompson seems consistently evil. He has no hesitation to kill anyone who gets in the way of The Company and, in the end, receives no mercy from former employee HRG. Bennet shoots Thompson point blank and shows no remorse in killing a representative of The Company out to capture Claire.

Even Linderman, long built up as the evil mastermind behind The Company, occasionally shows a softer side. He collects and protects cultural artifacts (or, on the flip side, keeps them from the rest of the world); gardens and cooks, both genteel hobbies; and heals Nathan's paraplegic wife, Heidi, on election day. Although this kind act is a gift both to Heidi and Nathan, Linderman realizes that it also binds Nathan even more closely to The Company. (Nathan, however, remembers that Linderman's goons caused the car accident in which Heidi was paralyzed. By healing Heidi, Linderman merely rights one of his earlier wrongs.) Linderman can do something nice, but each act is carefully calculated; kindness and assistance are tools to be used to further his, and The Company's, objectives.

The Company appears highly successful, legitimate, and well invested in international businesses. Like many large corporations, it becomes an entity to admire or fear. The people behind the corporation, whether a CEO such as Linderman, part of the ostensible board of directors (as apparently are Angela Petrelli, Charles Deveaux, and Kaito Nakamura), or lackeys like Noah Bennet, display varying degrees of culpability in the way The Company operates and how efficiently it advances its agenda.

For many viewers, such an institution invites suspicion just by its existence. Many real-life large corporations seem to have undue lobbyist influence on the U.S. government; international business, including outsourcing and trade conglomerates, often seem to work only for the best interests of wealthy CEOs or exclusive boards of directors. Corporations' products may hurt consumers instead of making their lives easier. Profit, rather than public interest, is a prime motivator, and many viewers, such as the "heroes" struggling to make a living (e.g., police officer Matt Parkman, single mom Niki Sanders), resent and suspect the wealthy behind such corporations. To many viewers, Linderman is a "typical" depiction of a modern CEO. The Company looks out for The Company, and anyone who gets in the way is likely to be squashed.

Jessica may be a surprise addition to this list of bad guys because of her sweeter, gentler alter ego, Niki. If the Jessica personality is perceived as a separate character, however, she easily falls into the villain category. She unhesitatingly kills those who get in her way (Linderman's loan collectors, poker players, D.L.'s gang members, Aaron Malsky, law enforcement agents). She steals money. She sets up Nathan to be blackmailed for extramarital sex. She is sorely tempted to take Linderman's cash in exchange for killing her husband, confessing to D.L. that the "Jessica" persona who would take the money won't do that because "Niki" truly loves her husband ("The Hard Part"). Jessica protects herself and uses her strength and beauty to get what she wants. Her one redeeming act is to merge with Niki, allowing this caring, nurturing personality once more to prevail in their combined life and reunite her family ("Landslide").

Unlike Jessica, a personality generated from abuse who seems born to be bad, Sylar, né Gabriel Gray, merely lives up to his name. He likes to "blow his own horn" about his achievements in order to gain his mother's approval and lives in the gray world of mediocrity and moral ambiguity until he develops the ability to gain others' superpowers. Although Sylar unflinchingly kills those whose powers he wants to assimilate, he confesses to his mother that he might kill millions and wonders what might make him do such a thing. Actor Zachary Quinto describes his character as "'somebody . . . overtaken by a desire that he didn't expect to overtake him as powerfully as it does . . . it starts from a place of really just wanting to be valued and desired, and it evolved into something . . . insatiable." Gabriel/Sylar hurts his mother physically and emotionally but then begs her forgiveness; when she becomes afraid of him and declares he's not her son, he tries to stop her from running away, resulting in her death. With no family or friends — only people who fear and hunt him are left in his world — Sylar plans to become the son his mother wanted. He will grow up to be president, that is, killing future world leader Nathan and others with superpowers to become the most powerful man in the world. Then he can do whatever he likes, and no one will be able to stop him. In "Five Years Gone," his plans have come to fruition.

Although the "bad guys" can be really bad, *Heroes* also presents some redeeming qualities in each or tries to rationalize their behavior. After all, if Gabriel hadn't come from a dysfunctional family and desperately needed approval to feel special, he might not have turned into an (apparently) brain-eating murderer. If Niki's abusive father hadn't killed her sister, the personality of Jessica might not have emerged with such fury. If Linderman and his cohorts had been able to achieve their vision of a peaceful world early in their lives, they might not have resorted to underhanded manipulation. Evil may take many forms as it operates in a world of (Gabriel) Gray.

"GOOD GUYS": CLAIRE, HIRO, AND PETER

Three characters begin season 1 as innocents, naively exploring their burgeoning superpowers and gradually realizing that their desire to do something good with their special gifts requires a great deal of sacrifice. As these heroes mature during a series of mishaps and adventures, they become desensitized to violence to the point that they can wield weapons and at least offer to kill someone else. Even the good guys realize that sometimes they may have to go against their better nature in order to protect either the ones they love or the population at large.

Claire isn't afraid of hurting herself; after all, she initially attempts death-defying acts to document her unusual ability to heal. This ability makes her feel like a freak rather than a hero; even when she saves a man from a burning train wreck, she allows cheerleader Jackie to take the credit. Being a hero isn't something she wants.

Claire has enough on her mind already. Between homework assignments and extracurricular activities such as making the cheerleading squad and being elected homecoming queen, she survives a series of personal shocks. Her adoptive father is part of The Company and can't be trusted, but then he breaks away from The Company and sacrifices his memory and body in order to protect her. She learns that her biological parents also have superpowers, and that her father, Nathan Petrelli, is part of a wealthy, politically important family. Claire sees his duplicitous nature and fears to trust him, although he, too, later redeems himself by flying Peter far enough from New York to protect it from nuclear fallout. Probably the most difficult decision for Claire, however, is Peter's request that she shoot him if he becomes a nuclear threat. "The universe can't be that lame," she argues ("Landslide"), although when Peter encourages her to kill him in Kirby Plaza, she shakily picks up a gun and readies herself to do so. Fortunately, Claire isn't forced to shoot, but she knows that she is capable of killing the one person she has been able to trust completely: her hero and biological uncle, Peter.

Hiro (whose development is explored in depth in "The Making of a Hiro") at first worries about every rule infringement, but before long he cheats at dice and cards (although he rues this deception soon enough), steals swords, and agrees to kill Sylar. Killing even a bad man proves difficult for Hiro, but the very real possibility that Ando will die unless Hiro kills Sylar motivates him to action. Once he gains skill using a sword, he safely teleports Ando back home to Tokyo before returning to New York to complete his mission. Stabbing Sylar, however, doesn't avert the nuclear crisis, and Peter asks Hiro to kill him. Before he can accommodate this request, Sylar banishes him from the square, forcing Hiro to teleport hurriedly.

Like the audience, Hiro needs to come to grips with some important questions, such as whether it is wrong to kill an enemy when it's not in self-defense. (Hiro isn't directly threatened by Sylar. Ando is safely back in Tokyo, and Hiro could let someone else stop the exploding man, which happens anyway when Nathan flies Peter out of New York before he detonates.) In hindsight, is Hiro justified, even glorified, for overcoming his reluctance to kill? His action may rid the city of one bad guy, but it doesn't effectively stop all evildoers. Do Sylar's previous murders justify his death at the hands of a "hero"? If it turns out that Hiro acts primarily to avenge girlfriend Charlie's death, does that make him less or more of a hero? Should vigilante justice be encouraged? His actions may prompt audiences to ask some tough questions regarding even as lovable a "hero" as Hiro.

Peter, too, seems imminently likable as well as ultimately deadly. He first serves Charles Deveaux as a hospice nurse/companion; Peter's noble career ambition is to help the terminally ill die gracefully. He also gains viewer sympathy or empathy as the less loved and misunderstood second son in a powerful family. Peter is identified with hope in the series' finale; his ability to love unconditionally and to want to make the world a better place lead Deveaux to believe that Peter, not brother Nathan, would make a better world leader/savior. Hoping he can stop Sylar and avert the predicted destruction of New York, Peter takes him on in a fistfight. Unlike Future Peter, a scarred, hardened man who easily uses his many superpowers in a fight to the death with Sylar, Present Peter chooses not to use the superpowers under his command in order to fell his nemesis.

The challenge of becoming heroes on a mission apparently kills these characters' innocence and changes their perceptions of who they must be if they are to act heroically.

LIVING IN A MORALLY GRAY WORLD

To become more effective heroes, even good characters must embrace their darker side, a fact that Joseph Campbell notes in all hero myths. This raises the question whether, in today's complex world, anyone can accomplish great deeds or humanitarian works without selling out to a certain extent. The people who get things done know how to manipulate a system politically and financially for their best interest — with the intention that what's best for them allows them to act on behalf of others. On *Heroes*, acting "for the greater good" usually supersedes what is lawful; legality becomes another gray area.

During season 1, the most effective heroes merge their good intentions with the ability to back them up however necessary, preferably while causing no harm to innocents. Jessica embraces Niki, and the two merge into a kick-ass personality tempered by motherly love. Hiro runs Sylar through with his sword and even smiles afterward, a big change from his joyous naïveté when he first discovers his ability to bend time and space. Claire accepts her adoptive father, hugging him and planning to return home, whereas a few weeks earlier she despised him for being a Company man. She has become a daddy's girl again, with a better understanding of who's her daddy.

Even though several characters, including Hiro and HRG, have broken laws, they get away with their crimes. The series emphasizes bigger issues — whether New York City can be saved, whether a superkiller can be stopped. Some form of lawlessness is expected; a world free of crime isn't realistic. For society to survive, it may need to live with lower expectations of goodness. Perhaps Mohinder Suresh is right — only cockroaches ultimately survive (and the cockroach sometimes symbolizes Sylar's ability to slink away to fight later battles). Whether viewers want to embrace their "inner cockroach," however, is another matter.

The *really bad* "bad guys" do get their comeuppance by the finale. Thompson is murdered by HRG. Sylar is stabbed and appears to die. D.L. dispatches Linderman with apparent poetic justice by ripping out the brain of the man who seems to have masterminded much of the world's fate. Linderman's death brings up another issue: is The Company self-perpetuating even without Linderman's direct supervision? Evil, like nature, abhors a vacuum, and the power vacuum in The Company will likely soon be filled, probably by someone even more sinister. Early hints about season 2 indicate at least one likely new villain, an "Irish mobster." Molly foreshadows an even greater evil, one that she's afraid will see her if she tries to locate him.

Heroes suggests that characters and viewers alike have become somewhat jaded by the prevalence of evil. To combat it, audiences, like these superheroes, may need to get dirty. To become effective heroes, Hiro, Peter, and Claire, three of the best-liked characters at the beginning of the season, show that they have the capability to kill others; they are more powerful than ever, and they believe they've sworn allegiance to a mission greater than themselves. In the fight for what's good, these and other characters may feel compelled to do bad things for the greater good. The trick is to stay grounded on what quickly becomes a very slippery slope.

LIGHT AND DARK

GOING DARK IN HEROES

STEVEN PEACOCK

> A hero's journey takes him down many dark paths, before returning to the light.
>
> — Hiro ("The Hard Part")

DARKNESS CLOAKS THE MODERN SUPERHERO, on screens big and small. As *Batman* begins again, bleakness and blackness replace the day-glo rainbow of the Schumacher years. The inhabitants of *Sin City* skulk in the gloom, and the *X-Men* pitch a somber final battle under dulled skies. *Buffy the Vampire Slayer* dies to revive the franchise; even Spider-Man goes dark in his third outing under director Sam Raimi, donning a black costume (and, it seems, charcoal eyeliner) to scowl at the world. *Heroes* follows suit, pitch-black to its core. Dark tones pervade the series' plot, mood, and palette. Characters constantly lurk in the shadows, absorbed in shady dealings. A sense of dread suffuses the storylines. Sequence after sequence plays out in pools of darkness. Above all, there is the looming threat of the coming apocalypse, the destruction of New York City, the end of the world. Yet, unlike some of its counterparts, the darkness at the heart of *Heroes* is not oppressive. While exploring the murky mysteries of superhuman abilities, the series takes care not to let its grim disposition *overpower* the drama. In the world of *Heroes*, bleakness is not burdensome. One of the series' central features, and pleasures, is its handling of darkness with a light touch.

SOMETHING WICKED THIS WAY COMES

Initially, the omnipresent darkness of the series *threatens* to engulf all in its path. In many ways, the first sights and sounds of *Heroes* act as a harbinger of things to come. At the start of the first episode, white lettering on a black background scrolls to announce an ominous premonition:

> In recent days, a seemingly random group of individuals
> has emerged with what can only be described as "special"
> abilities. Although unaware of it now, these individuals will
> not only save the world, but change it forever ("Genesis").

The slow-burning drama promised by these portentous words ("the transformation . . . will not occur overnight") matches the menacing pulse of the music. Chords of jabbing strings loop round and gradually meet with a protracted, high-pitched howl. As Shankar's cry sounds out, high and plaintive, the sight of the scrolling words gives way to that of a huge, turning Earth-globe. The yowling sound combines with the spinning Earth; the world, it seems, is crying.

Suddenly, darkness falls over the entire globe. Perhaps it is the solar eclipse, the sight shared by all characters in the first episode, connecting them across the world, or perhaps the bomb, casting its pall. A world shrouded in blackness provides the signature image of the entire series. Presenting the Earth in silhouette, the show forms a stark *outline* of its concerns. The shadowed globe appears again at the start of each episode, and as a painting in Isaac's apartment, itself a dark centre of the *Heroes* universe. In global terms, the image encapsulates the series' status as a post–9/11 drama, gravely reflecting on the dark days of a new world order — a world "changed forever." The recurring sight of the eclipse binds the series as tightly as the twisting Helix symbol. Both appear in the first moments of volume 2 ("Generations"), as a befuddled Hiro crashes into Japan, 1671. Here, the spreading darkness of the eclipse *diffuses* a moment of conflict. The feudal army and Hiro join in casting their eyes skyward, as the darkness of the eclipse shrouds the heavens across space and time.

More locally, within the world, a dark presence haunts each of the characters. In both their ordinary and extraordinary lives, fate traps the protagonists. The series is distinctive in exploring the dubious gifts and dark twists of its heroes' superpowers; yet, even before this, it presents domestic lives tainted with violence, doubt, and death. It is fitting that *Heroes* begins by introducing (the *fall* of) Peter Petrelli, not only as events will gather around this figure, threatening to bring fiery destruction to all, but also as a man who has daily dealings with death. As a hospice nurse, Peter is in constant contact with the trappings of mortality. Watching over Simone's dying father, he observes, "he's close . . . couple more days maybe." From the beginning, Peter is vital to the end of things, offering his dark prophecies. Both the character and the series are acutely sensitive to a patterning of actions and *reactions*. It is no accident that Peter's early fall couples and contrasts with his final ascension in the season 1 finale.

In this first hint of a bleak future, and to match the mood, darkness spills into sound and image. The howl and pulse of the opening music carries into the fleeting scream of a police siren and the persistent blip of the patient's heart monitor. Peter and Simone's gloomy conversation unfolds in the shadows of the shrouded room. Amber lights smolder at the corner of the frame. In a color scheme that will carry across the entire season, steely blues, earthy browns, and stabs of crimson shade the scene. Hinting at the characters' future connection, the same colors gather across the globe in India, in the classroom, neighborhood, and apartment of Mohinder Suresh. Inside, thick curtains shroud gray windows, lit by low, flickering bulbs. Outside, incessant rain drives down. The dim vision is more *Blade Runner* than Bollywood. A threat lurks nearby, in the shifty shape of Bennet, yet to reveal himself to Mohinder or the viewer. The same sort of distressing news connects Peter and Mohinder in unhappiness, as *Heroes* announces (in a field day for psychoanalysts) the death of the father, to the power of two: Papa Suresh dies "driving a taxi in New York City . . . a very dangerous job," while Deveaux Senior ebbs away. Peter and Nathan's father passes, too, albeit off camera, in a dark corner of the series' story line.

GOTHIC NOTES AND GORY SPIKES

The twinning of these two scenarios reveals *Heroes'* interest in the Gothic. Throughout, Gothic elements inspire the decor, architecture, tone, and approach of the series. *Heroes* envisions the exploding skyline of future New York from the Deveaux roof, crowned by the pointed archway of two stone gargoyles. The Petrellis consistently dress as if for an elegant funeral: a Manhattan Addams Family. As noted in Peter's and Mohinder's like situations, *Heroes* embraces the Gothic concern of *doubling*. The notion lies at the heart of all superhero myths, as the extraordinary seeks refuge in an ordinary alter ego.

In Niki/Jessica, this series takes the notion to bleak, physical extremes. The introduction of Niki gives us the first hint of a dark superpower, glimpsed in the doubling reflection of a mirror ("Genesis"). Typically, the series folds the ability into a shady domestic routine. Niki performs a sleazy striptease to the raunchy chords of "Mustang Sally" for her invisible, Internet audience. Red drapes in a darkened room shut out the natural morning light. Just as the sinister undercurrent of the situation will surface when Linderman's henchmen force a disturbing repeat performance, darkness comes to the fore in the form of Jessica. For now, a fleeting glance suffices, a mirror's image of the mirror image. Later, Jessica's killing sprees release the force contained in the frame. *Heroes* is cut through with shards of violence, often manifest in Jessica's actions: the slaughtering of a gang, the sniper's callous precision, the body in the trunk. Whereas the character first controls the shady pleasures of the striptease, stopped in the clinical click of a mouse, violence begets violence, and darkness begins to bleed through.

Violence also heralds the arrival of another pivotal player in the series, Claire Bennet ("Genesis"). Yet, although shocking and bloody, the introduction of the cheerleader is far from cheerless. In Claire's grisly plummet, *Heroes* points up its plans to touch darker designs with lightness. We look through the shakily held viewfinder of a camcorder. A young male voice provides the commentary as a teenage girl, dressed in a cheerleader uniform, clambers to the top of a high industrial scaffold. To the distress of the cameraman (and perhaps the viewer), the girl suddenly jumps, shrieking and thudding down. The camera rushes toward the broken body; the girl slowly lifts herself up, rising from the dead, setting her shoulder back into place with a morbid click. This, we are told, marks attempt number six. The use of the word attempt points the way to the darkness of a failed teen suicide; yet the girl's miraculous (and nonchalant) recovery suggests otherwise.

In Claire, *Heroes* performs a somber turn on traditional superpowers, skewing the impenetrability of, say, Buffy or Supergirl. The series revels in the violence inflicted on the body before it inevitably heals, showing Claire fussily tidying away snapped ribs sticking out of her gut and, later, the bloody grin of her open chest cavity as she "plays dead" on a gurney ("Collision"). The handling of the scenario and the superpower reveal something of the series' black humor. The documentary-style presentation of "attempt number six" calls to mind the masochistic foolery of MTV's *Jackass*. At the same time, the invincibility of a body tossed off buildings and thrown into flames has a Looney Tunes quality to it. At home, Claire absentmindedly retrieves a ring from the rotating blades of a waste-disposal unit ("One Giant Leap"). While Claire's hand as a gory stump sprouts new fingers, her mother's Pomeranian Mr. Muggles licks up the blood spatters on the floor. The moment echoes that of another masterstroke of black humor, in David Lynch's *Wild at Heart*, when a stray dog makes off with a recently decapitated bank robber's head.

TAKING WING

Like the gallows-style humor of Claire's ability, *Heroes* presents powers with flair and agility. A good example is the lightness found in the Petrellis' power of flight. After the initial dramatic climax of Peter's fall and Nathan's swooping catch comes out of nowhere ("Don't Look Back"), the treatment of this superpower delicately lifts the series. Rather than heavy-handedly building up dramatic tension, charging events around instances of flying with shock and awe, this superpower nimbly flits into and out of the narrative. At points, *Heroes* and Nathan make light of their ability. There are humorous examples of the Petrelli brothers finding their feet, of tottering baby steps off a climbing frame ("One Giant Leap") and a hotfooted landing in the desert ("Hiros").

Alongside the lightness of comic relief, there is the slightness of the act. The series is agile in capturing the dexterity of flight. When put to use (by the show and by the character), this superpower is remarkable in the brevity and delicacy of its appearance. Cornered by Bennet and the Haitian, Nathan instinctively flies away ("Hiros"). Rather than appearing as an eagerly awaited upsurge to the scene, the act of flying releases the dramatic pressure. Nathan escapes in a flash, tracing a thin white line in the sky. The expression on Bennet's upturned face captures the effect of the moment, quietly appreciative of its effortless flair, of a sudden and successful act of flight.

DARK INTO LIGHT

Heroes abounds in light touches of decidedly darker powers too. The Haitian is capable of creating a dark mist in the mind, erasing all memories by a single, delicate push of his palm. The sudden appearance (and disappearance) of Claude Raines is as fleeting as it is pressing.

When not landing fierce blows to Peter in training, compelled by his own manic bluster, the invisible man is gone in the waft of a breeze ("Distractions"). Even the most sinister "big bosses," when revealed, step lightly out of the gloom. Emerging from the plotline's shadows, the kingpin Linderman finally introduces himself chopping vegetables in the brightly lit space of his hotel kitchen ("Parasite"). Again, *Heroes* brings together the everyday with the extraordinary.

More precisely, the moment echoes the arrival of Bill (David Carradine) at the end of Quentin Tarantino's *Kill Bill: Vol. 2*, making sandwiches for his daughter. Rather than declare the dark presence of chief villain in doom-laden terms, the film and series tread more lightly. The menace of the meeting catches in the glint of the blade, in the fastidious preparation of food. Even Sylar, the most menacing and explicitly violent of *Heroes'* supervillains, comes close to lightheartedness before a descent into total darkness. With a twinkle in the eye, the series presents Sylar's tragicomic relationship with his mother, aping Norman Bates ("The Hard Part"). As the threat of the coming apocalypse grows nearer, the blackness of Sylar's soul deepens in the brilliance of a hundred swirling snow globes. This playful attitude comes to the fore a last time in the finale battle, as Sylar bats around Bennet and Hiro with effortless aplomb: a ballistic ballet.

In other moments, *Heroes* moves between particular characters to create tonal counterpoints, shifting from dark to light across the edit. Most often, such instances involve Hiro. In his relationships, appearance, performance, and powers, Hiro provides light relief. There is a gentle humor at the heart of his double-act with Ando, in their constant bungling of the mission and close relationship to farce, fixing cards to gamble with their lives ("Collision"), hiding under beds and behind clothes racks, offering a helping hand to Hope ("Run!"). There is lightness found within Hiro's frothy enthusiasm for his powers — "Yahooo!" — and those of others — "Hey flying man!" Whilst showy, the character is also prim. Dressed in a crisp white shirt, fussily pushing up his spectacles, exactly quoting from comic books or *Star Trek*,

Hiro is, in many ways, a precisely drawn character. His musical motif fits his twinkling sensibility, tinkling and lightly lilting. His power is as delicate: a moment's effort stops the second hand. Hiro's lightness is crucial to the agility of the series, and to its weightier concerns.

As well as balancing light and dark tones in its treatment of individual characters, *Heroes* also achieves a delicate touch in its arrangement of a vast ensemble cast. Following the trail blazed by *Lost*, the series introduces and moves among many different key players. Crucially, it presents the repeated scenario of characters discovering and dealing not only with their superpowers but also their fateful role in a much bigger picture. A lesser series could easily have made the process laborious and overbearing, as the same dismal tune recurs, building to a doom-laden climax. Yet *Heroes* arranges all as intricate parts of a single mechanism, attended to with the same care and precision that Sylar brings to each watch repair.

The series itself is a delicate timepiece ticking toward the season's conclusion. The episodes' series of connections among events and characters are finely interwoven, with the likelihood of a happy ending hanging by a thread. *Heroes* manifests both metaphors throughout the season, in the repeated sound of a ticking clock accompanying Sylar's movements and in the timeline made out of string in Isaac's apartment, each action and scenario intricately connected ("Five Years Gone"). Following each tightly entwined strand, the series moves deftly between yarns. One example shows *Heroes*' interest in patterning gestures and scenarios to connect them closely. As Claire's mother struggles to recover from her memory-wipe, the series moves to focus on Jessica's appearance. To mask the sight of the mysterious dark (Helix) tattoo on her arm, Jessica carefully wipes a measure of make-up over the spot ("Run!"). Here, aspects of concealment combine in a light application.

FUTURE IMPERFECT?

Yet it could all have been, could still be, so different. In "Five Years Gone," *Heroes* presents an alternative future vision not only of the characters' world but also of the series itself. In terms of the season's story line, the episode reveals a dystopia that is yet to come, where Future Hiro meets with Possible Peter in a radically different world order. At the same time, in its tone and approach of the material, *Heroes* shows how a substitute set of decisions by Kring and company could have led (could lead) to a radically different series.

In this alternative terrain, darkness is desperately dour. The possible-protagonists constantly act out, performing earnestness in each glowering glare and meaningful glance. A snarling, scar-faced Peter plays at being bad, while Parkman works for The Man. Rather than being opaquely addressed, references to terrorism are hammered home. After the introduction of the Linderman Act, Homeland Security is called upon to clamp down on attackers "acting against America's interests." Dark allusions are forced to the surface: as a boy shows signs of (outlawed) superpowers, Bennet gives the family false IDs, to prevent them being "marched off to the gas chambers." The color scheme matches the heaviness of tone: all scenarios are beaten to submission in swathes of black and blue.

The episode treats the characters' superpowers with an equally heavy hand. Abilities are put to use in declamatory blasts: Peter makes an invisible entrance, stops time, and throws assailants into the air in a triple whammy. Heavy-duty artillery provides a constant hail of bullets, while the bombastic final battle buckles under the strain of its own biblical proportions. As "America remembers" the explosion of the city, bells toll in dull tones.

A return to the present releases the hold of the alternate vision and restores the series' buoyancy. A sense of relief is immediately palpable. Hiro and Ando stand in the open air, on the Deveaux building rooftop, free from the tight confines and restricted settings of the future in "Five Years Gone." Gloominess remains, but with an air of possibility, room to breathe. Pleased to be back on familiar ground, Hiro raises his head, delicately and customarily propping his glasses up on his nose: the (slightly) lighter designs of the present welcomed back in a light touch. In giving us a glimpse of a dreadful alternative, *Heroes* throws its skills into relief. Dealing with darkness in a seemingly effortless manner is no easy task. As Hiro declares, standing toward the future on the edge of the roof, in order to continue to achieve remarkable things, now comes "the hard part" — seeing things through. As the final moments of season 1 flit swiftly into the darkly tinged, lightly played past of "Generations," the future looks bright.

THE HEROES KALEIDOSCOPE

MARY ALICE MONEY

HEROES PRESENTS A TELEVISUAL KALEIDOSCOPE of characters, themes, structure, and images — images as pictures, images as reputation, and, most important, images as mirrors or shadows. Just as bits of mirror within a kaleidoscope form different images as the device is turned, so do the bits and pieces of the Heroesverse morph as the episodes unfold. The ever-changing images reflect different literary worlds from which the elements of *Heroes* arise: from cult TV, horror films, superhero comic books, and science fiction to the more rarified demesne of Nathaniel Hawthorne. As the season turns, the characters' identities mutate to reveal shadow figures, mirror images, warped reflections of evil twins, and ever-shifting alliances. Not only are viewers kept off balance as each character develops, hides, or reverses identity, sometimes even the character questions who he or she is. In an evolution of past, present, and future narratives spun on our television screens and in a series of online graphic novels, we see the story unfold and eventually are shocked to see ourselves reflected in those mirrors.

"Genesis," the first episode of *Heroes*, occurs on the day of a solar eclipse. The series' logo or identifying symbol is the circle of the eye of heaven darkened in that total eclipse with only a golden rim and tiny fragment of light showing. (Revealingly, it is here, on this image, that Tim Kring chooses to place his creator credit.) The entire first season determines whether that bit of sun is the final glow about to be swallowed by the black or the first light beginning to emerge as darkness ends. To stand outside during a summer's solar eclipse is to shudder in that unnaturally cold wind, physically and psychically, a moment in a suddenly cold, shaded world so unreal that even a rational modern human feels all order is gone from the time-space continuum. Thus the stage is set.

The entire series seems to take place within an eclipse where all anomalies and all futures are possible. The rimmed circle of the eclipse also suggests the eye of a kaleidoscope through which viewers experience the story, and the motif is echoed in the two-thirds circle (almost like two arms embracing the city view) of the architectural trim on the roof of the Deveaux building. Inside the building both Charles Deveaux and Isaac Mendez live and die, but the rooftop is most significant. There, the characters and thus the viewers return many times, often seeing New York framed within the circle. In the present, when Bennet and the Haitian attack Peter and Claude on the roof, Peter flies them both to safety ("Unexpected"); in a dream-vision of the past, Peter gains Charles Deveaux's approval ("How to Stop an Exploding Man"); and in the post-apocalyptic future, Hiro and Ando look through the circle at a devastated city and vow to change the future (".07%"), soon returning to see the city whole again in the present ("Five Years Gone"). The circles of eclipse, kaleidoscope, and architecture all suggest cycles of change and return, uniting the many threads of plot, character, and theme throughout season 1.

ELEMENTS OF CULT TV

Heroes uses the elements of cult TV very effectively, beginning with various structural elements from the worlds of TV series. The first season (twenty-three episodes, 2006–07) is one "novel" or serialized story arc with no stand-alone episodes. One of the first prime-time series to use story arcs was Stephen J. Cannell's *Wiseguy*, 1987–90, whose hero was an FBI agent working undercover in organized crime with two or three arcs each season. More recent cult TV series — among them *The X-Files* (1993–99), *Buffy the Vampire Slayer* (1997–2003), *Angel* (1999–2004), *24* (2003–present) and *Lost* (2004–present) — have included varying numbers of stand-alone episodes, flashbacks, alternate realities, and/or concurrent subplots in addition to the long-range series myth or conspiracy to unify a season or the entire run of the show.

Some dangers are inherent in shows with series' mythologies or conspiracies. If the series tantalizes the viewers too long without a payoff or solution to the mystery, many annoyed viewers will quit watching the castaways explore hatches and find the Others, as occurred in the second season of *Lost*. In *The X-Files*, even the most fanatical viewers — especially the most fanatical viewers! — were outraged by the final seasons' changes to the series myth (Mulder's sister wasn't really abducted?) and a Mulder-Scully sexual liaison that defied the logic of all earlier seasons of the series. The question of whether Tim Kring will remain true to the heart of *Heroes* throughout a long run will be answered in the future. However, Kring has stated that *Heroes* will answer the questions raised each season and something significant will happen in every episode, and in season 1 he has kept that promise: the cheerleader was saved, the list was found, and the exploding man was stopped.

At the same time, the finale suggests plotlines for season 2: the fate of Peter and Nathan; the return of Sylar; the identity of the supervillain who can see Molly; the continuing conflict with The Company; the role of Angela Petrelli; and the instant rapport between Micah and Molly — all will be part of "Generations." (Perhaps this is the first hit cult TV series about the human genome, and the mysterious symbol that appears from time to time seems to be a Helix, part of the double Helix genetrix of the human race.) Best of all, season 2 will surely follow the adventures of Hiro and Takezo Kensei (perhaps Hiro's ancestor) in 1671 Japan. Samurai swords, teleportation, and time travel, all under Kensei's Helix banner — what more could any cult TV fan ask?

In other significant ways, *Heroes* uses many elements of the cult TV world that Joss Whedon popularized, especially in *Buffy the Vampire Slayer*, and not just the obvious protagonists with superpowers, a series myth, complex characters, and serialized stories. *Buffy* is justly famous for Whedon's respect for the audience, a rare quality in network television. Both Whedon and Kring assume that viewers are willing and able to remember details, follow multiple storylines, and assemble all the bits and pieces over twenty-three hours (or seven seasons, in the case of *Buffy*) of story, and both assume that viewers will see more than just blonde cheerleaders and exciting fights.

When *Heroes* began in fall 2006, *TV Guide* critic Matt Roush accurately praised the show for "some awesome cliff-hangers" and Masi Oka's breakout role as Hiro, but ultimately dismissed it as an "overly sprawling show. . . . [with] too much pretentious hooey," obviously targeted at "comic-book geeks." His score: five out of ten. But those comic-book geeks and a few million other viewers seem to compose a fairly intelligent audience.

When Company man Thompson persuades Mohinder to find a cure for super-finder Molly in "The Hard Part," the audience is expected to recognize her as the child whom Parkman rescued when he was first developing his telepathy nineteen episodes earlier in "Don't Look Back." As soon as Thompson mentions Molly Walker's surname, the viewer should figure out that she is the so-called Walker Tracking System that Bennet, Parkman, and Sprague have been searching for since ".07%." Then for the last two episodes of the season, viewers fear that Bennet and Parkman will lose their heroic status by murdering Mohinder and the child, all for family values and the greater good. The heroes' decision in the last half hour of the finale rewards the true fans' understanding of each hero's motivation and character from the entire season.

In a question-and-answer session with *Sci Fi* magazine, Tim Kring, coproducer Aron Coleite, and writer Joe Pokaski (of "Five Years Gone") comment on the show's fans:

> We have the smartest fans on television, that's for certain.
> They pay attention and absolutely nothing gets by them.
> We'll lay in a subtle line or look setting something up for six
> episodes from now, and the fans always seem to find the
> meaning in it. It's pretty amazing.

Disregarding Kring and company's intentional flattery of their audience, they demand and receive such attentiveness. For instance, director-producer Greg Beeman's detailed blog on "Five Years Gone" quickly elicited forty-nine fan postings of intense, even obsessive, analysis of every act and word on screen.

Another *Heroes* cult TV element that Joss Whedon popularized is the willingness to kill some major characters despite the audience's investment in them — and sometimes to bring them back. In seven seasons of *Buffy*, Whedon at various times killed Buffy (twice), Angel, and Spike, and resurrected each, but in "The Body," one of the finest hours in all of series television, Buffy's mother dies an unspectacular and realistic death. Among other cult TV series, *Lost*, another "sprawling" series with "awesome cliff-hangers" (to echo Roush), several main characters have been killed, including the popular Charlie in the third season finale. The makers of *Heroes* have often said that any character could be killed off and some would die in the first season, although death might not preclude later appearances. As of the end of season 1, the casualties (varying degrees of deadness) include Peter, Nathan, and Sylar (apparently dead but surely not); Mr. Linderman (apparently dead but perhaps not), Isaac Mendez, Eden McCain, Ted Sprague, and Charlie Andrews (probably permanently dead); and a few minor specials such as Brian Davis and Dale Smither (well developed characters but still the equivalent of red shirts who beam down with the Captain on *Star Trek*). After so many years in which hardly any main character ever died in prime-time television, the creators of cult TV shows have added a note of reality and discovered a way to shock and surprise the audience. Yet here, too, are dangers. Too high a mortality rate on series television will begin to alienate many loyal fans and soon become a cliché.

Above all, any good series from the world of cult TV must be committed to presenting moments of wonder, those sudden, unexpected, off-the-wall events or scenes that shock and awe the engaged viewer. *Buffy the Vampire Slayer* had many such moments, but it would be difficult to top the fifth season finale, in which Buffy dives to her death to save the world. *Heroes* repeatedly provides moments or scenes conveying that sense of wonder: Hiro teleporting into Times Square, overwhelmed with wonder and joy ("Genesis"); Nathan flying away from Bennet and the Haitian ("Hiros"); Claire gluing herself back together and getting up from the autopsy table ("Collision"); bad-ass Future Hiro appearing on the time-frozen subway to tell Peter to "Save the cheerleader; save the world" ("Collision"); and virtually every scene in "Five Years Gone." In each instance, the viewer thinks or says: "Do it again! Surprise me again! Top that! I want more!" Achieving that effect helps every cult TV series to achieve its most necessary goal: to stay on the air by whatever prestidigitation is possible.

THE HORROR OF IT ALL

Heroes also utilizes elements from the world of horror fiction and film. Claire's regenerative superpower requires vivid images of her burnt alive, cut upon for an autopsy, or with bones protruding. However, the prime example is Sylar's practice of cutting open other heroes' skulls and (off-screen) eating/ingesting/injecting the brain to obtain each hero's power. These scenes, though a bit over the top, are a clear-cut nod to one of the clichés of old horror movies and comic books.

At a deeper level, the action is a return to a primitive — or archetypal — concept of many cultures, the idea that by eating some

156

significant chunk of an enemy one has killed, one can absorb that enemy's desirable quality or power, as Sir James Frazer delineated in *The Golden Bough*. That power was more often bravery or strength (or perhaps wisdom or skill with weapons) in the *old* old days, but here it is the specific superpower of the person killed. According to *Time* magazine, the Parents Television Council recently cited the vivisection scenes among examples of violence that should be censored by the Federal Communications Commission in order to protect children. Gruesome as Sylar's scenes are, they pale before the new horror movies (*Hostel*, *Wolf Creek*, etc.) available today.

LITERARY INFLUENCES

Although cult TV and horror seem not to fit into the literary world, *Heroes* consistently builds on ideas from both Nathaniel Hawthorne and archetypal criticism. Northrop Frye would particularly approve of "Five Years Gone," for it presents a fine example of his demonic world as a perverse dystopia contrasting with the apocalyptic world in *Anatomy of Criticism*. Each hero is following the steps of Joseph Campbell's hero's journey as analyzed in *The Hero with a Thousand Faces*, and Hiro and Ando both refer to the hero's journey at some points. (See Chapter 6: "The Making of a Hiro.")

Rather surprisingly, the canonical writer who is echoed frequently in the themes of the series is Nathaniel Hawthorne. The show is clearly in Hawthorne territory: The Company (whatever it is) is committing the unpardonable sin of letting the intellect rule the heart. Hawthorne's Ethan Brand is the character who studies people around the world to determine the one sin that cannot be forgiven and eventually finds it in his own marble-hard heart: treating people as objects to be experimented on instead of as human beings ("Ethan Brand"). Similarly, Hawthorne's Dr. Rappaccini, a professor at the University of Padua in Renaissance Italy, somehow creates his daughter with the power to poison anyone she touches and ends up destroying her and her lover ("Rappacinni's Daughter"). One artist-scientist devotes years to creating an improvement on nature: a gorgeous mechanical butterfly that lives for only one brief flight ("An Artist of the Beautiful"). Another scientist is obsessed with finding a potion to remove a facial birthmark from his otherwise perfect wife; he finally succeeds, but the potion kills her as it "cures" her ("The Birthmark"). Throughout most of Hawthorne's fiction, the characters who live their lives most honorably are those who live as their hearts, their innermost conscience, dictate, instead of ignoring the heart and rationalizing weakness and cruelty.

Hawthorne's theme is reinforced throughout the first season of *Heroes* as well. The Company consistently sacrifices humans and humanity to gain power by tracking, controlling, and experimenting on the heroes. In the finale, Linderman tells Niki/Jessica and D.L. that he set up their entire relationship, guiding them to "breed" to discover what superchild they might bear. Apparently, other potentially special children (perhaps stolen, perhaps bred — their source is not yet clear) are taken from their parents and assigned to Company men to rear, as Claire was assigned to Bennet by Kaito Nakamura ("Company Man"). All of this baby farming is logical and will lead to a great future — if one disregards its heartlessness and the resulting absolutism implied by The Company.

The situation suggests a mixture of George Orwell's *1984* and Aldous Huxley's *Brave New World*.[1] In the first episode of Heroes, when Peter expresses regret that his parents never seemed to love him, his mother Angela dispassionately replies that "love is overrated." She arranges for Nathan to win election by a landslide and is generally capable of anything that will forward her goal of uniting the nation — under The Company's control, of course. She arranges for Nathan to steal an election; selects, then discards, Claire to die in the coming nuclear blast; and refuses to attempt to change the future in which her "weak" son Peter will explode. After all, he will kill only .07 percent of the population, and it will all be for the best.

In Peter's dream-vision on the Deveaux roof, Charles Deveaux tells him that he has the heart to be the best of the Petrelli family even if Angela does sneer at his sensitivity. Of course, Angela is wrong and Charles is right. Peter is strong enough to think with his heart, as are the other true heroes, and they triumph. During the final episodes, each one makes a critical decision from the heart — and saves New York. Mohinder risks his life to protect Molly and persuades Bennet to save her; Parkman refuses to kill Molly no matter what the cost; Niki uses her love for D.L. to overpower Jessica and trade $20 million for the man she loves; Peter asks to be killed rather than destroy the city and his friends; Claire jumps off a building to escape from Nathan and her grandmother and keep her word to Peter; Ando challenges Sylar when he thinks no one else will; Hiro risks all to save Ando and thus is strong enough to run Sylar through; and Nathan returns from safety to fly Peter into space and die (apparently) with the brother he truly does love. Any one of the heroes could have logically justified escaping to safety and letting the dystopian future occur; most heroes could have easily stayed with The Company and the winning side in that future; but all of them decide with their hearts. *Heroes* definitely reveals one of Hawthorne's favorite themes.

COMICS AND SCIENCE FICTION

Most obviously, and most often, the kaleidoscope of *Heroes* focuses on the overlapping worlds of superhero comic books and science fiction, the heroes of which are themselves based on archetypal figures of legend. Because much has been made of this connection in earlier chapters (see Chapter 4: "Comic Book *Heroes*" and Chapter 5: "Growing Pains: *Heroes* and the Quest for Identity"), no further discussion will be included here.

KALEIDOSCOPIC CHARACTERS

As the turning kaleidoscope reveals many overlapping worlds of cult TV, horror, Hawthorne, and comics, so does it reveal many fragments and views of the characters. Often the viewers are not quite sure of a character's identity or motive; almost as often, the characters are also trying to determine who they are. Their self-conceptions reveal or revise their actual identities. Because every hero is dealing with a mysterious new power without an instruction book, each one has the right to reinvent himself or herself.

Every character and every episode presents new examples. Bennet changes loyalty several times but always remains committed to protecting Claire, who searches for her identity and the reason for her superpower throughout season 1. She laments her loss of identity when Bennet and the Haitian conspire to let her escape and finally refuses her fake Canadian passport and her fake new life. But then she finds her way to her grandmother's house, the Petrelli apartment presided over by Angela. Claire's final choice is to leave her blood relatives Nathan and Angela to return to her adoptive father and Peter. (The conflict between blood relations and chosen families [especially in light of the apparent hereditary nature of superpowers] should continue as a theme in season 2, "Generations.")

Early in the series, Nathan was a double agent, working for the FBI in order to trap Linderman; then he passes up a chance to shoot Linderman and succumbs to the temptation of the presidency, truly becoming the conniving politician that he had earlier appeared to be. Fortunately for New York, he changes sides again in time to stop the bomb in the finale.

As might be expected of a story seen through a kaleidoscope, many characters are mirror images of one another. Niki and Jessica play out the mirror relationship most obviously, but many other pairs are important. Peter and Sylar both assume the powers of other specials, one by empathy and the other by surgery and ingestion.

Season 1's best use of mirror identities is in the splendid episode "Five Years Gone," which reveals the consequences of a few mistakes that would have delivered the characters into a post-apocalyptic, jackbooted dystopia. That episode also reveals the evil potential within each human that could twist even the best intentions into darkness.

The viewer experiences whiplash trying to follow as one character after another — Parkman, Hiro, Niki, Peter — enters in some new, shocking permutation of his/her original identity. All characters are darker. Future Claire has even dyed her blonde hair brown and assumed a new identity, as a waitress called Anne.[2] Future Parkman (in a very expensive coat) is the brutal commander of Homeland Security; but no, he's working with Bennet in the resistance, and his wife and super daughter are in hiding; or maybe he is both The Man and the rebel. Future Peter, the rock of the series, is scarred by a blade (Hiro's?) and has learned to slick his hair back; he looks tough, dangerous, damaged — like an outlaw (which he is) hanging out with his woman, Niki, just as dark as he is. Future Hiro looks like a samurai Clint Eastwood. He is the most changed and embittered of all, partly because he could not save Ando and the others from the bomb. Present Hiro and Ando teleport onto the scene, only to be arrested by Parkman and rescued by Future Hiro. Ando prompts Hiro, "Talk to yourself"; but Hiro refuses, saying, "I scare me." This comment says it all. At some time in season 1, every hero reaches the point at which he or she scares himself or herself. Every hero must decide once, or several times, which image in the mirror is the person to become.

THE DESIRE TO DO OVER

Tim Kring's *Heroes* assembles and reassembles many worlds of literature, peopled by memorable characters with shifting identities. In the final analysis, perhaps this kaleidoscopic series suggests something about the twenty-first century's surface and its collective unconscious. The old sci-fi cliché of foreseeing the future and changing it by adjusting the past or present is becoming omnipresent in fiction.

As an example, I give my experience on one day in March. I went to a movie, *Premonition*, in which wife Sandra Bullock adjusts her past to make the best of her husband's horrific death. One of the previews touted *Next*, in which hero Nicholas Cage can dream various versions of the future, all containing his lover's death *or* the end of the world —

his choice. At home that night I watched an episode of *Medium* on television in which Allison's dreams allow her to return to the past and *not* interrupt when a serial-killer-to-be was planning to commit suicide.

That heavy dose of future-changing reminded me of recent-past examples from movies (*Groundhog Day, The Jacket*) to television series (*The Dead Zone, Tru Calling*) to science fiction novels (Jane Lindskold's *Child of a Rainless Year*), back to classic Hollywood (*It's a Wonderful Life*), and many more. Sometimes a trend is just a trend: it works in one movie/television show/novel, so everyone else steals the stunt. Predictably, *Heroes* has inspired a surge of pilots based on supernatural and science fiction elements for the 2007–08 television season, including at least one centered around a hero changing past incidents to save the world. Granted, there is probably no human who has not sometimes thought, If only I could live that over and do it differently. But the feeling is too creepily pervasive in recent years to be a simple trend.

Perhaps there are reasons for our increasing fascination with the theme. One of the most memorable examples is in the 1978 film *Superman*, in which the hero reverses the rotation of the Earth in order to turn back time and bring Lois Lane back to life. At about the same time, the late 1970s, video tape recorders were becoming available to the public for under $1,000, and television buffs were first experimenting with those fascinating buttons labeled fast forward, rewind, and record. In effect, Superman rewinds the tape and records another event: the saving of Lois. Barely thirty years later, Americans are so accustomed to controlling and rescheduling their own lives by PDA, cell phone, TiVo, and DVR — replaying, saving, rerecording, etc. — that perhaps, subconsciously, we have the hubris to almost believe we *can* rewrite our own existence. A deeper reason might be that since 9/11, we are perhaps collectively foreseeing a terrible future and shuddering at the view. Now the kaleidoscope turns into a mirror, and in "Five Years Gone" we are suddenly looking at a distorted image of ourselves, at what we could become in the aftermath of 9/11.

Viewers experience a shock of recognition when President Nathan Petrelli (actually Sylar) appears in front of a devastated New York landscape to speak inspirational platitudes designed to unite Americans and prevent another disaster. The scene is a slightly twisted reflection of ceremonies upon the fifth anniversary of September 11, 2001. *Heroes* is successful cult TV not only because Tim Kring engages the viewer with complex characters enmeshed in the worlds of comics, science fiction, horror, and Hawthorne. The series also fascinates viewers because its people and worlds reflect our own twenty-first century realities.

THE FINALE

FINALE FACE-OFF:
NIKKI STAFFORD VERSUS DAVID LAVERY ON "HOW TO STOP AN EXPLODING MAN"

> **IN THIS CORNER: NIKKI STAFFORD**
> *Nikki Stafford posted this critique of "Exploding Man" on her blog (nikkistafford.blogspot.com) within ninety minutes of the episode's broadcast on May 21, 2007. The "Postscript" that follows was written by her in June 2007 after reading David Lavery's comments.*

We've seen twenty-two chapters building to this final one of Volume One. We've seen characters go from ordinary people to superheroes, slowly master their powers, realize what their callings were, and look within themselves to see what truly mattered to them. We've waited all season for all of them to finally end up together in one spot, and we know the fate of 0.07 percent of the entire world's population hangs in the balance, and Tim Kring said this finale would be like a big-budget summer film in the final moments. This was going to be the biggest season finale of 2007 . . . and then . . . thud.

I can't remember the last time I was this disappointed in one of my shows.

I'm not saying it was all bad. The episode had some great moments, but the writers and producers have been filling their heads all season with the lavish praise poured on them by the fans, the critics, and everyone in Hollywood. It's the highest-rated new show. There was *so* much excitement all year:

- Save the cheerleader; save the world.
- The unveiling of Sylar
- The journey of Hiro Nakamura
- The glimpse of the apocalyptic future
- Mohinder finally getting a clue (Oops, sorry, that didn't happen.)
- The heroes slowly coming together and crossing paths
- Bennet going from evil to good

The writers had *so* much riding on this finale that it *had* to be superb or it was going to fail. Could they do it?

Well, actually, they should have. *Buffy* had several fantastic seasons, all with self-contained arcs, and Joss Whedon always managed to pull out all the stops to have mind-blowing finales. The writers on *Heroes* have been comparing themselves favorably to *Lost* all season because they've borrowed so much from the series, talking about how their numbers are up rather than down (though they had nothing to compare it to from last year), and how, unlike *Lost*, they'll reveal all the answers and won't keep you guessing.

But guess what? I like guessing. A lot has been wrapped up, and they've given me a little teaser at the ending, but what about the journeys of the season? Of *course* I'll be tuning in next season, and the next, and buying the DVDs the second they come out. I love this show. But this was just a disappointment. I think Tim Kring and company let the praise get to their heads, and just didn't try very hard. So here's the wrap-up:

Sylar does his psycho painting — only he doesn't actually have to make any brush strokes — and realizes Peter will be his adversary in the final battle. The opening title is embedded in Sylar's paint palette. I know I've said this before, but they are so brilliant with these opening titles.

Parkman stops Bennet from killing Molly, which is unbelievable. One minute Bennet's holding a gun to her head while Moronder holds a gun to his, saying that he will kill her no matter what. Then Parkman says he won't let anything happen to her, and Bennet drops the gun like, "Oh, okay. If you say so, no probs!"

Meanwhile, D.L. helps Niki go through a wall and then tells her to save Micah, so she leaves him by the elevator and runs away. So is Linderman really dead? If so, his death was about as anticlimactic as the final scene of this episode.

Bennet tells Peter that he's the only person who can stop Sylar. Peter takes Claire to Nathan, which is a surprise twist, because he says his brother has never let him down (except, of course, throughout most of this season), but he reads his mind and realizes Nathan thinks there's no way out of this, that the bomb is inevitable, and it's not worth trying to stop it. Claire runs away, but Granny catches her. Peter runs after her, and ends up out in the street with his hands going all radioactivey. He passes out.

Molly suddenly seems to be sick, so they hook her up to an IV and Moronder gives her another transfusion. She tells them that if she thinks about someone and points to the map, she can find them. There's only one person in the world that she can't find, and this person is even worse than Sylar. If she thinks about this person, the person will be able to see her. Here's our first setup for season 2. She locates Sylar in Isaac's apartment.

Bennet calls Claire, and Gran picks up the phone and tells him that they're Claire's birth family and will get her safe. Bennet tells Claire that they're right, let's let them do this, but he has a plan and will see her again.

Peter, lying on the pavement, suddenly wakes up in the greenhouse on the top of Isaac's building, and Simone and her dad,

Charles, are there, with Peter as his nurse. It's not clear (even at the end of the episode) what exactly happens here, other than I always suspected that Charles had some sort of power too. I think he can con-trol dreams somehow, and it's being around him that allowed Peter to have his prophetic dreams. He meets with Peter's mom and says that Nathan isn't the one who should be treated like the man who will save the world, but Peter. Then he starts talking to invisible Peter, and knows he's there. Inside the greenhouse there's some cheesy dialogue delivered by nurse Peter to Simone about how all that matters is how much we love and care about people and, in the words of Anthony Cooper on *Lost*, "blahblahblahblah."

Ando enters Isaac's apartment and slips on blood; Sylar is sud-denly behind him. Sylar throws the sword away, pins Ando in a neck hold against the wall (without using his hand, of course), and sees the future comic book. He finds the final page and laughs, saying, "You're kidding. This is how Isaac thought I'd die, stabbed by a silly little man!" (Good point, there, Sylar. After seeing the scene, I agree with you.) Sylar begins cutting his throat, until Hiro morphs into their presence, and Sylar wonders aloud if he can stop time before Sylar slashes Ando's neck. So Hiro instead disappears, reappears beside Ando, and then disappears the both of them. AMAZING. I loved this moment.

Niki comes into the room where "Jessica" is sitting (seriously, I doubt *anyone* could have possibly believed that was Jessica and dead Micah, and not Candice doing her illusioneering). Candessica kicks Niki in the head.

Parkman comes into Isaac's loft, finds the paintings everywhere, sees the oozing blood on the floor, and sees the painting of Sylar and Peter facing off, with "Kirby Plaza" in the back of the painting.

Moronder tells Molly that they have to go — the bogeyman is on his way. Molly says nope, he's already here.

Granny and Nathan talk to Claire about what's going to happen tomorrow, but that she'll be safe. She asks them how they could do this, how Gran could let her own son be such a villain and kill so many people, and how Nathan could allow that to happen. Claire tells Nathan if things were inevitable, then why did Gran try so hard to keep them apart for all these years? Nathan looks like he's finally thinking, "Uh . . . hm . . . good point?" But instead he tells her everything will make sense very soon. Gran says they're offering Claire everything she always wanted, a place to belong, a family, etc. and Nathan gives her a big ol' hug. So Claire does what any daughter would do in that situation. Jumps out the window. (The *thunk* was particularly cool.) Gran tells Nate to let her go.

Candessica and Niki conduct an Ali Larter on Ali Larter fight scene (the editing team must have *loved* doing this scene) and it's pretty cool. Niki sees Jessica in the mirror and explains that's not her. Niki worries she's not strong enough, then stands up, pummels Candessica with one blow, and she turns back into Candice. Micah calls from the closet, and she finds him. Wow. Had to work hard for that one. An entire season of Niki whining that she's not strong enough, and apparently after she hears for the eighteenth time that yes, she is, she listens.

Moronder and Molly find D.L. in the hallway, Molly tells him to wait, Moronder says, "But he needs my help" and runs out, D.L. morphs into Sylar and sucks his brain . . . okay, that didn't happen, but it would have been awesome. This scene just shows once again that no matter what, Moronder will do the stupid thing. In the last half hour, he's seen people die, had a gun held to Molly's head, found out Sylar was in the building, and getting Molly out of the building is of the utmost importance to guarantee the safety of the heroes, and . . . oh, look, there's a guy who's bleeding. I must go help him. Idiot.

Hiro transports himself and Ando to the office headquarters in Japan, and tells Ando he's leaving him there, gives him the Kensei sword and takes the other one. He tells him it's the man who will do it, not the sword. Ando tells him he looks bad-ass. Hiro looks pleased. This was a great scene, and a perfect throwback to the early episodes.

Peter talks to Charles, and Charles says that Peter's true power is to love unconditionally. Then he tells him that all he needs is love, and you can suddenly hear the Beatles behind him singing. A bunch of hippie flower children appear in the air, singing in a purple sky with stars falling all around them. Oh, and that sound you heard was me gagging.

Bennet shakes Peter out of his reverie, and tells him that he will be here to save him if he goes kablooey. And by save him, he means put a bullet in him. This raises an interesting question: Can Peter be killed at all? We know that as long as the thing that killed him remains inside, then he'll stay dead. So if Peter is shot in the head, and the bullet remains lodged, he's dead. Someone buries him, he's put underground, begins decomposing, and somewhere, years later, the bullet just pops out of the skull because a worm dislodged it or something. Does he suddenly come back to life? Hmm . . . Anyway, Peter thanks "Bennet," who finally reveals that his name is Noah. He's been sent by God to collect the heroes and load them onto an ark two by two, and it won't be Sylar or Peter who blow up the world, but God, angry that people haven't been listening to Him. Only the people in the ark will live. Or something. It was exciting to finally hear his name, but *Lost* has cornered the market on characters with biblical names.

Moronder continues to try to save D.L. rather than get Molly out of harm's way. Micah and Niki run into the hallway. Micah talks to the elevator and makes it work, and Molly, D.L., Niki, Moronder, and Micah get onto the elevator.

Peter and Bennet are in the courtyard in front of the Kirby building. Sylar suddenly shows up, zaps Bennet across the yard, and knocks the gun out of his hand. They exchange a few verbal barbs. Suddenly all the heroes are there. We *finally* have them all together, and as we've been told all season, when the heroes are all together, it will be like the Justice League of America. So let's break down what each of them does, then, shall we? I mean, awesomeness of this magnitude has to be looked at closely:

Parkman: Shoots at Sylar, who turns the bullets on him and shoots him back. Parkman lies there bleeding for the rest of the scene.

Niki: Grabs a parking meter and whacks Sylar hard, but then Micah shouts that Daddy needs tending to, and she runs back over to D.L. What the hell was *she* going to do to "tend" to him??

D.L.: Lies there bleeding the entire time.

Micah: Stands there yelling about how Daddy is bleeding.

Molly: Nothing.

Bennet: Lies against the building, useless.

Moronder: Sits with D.L., "tending" to him.

Peter: Held in a grip by Sylar, helpless until he absorbs Niki's strength, then he beats up Sylar. Suddenly he goes radioactivey, and he becomes the liability, not the strength.

Hiro: Time travels into the scene, runs toward Sylar with the sword, and seemingly kills him. Uh . . . okay? The greatest villain I've seen in *years* and he goes that quickly, without a fight?? What happened to the whole, "This ending will be like a big-budget summer movie" that we were promised? Peter asks Hiro to kill him, but Sylar, in his final moment, shoots Hiro into the building, but Hiro teleports from the scene.

Claire: *Finally* shows up, runs to Daddy, grabs the gun, and . . . can't do a damn thing. Great.

So there are your heroes for ya. Looks like Hiro was the only one worthy of *anything*, but in the end didn't really do much. Sylar ain't dead, and he couldn't stop Peter.

Peter stands there, glowing and getting worse, and it sounds like the opening strains of U2's "Where the Streets Have No Name" start up.

Nathan suddenly shows and says, "You saved the cheerleader. So *we* could save the world." (Oh, that sound was me gagging again.) They exchange verbal love for each other, then Nathan grabs him and flies up into the sky. And somewhere, out in the Earth's stratosphere,

Peter explodes. Instead of killing everyone in New York City, he possibly takes out the *galaxy*. Nice. Then radioactive rain begins falling, and the world melts. But don't worry . . . probably 0.07% of the world will survive. Ahem.

Claire hugs her father and smiles. Why does she smile??? Because she couldn't pull a trigger, *both* the Petrellis died!

Cut to montage of Moronder talking, saying we have a simple human need to find a kindred, and know in our hearts we are not alone. We see people move on, everyone seems so happy, and then we see a trail of blood showing Sylar apparently wasn't dead, and slouched into the nearest sewer.

But Kring doesn't end it there. He cuts to Hiro landing in a field, and we're told this is actually the beginning of season 2. He's trapped between a gang of warriors and the kensei warrior, and then suddenly the world goes black, and a huge eclipse happens. The end.

I've watched it twice, and still found the Sylar/explosion ending to be anticlimactic, but like I said, had good moments in it. Did they try to cram too much into it? Did they rely on too much cheesiness about how we just need to love ourselves and love the world and everyone in it and find kindred spirits and know we're not alone and . . . blahblahblahblah?

Are Peter and Nathan dead now? How did Sylar survive? Is Linderman dead? Will Mohinder get a clue? Is Niki cured and now just a strong bad-ass? Will Hiro ever find his way back to our time? Will D.L. die? Will Parkman be saved?

How will season 2 tie in to season 1? I'm definitely intrigued, and because it's called "Generations," presumably we'll find out who Gran is (could she be the person that Molly won't even picture in her head?), where Linderman came from, Charles, Mr. Petrelli . . . all the previous heroes. While I found tonight's ep to be a disappointment, I definitely can't wait for season 2. Here's hoping they map out the full season ahead of time so they don't disappoint as much with *next* year's finale.

"Damn season finales."[1] The finales of two of television's most talked about shows, NBC's *Heroes'* "How to Stop an Exploding Man" and ABC's *Lost's* "Through the Looking Glass," generated tremendous fan anticipation prior to airing on (respectively) May 21 and 23, but while the latter was almost unanimously well received, the former met with very mixed reviews, including such derisive scorn as Nikki Stafford's. A few weeks later (June 10) "Made in America," the season- and series-ending episode of HBO's *The Sopranos*, with its brilliantly inconclusive supply-your-own ending, left many fans feeling shortchanged. "Damn season finales." Though perhaps not deserving of eternal fire and brimstone, season-enders do present formidable challenges. If the season has been any good, the last episode before a long summer (or, in the case of a series-ender, a long forever) without a favorite show (especially a favorite serial) must clear a very high bar.

Asked (by *TV Guide*) to answer viewer complaints such as Nikki Stafford raises in the previous section about credibility, in particular the question why Peter didn't fly himself away from Kirby Plaza, Tim Kring's response is quite fascinating. While willing to "admit that there's a very tiny window of logic there," he insists that doubting fans broke the rules: "Theoretically you are not supposed to be thinking about that," he gently scolds, and this man who, as we saw earlier, happily cited Charles Dickens as an inspiration and a model, then evokes (with a laugh, *TV Guide* notes) an even older nineteenth-century British writer: "But what can I say? It's requires the proverbial suspension of disbelief."

The concept, of course, comes from the great Romantic poet, philosopher, and literary theorist Samuel Taylor Coleridge (1772–1834) and first appears in *Biographia Literaria,* where it is described as an essential "poetic faith" elicited from a reader by "a human interest and a semblance of truth sufficient to procure" it.

Kring, however, has left off an important word in the original formulation: for Coleridge was describing the *willing* suspension of disbelief. A writer (or filmmaker or television showrunner) cannot *demand* it of an audience. It must be established by "best laid plans."

Unlike the unwilling, gagging Nikki, my disbelief was willing, at least at first. My "crap detector" (the original phrase was Hemingway's) was registering inconsistencies and disappointments as the scene in Kirby Plaza unfolded. I didn't understand why Jessica didn't stay there and fight out with Sylar — why she lamely had to go tend to D.L. Only the needs of the script made that the right thing for her to do (she had to get out of the way, to make room for Peter and Hiro).

Nor did I buy (and never did) why Claire had to be the one to off Peter. Claire was the only one who could plunge a syringe into Ted Sprague in "Company Man," of course, because only she could get close enough to the original exploding man, but could not Bennet (who seemed more hobbled by the thematic needs of the screenplay than by Sylar having tossed him aside) or even Mohinder have shot Peter at a distance pre-explosion? Couldn't Niki/Jessica have swatted him as well with that parking meter?

And yet when Nathan flew in — Nathan, a character I had never been crazy about and who I believed, with Hiro, to be a "villain" — Kring had me at Flying Man's arrival. At "You saved the cheerleader, so we could save the world," I cried.

Now granted that I am, by admission, an easy mark,[2] I find it interesting that the scholar-fan (in Matt Hills' terminology) was so much more willing to suspend, to respond as it was written, than was Nikki, the ultimate fan-scholar, as her first-rate books on *Buffy, Angel,* and *Lost* have demonstrated.

This wasn't the first time that I was the one being less objective about a finale. When the series-ending "Chosen" completed the seven-season, 144-episode run of *Buffy the Vampire Slayer*, I was stunned to find fans carping over scores of questions regarding continuity, while I loved every minute of it despite its clear incongruities.

The unanimously praised finale of *Lost*'s third season, "Through the Looking Glass," was, like those of its two previous seasons, a two-hour episode, allowing ample time for its complex on-island and its flash forward off-island narrative to play out. *Heroes'* was only one hour, though Kring and company conceived of the last three episodes — "The Hard Part," "Landslide," and "How to Stop" as of-a-piece, but they were not packaged or promoted as such.

If they had been — if we had seen them in a single sitting (a hypothetical precluded, of course, by broadcasting needs and economic reasons) — would we experience "How to Stop" differently? We will all have the opportunity to repackage when we are in possession of the season 1 DVDS. Will Nikki still be gagging then?

Perhaps the real problem, however, was "Five Years Gone," the episode that immediately preceded the closing three-parter. A sensational, bad-ass episode, complete with a too-brief face-off, all powers at-the-ready, between Sylar and Peter Petrelli, episode 20 created expectations for episode 23 that couldn't be met. After "Five Years Gone," "How to Explode" was probably pre-ordained to be anti-climactic and unsatisfying.

In an end-of-the-year retrospective interview, Kring the veteran screenwriter offers a detailed writerly rationalization for the problems he faced in writing the finale: "The final episode was so predetermined by the events that came before it," he insists, "that writing it was a very complicated thing. . . . In some ways, for me it was more like taking dictation than writing an episode of television. Everything was so slotted in. You were dragging so much story behind you that you had very little wiggle room as to what people could say and how they could say it and what their attitudes were. It was all predetermined."

One facet of "How to Stop" was new, however. "The idea of the flashback or the dream sequence of Peter going back to the rooftop and seeing himself" was added in order to provide breathing room in an episode that had become "a freight train."

The scene's inclusion served another purpose, however, as Kring admits: "I also felt very strongly that *the message of the show* had to be imparted by one of the characters, so that scene delivered that message" (my italics). In case you've forgotten, the message, "the truth" (as Deveaux deems it) delivered by Peter to Simone and Shaft (or rather Deveaux) to Peter, is that "we have to be good to one another," "what we really need is heart," "all that really matters is love." (You know, the Beatles-echoing "blahblahblahblah" that made Nikki anything but willing.)

Appalled at the didactic nature of one of his studio's recent films, infamous Hollywood mogul Samuel Goldwyn purportedly quipped, "Pictures are for entertainment, messages should be delivered by Western Union." Kring, however, apparently thinks *Heroes* — or at least its final rookie season outing — is and should be a delivery system, even if lovers of his creation gag on the message. (Revealingly, this frequently dark series — see Steven Peacock's essay on page 141 as well as "The Ambiguity of Evil" — had exhibited little tendency toward the didactic in its first twenty-two episodes.)

Perhaps Kring should have listened to the critical maxim of yet another nineteenth-century British writer, Coleridge's contemporary poet John Keats, who reminded us that we must always mistrust art "that has a palpable design upon us." Was not Kring's "palpable design" upon us precisely what painted him into a corner in writing "How to Stop an Exploding Man"? If the episode had stayed dark, as its competition in the on-air finale faceoff *Lost* most certainly did, it might not have induced tears, but it might have inspired cheers — even from a nongagging Nikki.

POSTSCRIPT (NIKKI STAFFORD)

I e-mailed David Lavery the day after "How to Stop an Exploding Man" aired, asking if he'd seen the episode yet but not giving him my take on it (I didn't want to sway his opinion). Because he's overseas, it took him an extra day to get it, but when he did, he immediately e-mailed back with the brief, "OMG. Loved it." I was shocked, thinking he'd seen a different episode. He was shocked when he read my blog and saw how much I'd hated it. (Now, reading his response, it seems that multiple viewings have turned his love into a like.) He asked me if I'd be willing to do a finale face-off, in which my blog would represent the negative review, and he'd write the positive review. I was delighted that he'd asked, and joked that hey, it would definitely be more exciting than the Peter/Sylar showdown.

Now he's given me a chance to respond to his response (which seems overly obsessed with my gag reflex!). First, I just want to say to any reader who didn't see my twenty-two blogs that preceded this one, where I analyzed every episode and talked about how I loved it more than the previous week's, I am a *huge* fan of *Heroes*. I think the writing is brilliant, the storytelling moves at a brisk pace, the acting is fabulous, and it's the best new show I've seen since *Lost* premiered in 2004. That's why the finale was so painful for me.

While my adage is that everyone deserves an opinion, as long as they allow everyone else to maintain theirs without judgment (I was urging people to disagree with me in my blog comments afterward), I think David and I have different interpretations of what the phrase "suspension of disbelief" means. I've always taken it to mean one must suspend notions of what would exist in the real world to believe what is happening on screen. And despite what David says, I suspend my disbelief daily, while sitting before my television set. I believed in a young woman fighting vampires for seven years (and her vampire boyfriend running a detective agency for another five). I believed in a group of plane crash survivors battling a frightening monster on a possessed island. I believed in a superspy who could don a red wig and suddenly be unrecognizable to people. And I believed in a man who could fly, a girl who could heal herself, a guy who could teleport himself, and someone who could absorb all of these powers and more.

What David and Tim Kring (in the preposterous statement he made following this episode that David quotes) are suggesting instead is that I should suspend my *belief* in the quality of writing. When the fans say, "But, um, all season this character has done this, and that character has done that, and now they're . . . just kind of lame," Kring would apparently argue that I'm not supposed to be paying attention to details. It's like Buffy suddenly being played by a male actor one week, and I'm supposed to turn a blind eye and reason, "Well, maybe she has a cold and *that* is why her voice is so deep." Yet why would I assume the writers wouldn't deliver a knockout finale, when they'd given me the scene of Sylar shooting shards of glass throughout a room trying to find an invisible Peter; when I'd been on the edge of my seat when Claire had rushed back into her family home to stop Ted from obliterating himself and everyone else; when I cheered at Hiro screeching with unparalleled joy, "I love New York!" These were scenes of greatness, in which I recognized a group of writers that could tell a story I wanted to hear, and a creative genius at the center of it all. And then . . . this happened.

Yes, every show is allowed its slip-ups, and yes, there are limitations to the medium (which is the other half of what Coleridge's term meant), but as someone who has spent years writing about television, I cannot remember the last time I was disappointed in a finale the way I was in this one. It has nothing to do with me being an unwilling viewer — when audiences were dropping during *Lost*'s season 2 saying they couldn't follow the show due to the chaotic scheduling, I was the one saying, "No, wait, come back, you can't give up *now*! Try watching it back-to-back!" I allowed Joss Whedon an entirely bad season on *Buffy* (and then another one on *Angel*), confident that hey, he'll come back around, and all will be well with my shows again. I'm the kind of person who gets fifty pages into a bad novel, but feels compelled to finish it, hoping it'll get better. In fact, David asks at one point if I'd watched all of the final three back-to-back, would I still be gagging? And sadly, the weekend after the finale aired, I did go back and watch all three back-to-back on my DVR, thinking that maybe the finale could be saved because I wanted to like it *so* much but, I'm sorry to say, I didn't like it any more than I did the first two times. Yes, *Lost* had two hours in which they delivered their extraordinary finale two days after this episode aired, but their entire season was the same length as that of *Heroes* — twenty-three hours.

My vehement dislike of this episode, however, shows how much I care about the series. If I'd been watching a series that I didn't love, and it had given me a finale as unsatisfactory as this one, I'd have shrugged and changed the channel. It's my passionate belief that the writers of the show could have done *so* much better, that they had *so* much potential they'd shown us throughout the otherwise fantastic first season that renders it so disappointing to me.

And so, much to David's delight, I will never be able to watch this finale without gagging.

PART 2
ENHANCEMENTS

HEROES ENCYCLOPEDIA

#'s

".07%" — The nineteenth episode of season 1.

9th Wonders — Isaac Mendez comic book, featuring (among others) the adventures of Hiro, who buys a copy after teleporting himself to New York. Before Isaac is killed by Sylar, he sends a final issue to the publisher.

1671 — The year to which Hiro teleports himself in the final moments of season 1.

A

Activating Evolution — Chandra Suresh's book, first seen in "One Giant Leap," laying out his theory of emergent evolution.

Alexander, Jesse — *Heroes* writer ("Nothing to Hide" and "Landslide"). Previously wrote for *Alias*, co-authored the screenplay for *Eight-Legged Freaks* (2002), and worked on *Lost*. Also author/co-author of four *Heroes* graphic novels.

Ando — See **Masahashi, Ando**.

Andrews, Charlie (Jayma Mays) — *Heroes* character: a waitress at The Burnt Toast, and an evolved human with enhanced memory. Despite Hiro's efforts to prevent it, she is murdered by Sylar.

Andy (Kellen Lutz) — *Heroes* character: Claire Bennet's fiancé and fellow employee at the Burnt Toast in "Five Years Gone."

"Are you on the list?" — The second *Heroes* catchphrase, referring to Chandra Suresh's catalog of evolved humans.

Arkush, Allan — One of *Heroes'* go-to directors ("Don't Look Back," "Six Months Ago," "Company Man," "How to Stop an Exploding Man"), previously worked with Tim Kring on *Crossing Jordan* (twenty-two episodes) and, since 1970, on such shows as *Snoops, The Practice, Dawson's Creek, I'll Fly Away, Parenthood, St. Elsewhere, L.A. Law, Fame,* and *Moonlighting.* Also an occasional actor.

Armstrong, Matthew John (Ted Sprague) — *Heroes* actor.

Armus, Adam — *Heroes* writer ("Run," "Homecoming"). Previously wrote for *Night Stalker, Kevin Hill, Birds of Prey, Glory Days, The Practice, Boston Public, Xena: Warrior Princess* (fourteen episodes), *Hercules,* and *Snoops.*

Avari, Erick (Chandra Suresh) — *Heroes* actor.

B

Badham, John — British-born *Heroes* director ("Fallout," "The Hard Part"), who has also worked on other TV shows (*Crossing Jordan* [with Tim Kring], *Blind Justice, The Shield, Kung Fu, The Streets of San Francisco, Cannon*) before and after a career as a feature film director (*The Hard Way* [1991], *Bird on a Wire* [1990], *Stakeout* [1987], *Short Circuit* [1986], *American Flyers* [1985], *Dracula* [1979], *Saturday Night Fever* [1977], and *The Bingo Long's Traveling All-Stars & Motor Kings* [1976]).

Beckel, Graham (Hal Sanders) — *Heroes* actor.

Beeman, Greg — One of *Heroes'* go-to directors ("Better Halves," "Homecoming," "Unexpected," "Landslide"), after previously directing fifteen episodes of *Smallville,* eleven episodes of *JAG,* and working on such shows as *Providence, Nash Bridges, The Adventures of Brisco County, Jr., The Wonder Years,* and *Eerie, Indiana.*

Bennet, Claire (Hayden Panettiere) — *Heroes* character: the adopted daughter of the Bennets (her biological parents are Nathan Petrelli and Meredith Gordon), an Odessa, Texas, high school cheerleader and evolved human, capable of instant cell regeneration. In "Five Years Gone" she is apparently murdered by Sylar.

Bennet, Lyle (Randall Bentley) — *Heroes* character: brother of Claire Bennet.

Bennet, Mr./Noah (Jack Coleman) — *Heroes* character (a.k.a. HRG [Horn Rimmed Glasses]): an employee of The Company masquerading as a salesman for Primatech Paper. Claire Bennet is his adopted daughter. "Company Man" gives us his backstory. We learn his name at last in the final episode of season 1.

Bennet, Sandra (Ashley Crow) — *Heroes* character: Claire Bennet's adoptive mother, a homemaker devoted to her family and show dog Mr. Muggles.

Bentley, Randall (Lyle Bennet) — *Heroes* actor.

Berman, David (Brian Davis) — *Heroes* actor.

"Better Halves" — The sixth episode of season 1.

Bilderback, Nicole (Ms. Sakamoto) — *Heroes* actress.

bio-parents — In "Better Halves," Mr. Bennet arranges a meeting between Claire and her birth parents, but the sitdown is a ruse, intended to keep her in the dark about her true origins.

Boogeyman — Molly Walker's name for Sylar.

Bozeman, Montana — *Heroes* location, home to Dale Smither, killed by Sylar for her evolved human ability (enhanced hearing).

Brain Extraction — Through psychic surgery, Sylar removes the brains of his victims to steal their evolved human powers.

Bray, Kevin — *Heroes* director ("Parasite"), who has also directed episodes of such series as *Cold Case* (six episodes), *In Justice, Veronica Mars, Criminal Minds,* and *CSI: NY,* as well as the feature film *Walking Tall* (2004).

Burnt Toast Diner — The Midland, Texas, restaurant where Hiro falls in love with Charlie Andrews, Sylar murders Charlie, and (five years in the future) Claire Bennet works and meets her fiancé, Andy. Other visitors to the diner, now and in the future, include Peter Petrelli, Isaac Mendez, Mr. Bennet, Zach, Matt Parkman, and Ted Sprague.

C

Cabrera, Santiago (Isaac Mendez) — *Heroes* actor. Venezuelan-born London resident, Cabrera's previous U.S. television credit is *Empire*.

Candice — See **Wilmer, Candice**.

cell regeneration — Evolved human power exhibited by Claire Bennet, allowing her to recover from virtually any injury.

Chaidez, Natalie — *Heroes* writer ("Better Halves," "The Fix"). Previously wrote for *Cracker* (U.S. version), *Judging Amy*, *Profiler*, and *New York Undercover*.

Chamberlin, Kevin (Aron Malsky) — *Heroes* actor.

Claire — See **Bennet, Claire**.

Claude (Christopher Eccleston) — *Heroes* character: an evolved human — his power is invisibility — and former agent for The Company who escaped Mr. Bennet's attempt to terminate him ("Company Man"). Now living in hiding in New York, he helps Peter Petrelli ensure his powers are "housebroken."

cockroach — Primitive, repulsive, enduring insect, discussed in Mohinder's opening lecture in "Genesis" and associated with Sylar (during his captivity by The Company; after his apparent death in the season 1 finale). Creator Tim Kring notes in an interview that cockroaches are a symbol of evolution.

Cohn, Ethan (Zane Taylor) — *Heroes* actor.

Coleite, Aron Eli — *Heroes* writer ("Six Months Ago," "The Hard Part"). Previously wrote for Tim Kring on *Crossing Jordan*. Also author/co-author of twelve *Heroes* graphic novels.

Coleman, Jack (Mr. [Noah] Bennet) — *Heroes* actor. Previously known as Steven Carrington on the long-running *Dynasty*, Coleman's many credits include guest roles on series such as *CSI: Miami*, *Nip/Tuck*,

Without a Trace, and *Entourage*.

"Collision" — The fourth episode of season 1.

"Company Man" — The seventeenth episode of season 1.

Company, The — The organization housed under the cover of the Primatech Paper Company and bankrolled by Linderman that has been identifying and controlling the emerging evolved humans for decades.

Corinthian, The — The Las Vegas hotel that serves as Linderman's base of operations.

Crow, Ashley (Sandra Bennet) — *Heroes* actress.

cryokinesis — The ability to instantly freeze matter, an evolved human power possessed by Sylar (acquired from an unknown source), who uses it to freeze Molly Walker's father, James ("One Giant Leap"), turn his mother's apartment into a snow globe ("The Hard Part"), and prepare for combat with Peter Petrelli ("Five Years Gone").

cyberpathy — Evolved human power exhibited by Hana Gittelman, allowing her to communicate wirelessly with any computer.

Cypress, Tawny (Simone Deveaux) — *Heroes* actress.

D

Davis, Brian (David Berman) — *Heroes* character: an evolved human capable of telekinesis, a power stolen by Sylar (his first) when he kills Brian in "Six Months Ago."

Dawson, Roxann — *Heroes* director ("Run!"), who has also directed episodes of such series as *Cold Case*, *The O.C.*, *Lost*, *Enterprise* (ten episodes), *Charmed*, and *Star Trek: Voyager*.

Deitch, Donna — *Heroes* director ("Nothing to Hide"), who after a debut as a feature film director (*Desert Hearts* [1985]) and a widely praised made-for-TV movie (*The Women of Brewster Place* [1989]), became a busy television director (eight episodes of Tim Kring's *Crossing Jordan*, *Bones*, *NYPD Blue*, *Judging Amy*, *Law & Order: SVU*, *Murder One*, *ER*).

Dekker, Thomas (Zach) — *Heroes* actor.

Dennison, Oliver (Stephen Spinella) — *Heroes* character: a journalist who comes to a brunch at the Petrelli mansion knowing about Nathan's tryst with Niki Sanders/Jessica in Las Vegas.

Deveaux, Charles (Richard Roundtree) — *Heroes* character: father of Simone Deveaux, a wealthy individual dying as the series begins (Peter Petrelli is his hospice nurse), he passes away in "Nothing to Hide" but offers wisdom to Peter in a dream reappearance in "How to Stop an Exploding Man." Involved in a yet-to-be-determined way in the prehistory of evolved humans.

Deveaux Building — The New York building in which Charles Deveaux lives and dies. Many significant *Heroes* moments take place on the Deveaux Building roof: baby Claire's assignment to Mr. Bennet ("Company Man"), Claude's "encouragement" to Peter Petrelli to fly ("Distractions"), Mr. Bennet and the Haitian's attack on Peter and Claude ("Unexpected"), Peter's dream encounter with Charles Deveaux in "How to Stop an Exploding Man."

Deveaux, Simone (Tawny Cypress) — *Heroes* character: daughter of Charles Deveaux. An art dealer (she is Linderman's source for Isaac Mendez's paintings) and lover of Isaac and (later) Peter Petrelli, she is shot and accidentally killed by Isaac when he fires at Peter.

Dickerson, Ernest — *Heroes* director ("Collision"), who became a director of feature films (*Ambushed* [1998], *Blind Faith* [1998], *Bulletproof* [1996]) and television (*The Wire* [six episodes], *ER*, *Masters of Horror*, *CSI: Miami*, *Invasion*, *Criminal Minds*, *The L Word*) after first establishing himself as a cinematographer (often working with Spike Lee).

"Distractions" — The fourteenth episode of season 1.

D.L. — See Hawkins, D.L.

DNA — Chandra Suresh and his son, Mohinder, are both geneticists, and the former's *Activating Evolution* lays out his theory of changes in human DNA as the basis for the development, "the transformation from ordinary to extraordinary," of evolved humans who have become *Heroes*' major characters.

"Don't Look Back" — The second episode of season 1.

dream manipulation — Evolved human power exhibited by Sanjob Iyer, which he uses to enter Mohinder's unconscious and show him important scenes from his past.

DuVall, Clea (Audrey Hanson) — *Heroes* actress.

E

Eccleston, Christopher (Claude) — *Heroes* actor, best known for playing the ninth Doctor Who in the long-running British sci-fi series.

eclipse — Behind the title of the series in the credit sequence of each episode is an image of a total eclipse of the sun, a solar event witnessed by several characers in "Genesis." A second eclipse, in 1671 Japan, brings the season to a close.

Edwards, Paul A. — *Heroes* director ("Seven Minutes to Midnight," "Five Years Gone"). Formerly a camera operator, he has also directed episodes of *Lost* and *Drive*.

election — The congressional election in which Nathan Petrelli runs for a New York seat in the U.S. House of Representatives — and wins, thanks to Linderman's manipulation (via Micah Sanders) of the voting machines — takes place on November 7, the penultimate day of *Heroes*' first season ("Landslide").

empathic mimicry — Evolved human power exhibited by Peter Petrelli, which allows him to absorb the special abilities of others with whom he comes in contact.

enhanced memory — Evolved human power exhibited by Charlie Andrews (Sylar kills her for it).

enhanced strength — Evolved human power exhibited by Jessica (Niki Sanders' mirror identity).

episode titles — Unlike most television programs, whose episode titles can only be found in magazines or on the Internet, *Heroes* exhibits theirs openly, in frame, on screen. See "*Heroes* Season 1 Episode Guide."

erasing memory — Evolved human power exhibited by the Haitian.

evolved humans — Those individuals who exhibit special powers (invisibility, telekinesis, cell regeneration, flight, etc.) as the result of a not-yet-explained mutation/alteration of their DNA.

eyes — A visual symbol of precognition. Isaac, Peter, and Sylar have white, glazed-over eyes that reflect their second-sight ability. The first image of the series is of an eye (Peter Petrelli's).

F

Fagerbakke, Bill (Steve Gustavson) — *Heroes* actor.

"Fallout" — The eleventh episode of season 1.

FBI — The Federal Bureau of Investigation, led by agents Eliza Thayer and Audrey Hanson, is investigating the serial killer Sylar, but throughout season 1 they remain essentially clueless concerning what is actually taking place.

Feds — Nathan Petrelli is covertly cooperating with a federal investigation into Linderman's illegal operations. Jessica puts an end to it, slaughtering their agents in Las Vegas in "Parasite."

"Five Years Gone" — The twentieth episode of season 1.

"Fix, The" — The thirteenth episode of season 1.

flight — Evolved human power exhibited by Nathan Petrelli (and Peter Petrelli by contact with his brother).

Flying Man — Hiro's name for Nathan Petrelli after seeing him come in for a landing outside a diner in "Hiros."

Foster, Kay — *Heroes* writer ("Homecoming," "Run!"). Previously wrote for *Night Stalker, Kevin Hill, Birds of Prey, The Practice, Boston Public, Xena: Warrior Princess* (thirteen episodes), and *Hercules*.

Fuller, Bryan — *Heroes* writer ("Collision," "Company Man"). Previously created the two-season Showtime series *Dead Like Me* (and wrote ten episodes), *Star Trek Voyager* (twenty-one episodes), and *Star Trek: Deep Space Nine*. Now developing a new series, *Pushing Daisies*, for ABC.

Future Hiro (Masi Oka) — *Heroes* character: the advanced, fully heroic, more jaded version of Hiro Nakamura, transformed by five years experience, who teleports back in time to deliver a message to Peter Petrelli (in "Hiros") and meets his present day self (who finds him scary) in "Five Years Gone."

Future Peter (Milo Ventimiglia) — *Heroes* character: the advanced, world-weary version of Peter Petrelli who faces Sylar (in the form of Nathan Petrelli) for a final battle in "Five Years Gone."

G

Genesis — The name of Chandra Suresh's project investigating emergent evolution.

"Genesis" — The pilot episode of season 1.

Gilsig, Jessalyn (Meredith Gordon) — *Heroes* actress.

Gittelman, Hana (Stana Katic) — *Heroes* character: a cyberpath, who appears for the first time in "Unexpected." She is the hero with the greatest number of appearances in the graphic novels.

"Go deep" — Mr. Bennet's oft-repeated instruction to the Haitian to erase the memory of Sandra Bennet, Claire, and even (in "Company Man") himself.

"Godsend" — The twelfth episode of season 1.

Gordon, Meredith (Jessalyn Gilsig) — *Heroes* character: the birth mother of Claire Bennet. An evolved human, she is capable of pyrokinesis.

Gray, Gabriel (a.k.a. Sylar) (Zachary Quinto) — *Heroes* character: an obsessive New York watch-repairman until identified by Chandra Suresh as an evolved human. Although he appears devoid of powers, he discovers he can forcibly steal the powers of others by cutting off the tops of their heads and (presumably) ingesting their brains.

Gray, Virginia (Ellen Greene) — *Heroes* character: the unstable, snow-globe-obsessed mother of the boy who would become the serial killer Sylar. She is accidentally killed by her son in a struggle over scissors in "The Hard Part."

Gray-Cabey, Noah (Micah Sanders) — *Heroes* actor. The young actor already had a regular role in *My Wife and Kids*.

Green, Michael — *Heroes* writer ("Hiros," "Distractions"). Previously wrote for such series as *Everwood* (fourteen episodes), *Smallville* (six episodes), *Snoops*, and *Sex and the City*.

Greene, Ellen (Virginia Gray) — *Heroes* actress. One of her best-known roles was as Audrey in the off-Broadway and movie versions of *Little Shop of Horrors*.

Grunberg, Greg (Matt Parkman) — *Heroes* actor. Best known for his frequent collaborations with childhood friend J. J. Abrams, including playing CIA agent Eric Weiss on *Alias* (2001–06).

Gustavson, Steve (Bill Fagerbakke) — *Heroes* character: the former partner of Hope, with whom he battles over a suitcase of stolen money.

H

Haiduk, Stacy (Agent Eliza Thayer) — *Heroes* actress.

Haitian, the (Jimmy Jean-Louis) — *Heroes* character: an evolved human capable of altering minds and erasing memories. In "Company Man" we see him as a boy, working for The Company for the first time. We later learn that he does the bidding of Angela Petrelli.

Hanson, Audrey (Clea DuVall) — *Heroes* character: an FBI agent on the trail of serial killer Sylar, assisted for a time in her search by Matt Parkman.

"Hard Part, The" — The twenty-first episode of season 1.

Hawkins, D.L. (Leonard Roberts) — *Heroes* character: Niki Sanders' husband. Framed by Linderman for crimes he did not commit, he uses his evolved human ability to phase through matter to escape from prison. Shot in "Landslide," D.L. manages to put his hand into Linderman's skull before collapsing and remains alive at season's end.

healing — Evolved human power exhibited by Linderman. In "Landslide," he uses it to heal Heidi Petrelli's paralysis.

Helix, the — A mysterious symbol, looking like a strand of RNA, not yet explained but seemingly related to the worldwide development of evolved human individuals. Ando identifies it as a combination of ideograms that signify "great talent" and "godsend." The Helix appears as an Easter Egg in a number of episodes. (See page 233.)

Heroes **graphic novels** — A series of (so far) more than thirty online comic stories about the further adventures of *Heroes* characters, often providing backstories for both major and minor characters and expanding the series' mythology.

Heroes: Origins — The season 2 spin-off that will introduce new characters each week, allowing fans to vote on which will then be included in season 3.

heroin — Narcotic to which Isaac Mendez is addicted (he thinks it is the source of his prophetic painting) until he overcomes his habit thanks to a Company "intervention."

Hiro — See **Nakamura, Hiro**.

"Hiros" — The fifth episode of season 1.

"Homecoming" — The ninth episode of season 1.

Homeland Security — The U.S. government organization, created in the wake of 9/11, which takes in Ted Sprague as a potential terrorist and in one possible future ("Five Years Gone") treats all evolved humans as terrorists (Matt Parkman having become one of its key agents).

Hope (Missi Pyle) — *Heroes* character: a showgirl who procures Ando's assistance in getting back stolen money from her partner-in-crime Gustavson.

Horn Rimmed Glasses — The name Mr. Bennet was known by before (and occasionally after) we learn he is Claire's father. In "Company Man," we see his daughter help him pick out his signature spectacles.

"How to Stop an Exploding Man" — The twenty-third episode of season 1.

HRG — See **Horn Rimmed Glasses**.

Human Genome Project — The ambitious scientific undertaking that mapped human DNA. Chandra Suresh used this database in generating a formula to identify evolved human individuals.

I

India — Both Chandra Suresh and his son Mohinder taught genetics at the University of Madras in this southeast Asian nation. Several other minor *Heroes* characters are from India as well: Sanjob Iyer, Nirand, Mira Shenoy, Mrs. Suresh.

induced radioactivity — Evolved human power exhibited by Ted Sprague and, later, Peter Petrelli and Sylar, which uncontrolled can result in an explosion such as the blast that levels New York in one possible *Heroes* future or goes off harmlessly in the air in the season 1 finale.

invisibility — Evolved human power exhibited by Claude and, through contact, Peter Petrelli.

Isaac's studio — Many *Heroes* events take place at this New York location, including Hiro's arrest for the murder of Isaac, Isaac's accidental shooting of Simone Deveaux, Sylar's murder of Isaac, and Hiro's meeting with Future Hiro.

isotopes, radioactive — Implanted into evolved humans (leaving a telltale mysterious mark on the neck), these devices enable The Company to track their movements.

Iyer, Sanjob (Javin Reid) — *Heroes* character, an evolved human boy gifted with the ability to manipulate dreams. Mohinder tracks him down in real life after he first appears in his dreams.

J

Jaffrey, Sakina (Mrs. Suresh) — *Heroes* actress.

Japan — Home of several *Heroes* characters, including the Nakamura family and Ando Masahashi. Season 1 ends outside Kyoto, Japan, in 1671, where Hiro has teleported.

Japanese phrase book — Hiro gives Charlie Andrews one at the Burnt Toast Diner, and from it she learns to speak Japanese.

Jean-Louis, Jimmy (The Haitian) — *Heroes* actor.

Jessica — Niki Sanders' Mr. Hyde mirror-image, the product of childhood parental abuse by Hal Sanders. Gifted with enhanced strength, she murders many in *Heroes'* first season.

Jittetsu Arms — A repair shop Ando finds in the Yellow Pages in "Landslide." Kaito Nakamura trains Hiro for his showdown with Sylar there.

K

Kane, Adam — *Heroes* director (".07%"); a veteran cinematographer, working as a TV director for the first time after one feature film (*The Fix* [2005]).

katana — See **Sword**.

Katic, Stana (Hana Gittelman) — *Heroes* actress.

Kensei, Takezo — Legendary Japanese samurai, whose sword Hiro steals from the Museum of Natural History and who Hiro encounters in 1671 in the closing moment of season 1.

Kermit, Texas — The small town where Claire's birth mother, Meredith Gordon, lives in a trailer park.

Kim, Chuck — The writer of ".07%," his first exercise in television writing. Also the author of two *Heroes* graphic novels.

Kirby Plaza — New York locale named after comic book "King" Jack Kirby (1917–94), co-creator of such classics as Captain America, X-Men, and the Fantastic Four.

Kring, Tim — *Heroes* creator and writer ("Genesis," "Don't Look Back," "Seven Minutes to Midnight," "Godsend," "How to Stop an Exploding Man"). See the chapter on "The Creation of *Heroes*" for more on Kring.

Kurup, Shishir (Nirand) — *Heroes* actor.

Kyoto, Japan — The final scene of season 1 takes place near here, as Hiro finds himself caught in a conflict between samurai after teleporting himself away from New York.

L

Lackey, Elizabeth (Janice Parkman) — *Heroes* actress.

Ladnier, Kavi (Mira Shenoy) — *Heroes* actress.

"Landslide" — The twenty-second episode of season 1.

Lanter, Matt (Brody Mitchum) — *Heroes* actor.

Larter, Ali (Niki Sanders) — *Heroes* actress. Her film credits include roles in *Varsity Blues, Final Destination,* and *Legally Blonde.*

Las Vegas — Nevada city that serves as a base of operations for Linderman (in The Corinthian hotel) and is the setting for many events in the Heroesverse.

Lee, Stan — The famous Marvel Comics superhero creator (Spider-Man, the X-Men, the Incredible Hulk, the Fantastic Four), who makes a cameo as a bus driver in "Unexpected."

Lee, James Kyson (Ando Masahashi) — *Heroes* actor. Previous work includes ADR (voice work) on *Lost* and guest roles on *Las Vegas, JAG,* and *The West Wing.*

Linderman, Mr. (Malcolm McDowell) — *Heroes* character: a multi-millionaire, the mastermind behind The Company, who exhibits evolved human powers himself (he is able to heal). Killed, or so it would appear, by D.L. (who puts his fist through Linderman's brain) in "Landslide."

liquefaction — Evolved human power exhibited by Zane Taylor and (later) Sylar, who steals it after killing him.

List, the — Chandra Suresh's catalog, discovered by his son Mohinder on his computer, of individuals worldwide who exhibit extraordinary powers.

Loeb, Jeph — *Heroes* writer ("One Giant Leap," "Unexpected"). Award-winning comic book author, who had previously written for *Smallville.* For more on Loeb, see "The Creation of *Heroes.*"

Lubbock, Texas — The city where Claire and Zach tell her mother they are going on a school-related trip to the aquarium (a cover for their trip to Kermit to meet Claire's birth mother).

Lutz, Kellen (Andy) — *Heroes* actor.

M

Malsky, Aaron (Kevin Chamberlin) — *Heroes* character: a Linderman operative, whacked by Jessica (doing Linderman's bidding) in "Run!"

map — Chandra Suresh develops a map of the locations of people likely to have enhanced abilities. The locations of possibly evolved humans, indicated with push pins and connected with string, especially interests Bennet and Sylar.

Masahashi, Ando (James Kyson Lee) — *Heroes* character: a girl-obsessed Japanese cubicle worker and Hiro's super-powerless but always supportive and brave sidekick. Teleported by Hiro out of harm's way to Tokyo before the final showdown in "How to Stop an Exploding Man." In the possible of future of "Five Years Gone," he is killed in the blast that levels New York.

Mays, Jayma (Charlie Andrews) — *Heroes* actress.

McCain, Eden (Nora Zehetner) — *Heroes* character: recruited by The Company, which makes use of her evolved human power of persuasion. Murdered by Sylar, who uses her power to force her to kill herself.

McDowell, Malcolm (Linderman) — *Heroes* actor, who gained early fame for his starring roles in two Lindsay Anderson films (*If . . .* and *O Lucky Man!*) and as Alex in Stanley Kubrick's *A Clockwork Orange*, though reduced in the last two decades to playing a series of villains (including Linderman).

McHenry, Tom (Rick Peters) — *Heroes* character: one of Matt Parkman's fellow cops, who once had an affair with Janice Parkman.

Mendez, Isaac (Santiago Cabrera) — *Heroes* character: a New York artist capable, thanks to the power of precognition, of painting the future. Murdered by Sylar in ".07%," who steals his power.

Micah — See **Sanders, Micah**.

Midland, Texas — City in Texas, part of the same metroplex with Odessa.

Mitchum, Brody (Matt Lanter) — *Heroes* character: the quarterback of the football team; his attempt to rape Claire Bennet sends her to the morgue. Mr. Bennet orders his memory erased by the Haitian.

Mohinder — See **Suresh, Mohinder**.

Molly — See **Walker, Molly**.

Montecito Casino — Fictional Las Vegas casino featured in the NBC series *Las Vegas* and owned by Linderman, where Petrelli and Niki/Jessica Sanders have a one night stand and Ando and Hiro gamble and later meet Hope.

Muggles, Mr. — *Heroes* character: Sandra Bennet's beloved (except when her memory has been erased) Pomeranian.

Museum of Natural History — While visiting this New York institution, Hiro discovers and then steals the sword of the famous Samurai Takezo Kensei.

N

Nakamura, Hiro (Masi Oka) — *Heroes* character: Japanese cubicle worker, the son of the owner of the corporation (Yamagato Industries), who has the evolved human power of space-time manipulation. With the help of a legendary samurai sword and his father's training, he fulfills his dream of being a hero and runs Sylar through in the season I finale. At the end of the episode (and the season) he finds himself in seventeenth century Japan.

Nakamura, Kaito (George Takei) — *Heroes* character: Hiro's father, a key figure in the prehistory of evolved humans (he turned Claire over to Mr. Bennet for safekeeping), though his exact role remains unknown. He trains Hiro for his fateful confrontation with Sylar.

Nakamura, Kimiko (Saemi Nakamura) — *Heroes* character: Hiro's "hot" (according to Ando) sister. In "Distractions" Hiro recommends that she, not he, become his father's successor in running Yamagato Industries.

Nakamura, Saemi (Kimiko Nakamura) — *Heroes* actress.

Nathan — See **Petrelli, Nathan**.

NCC-1701 — The license number on Kaito Nakamura's limo (also the serial number on *Star Trek*'s *Enterprise*).

New York — The setting for many *Heroes* scenes. The Petrellis, Isaac Mendez, Simone Deveaux (and her father), Eden McCain, and Sylar all live there; Nathan Petrelli is running for congress from New York;

Hiro teleports himself to the Big Apple; Mohinder Suresh journeys there to investigate his father's death; the final confrontation of season 1 occurs in New York's Kirby Plaza.

Newsome, Paula (Dr. Witherson) — *Heroes* actress.

Niki — See **Sanders, Niki.**

Nirand (Shishir Kurup) — *Heroes* character: a colleague of the Sureshes, both father and son, although a skeptic concerning the idea of "activating evolution."

Noah — See **Bennet, Mr.**

"Nothing to Hide" — The seventh episode of season 1.

November 7 — The day of the election that makes Nathan Petrelli a congressman.

November 8 — The date of Hiro's arrival (via teleportation) in New York in "Genesis"; the day a blast levels much of the city.

O

O'Hara, Terrence — *Heroes* director ("The Fix"), a busy director as well on a wide variety of TV series (*Navy NCIS, Smallville* [eleven episodes], *CSI, Numb3rs, JAG, Angel, The Shield, Third Watch, Dark Angel, The Pretender, Star Trek: Voyager, Dr. Quinn, Medicine Woman*).

Odessa, Texas — City where the Bennets live. Location of Primatech Paper.

Oka, Masi (Hiro Nakamura) — *Heroes* actor. Also an employee of Industrial Light & Magic, Oka had recurring roles on *Scrubs* and *The Jamie Kennedy Experiment*, as well as numerous TV guest-starring roles.

"One Giant Leap" — The third episode of season 1.

Origin of Species — In "Don't Look Back" Eden McCain gives Mohinder Suresh a first edition (once belonging to his father) of this book by Charles Darwin.

P

Panettiere, Hayden (Claire Bennet) — *Heroes* actress. The child actress had roles on *One Life to Live* and *Guiding Light* before graduating to guest-starring teenager roles.

"Parasite" — The eighteenth episode of season 1.

Paris — French city to which Claire Bennet is supposed to travel (at Angela Petrelli's wishes) at the end of season 1.

Parkman, Janice (Elizabeth Lackey) — *Heroes* character: Wife of Matt Parkman.

Parkman, Matt (Greg Grunberg) — *Heroes* character: A schlub, dyslexic policeman who aspires to be a detective (regularly failing the exam) but discovers he is telepathic. Severely wounded (by his own bullets redirected by Sylar) at the end of season 1. In the alternate future of "Five Years Gone," he is a brutal enforcer for Homeland Security who kills Future Hiro.

Pasdar, Adrian (Nathan Petrelli) — *Heroes* actor. A veteran actor with numerous film and TV credits, Pasdar starred in *Profit* and *Mysterious Ways* and played recurring characters on *Judging Amy* and *Desperate Housewives*.

peak experiences — Psychologist Abraham Maslow's theorized highest moments of which a human being is capable; Sylar tells Mohinder about them in "Run!"

Peregrym, Missy (Candice Wilmer) — *Heroes* actress.

persuasion — Evolved human power exhibited by Eden McCain.

Peter — See **Petrelli, Peter**.

Peters, Rick (Tom McHenry) — *Heroes* actor.

Petrelli, Angela (Cristine Rose) — *Heroes* character: Petrelli matriarch, who morphs in season 1 from grieving widow to Angela Lansbury–in–*Manchurian Candidate* political manipulator; linked in the past, in ways not yet made clear, to Linderman, Kaito Nakamura, Charles Deveaux, and her husband in the prehistory of evolved humans.

Petrelli, Heidi (Rena Sofer) — *Heroes* character: Nathan's wife, who uses a wheelchair after an auto accident ("Six Months Ago") until healed by Linderman ("Landslide").

Petrelli, Mr. — *Heroes* character: the late patriarch of the Petrelli family, connected, in ways not yet revealed, to Linderman (in the *Heroes* graphic novels, he served with him in the Second World War) and the prehistory of evolved humans.

Petrelli, Nathan (Adrian Pasdar) — *Heroes* character: an evolved human with the ability to fly, who, thanks to Linderman's manipulation, runs successfully for congress. In the alternative future of "Five Years Gone," he has been killed by a now-able-to-fly Sylar who, masquerading as Nathan, becomes president. In the actual narrative he heroically saves New York by flying an about-to-explode Peter Petrelli into the sky and may be dead.

Petrelli, Peter (Milo Ventimiglia) — *Heroes* character: a hospice nurse, working for Simone Deveaux, who, after dreaming of flying, discovers he has the ability to absorb the powers of other evolved humans, becoming, once he has been taught to control the powers by Claude, the most powerful of the heroes next to Sylar. In his final encounter with the Boogeyman in season 1's final episode, he goes nuclear and explodes harmlessly high over New York, flown there by his brother Nathan. Whether he is alive or dead remains unknown.

phasing through matter — An evolved human power exhibited by D.L. Hawkins and (in "Five Years Gone") by Sylar.

pigeons — Birds tended by Claude on the Deveaux roof.

Pokaski, Joe — *Heroes* writer ("Fallout," "Five Years Gone"). Previously wrote for Tim Kring on *Crossing Jordan*. Also the author of ten *Heroes* graphic novels.

power of illusion — Evolved human power to change the surrounding environment exhibited by Candice Wilmer and, in "Five Years Gone," by Sylar (who passes himself off as President Petrelli).

precognition — Evolved human power to see future events exhibited by artist Isaac Mendez.

President of the United States — In ".07%," Linderman informs Nathan Petrelli he will become POTUS and reveals a Mendez painting predicting it. In "Five Years Gone," Sylar, disguised as Nathan Petrelli, has become POTUS, a plan he hatches in "The Hard Part."

Primatech Paper — The Odessa, Texas firm, Mr. Bennet's supposed employer, but in reality a front for The Company.

Pyle, Missi (Hope) — *Heroes* actress. Most famous for her role as an alien love interest for Tony Shaloub's character in *Galaxy Quest* (1999).

pyrokinesis — The evolved human power, exhibited by Meredith Gordon, to spontaneously generate fire.

Q

Quinn, Deirdre ("Texas" Tina) — *Heroes* actress.

Quinto, Zachary (Sylar) — *Heroes* actor. Perhaps his best known role before *Heroes* was *24*'s computer wizard Adam Kaufman.

R

Ramamurthy, Sendhil (Mohinder Suresh) — *Heroes* actor. He has numerous theatrical credits on both the London and New York stage, as well as TV guest roles on *Grey's Anatomy* and *Numb3rs*.

Reid, Javin (Sanjob Iyer) — *Heroes* actor.

Roberts, Leonard (D.L. Hawkins) — *Heroes* actor. Played Forrest Gates in season 4 of *Buffy the Vampire Slayer*.

Roberts, Eric (Thompson) — *Heroes* actor. Julia Roberts' brother and one time leading man (*Star-80*), now a busy character actor often cast, as in *Heroes*, as a heavy.

Rose, Cristine (Angela Petrelli) — *Heroes* actress.

Roundtree, Richard (Charles Deveaux) — *Heroes* actor. Most famous for playing Shaft in a series of Blaxploitation films in the 1960s.

"Run!" — The fifteenth episode of season 1.

S

Sakamoto, Ms. (Nicole Bilderback) — *Heroes* character: A Linderman assistant, manager of a Las Vegas casino, who undertakes such dirty work as blackmailing Nathan Petrelli.

Sale, Tim — Award-winning comic book artist, often working with

Jeph Loeb. For more on Sale, see the "The Creation of *Heroes*" chapter.

Sanders, Hal (Graham Beckel) — *Heroes* character: Niki and Jessica's deadbeat, abusive father, whose treatment of the latter (now dead) seemingly caused Niki/Jessica's Jekyll-and-Hyde split.

Sanders, Micah (Noah Gray-Cabey) — *Heroes* character: the young son of Niki Sanders and D.L. Hawkins, he is a technopath, able to communicate intuitively with machines.

Sanders, Niki (Ali Larter) — *Heroes* character: An Internet stripper and mother (of Micah), whose "mirror" double Jessica has superhuman strength.

"Save the cheerleader; save the world" — The message brought to Peter Petrelli by Future Hiro in "Hiros," which became one of the series' catchphrases. Echoed in Nathan Petrelli's final episode line, "You saved the cheerleader so we could save the world."

Savre, Danielle (Jackie Wilcox) — *Heroes* actress.

scar — When Future Hiro brings his message to Peter Petrelli in "Collison"/"Hiros," he is surprised by how different Peter looks "without the scar"; in "Five Years Gone" Peter sports a prominent scar, the source of which has not been revealed.

Schwimmer, Rusty (Dale Smither) — *Heroes* actress.

science experiment — When D.L. Hawkins and Jessica break into Linderman's suite in Las Vegas in "The Hard Part," they learn that their lives, and that of son Micah, have been part of Linderman's "science experiment."

Semel, David — *Heroes* director (he did the pilot, "Genesis"), a TV veteran of such shows as *Studio 60 on the Sunset Strip, House, American Dreams, Buffy the Vampire Slayer, Ally McBeal, The Practice, Boston Public, Dawson's Creek, Beverly Hills 90210, Chicago Hope,* and *Party of Five.*

"Seven Minutes to Midnight" — The eighth episode of season 1.

Shapiro, Paul — *Heroes* director ("Hiros," "Godsend"), who has worked on many shows since 1980 including *Smallville* (six episodes), *Criminal Minds, Tru Calling, Keen Eddie, Las Vegas, 24, Roswell* (six episodes), *Dark Angel, The X-Files,* and *Millennium.*

Shenoy, Mira (Kavi Ladnier) — *Heroes* character: a young Indian woman, who tries to persuade Mohinder not to follow in his father's footsteps.

"Six Months Ago" — The tenth episode of season 1.

Smither, Dale (Rusty Schwimmer) — *Heroes* character: a Bozeman, Montana, auto-mechanic cursed with superhearing (which she alleviates with rap music). Murdered by Sylar, who steals her evolved human power.

Sofer, Rena (Heidi Petrelli) — *Heroes* actress.

space-time manipulation — Evolved human power possessed by Hiro, allowing him to both teleport and freeze time.

Spinella, Stephen (Oliver Dennison) — *Heroes* actor.

Sprague, Ted (Matthew John Armstrong) — *Heroes* character: able to generate thermonuclear energy out of his body (he accidentally kills his wife with radiation, and almost explodes in "Company Man"). His power passes on to Peter Petrelli (who explodes in the season 1 finale) and to Sylar, who murders him in "Landslide."

Star Trek — Classic American cult sci-fi television series (1966–69) often referenced by Hiro and Ando.

"String Theory" — The rumored title of "Five Years Gone," the twentieth episode of season 1. The title, the name of an esoteric aspect of modern quantum physics, presumably would have referred as well to the elaborate timeline of the episode.

superhearing — Evolved human power exhibited by Dale Smither and stolen by Sylar in "Unexpected."

Suresh, Chandra (Erick Avari) — *Heroes* character: Indian geneticist who developed a formula for identifying emergent evolved human individuals, created a list of such people, and wrote *Activating Evolution*. Murdered by Sylar.

Suresh, Mohinder (Sendhil Ramamurthy) — *Heroes* character and frequent narrator, son of Chandra Suresh, like him a professor of genetics, who reluctantly (at first) takes over his father's work after his death.

Suresh, Mrs. (Sakina Jaffrey) — *Heroes* character: wife of Chandra Suresh and mother of Mohinder and Shanti.

Suresh, Shanti — *Heroes* character (seen so far only in a photograph): Mohinder Suresh's older sister, who died at an early age of the same genetic anomaly that caused her evolved human power. Like Molly Walker, who experiences the same power, she was able to pinpoint the precise location of anyone on Earth.

sword — After seeing Isaac Mendez' painting of him wielding a samurai sword (known in Japan as a *katana*), Hiro steals the sword of Takezo Kensei from the Museum of Natural History in New York. After it is broken by Sylar and repaired (at a handy samurai sword repair shop), Hiro is trained in its proper use by his father. The Helix symbol can be found on the sword's hilt.

Sylar (Zachary Quinto) — *Heroes* character: a serial killer systematically murdering evolved humans in order to steal their powers. He is run through with a sword by Hiro in "How to Stop an Exploding Man" but may still have escaped alive. See also **cockroach**.

Sylar Watches — A brand of timepiece from which watch-repairman Gabriel Gray takes the name of his serial killer persona.

Szwarc, Jeannot — Parisian-born *Heroes* director ("Distractions"), working in television since the 1960s on shows from *Without a Trace* (ten episodes), *Smallville* (nine episodes), *Bones, Cold Case, Boston Legal, Numb3rs, JAG, The Practice* (fourteen episodes), *CSI: Miami, Ally McBeal, Boston Public,* and *Providence* to the earlier *The Rockford Files, Night Gallery* (twenty-two episodes), *Marcus Welby, M.D.,* and *Ironside*.

T

Takei, George (Kaito Nakamura) — *Heroes* actor, most famous for his role as Sulu on the original *Star Trek*.

Taylor, Zane (Ethan Cohn) — *Heroes* character: an evolved human able to liquefy matter. Killed by Sylar in "Run!," who steals his power and assumes, for a time, his identity.

technopathy — Evolved human power exhibited by Micah Sanders, which allows him to communicate intuitively with machines of all kinds: computers telephones, ATMs, voting machines. Linderman coerces Micah to use his gift to fix an election, guaranteeing Nathan Petrelli's "Landslide" victory.

telekinesis — The ability, exhibited by Brian Davis, Sylar, and Peter Petrelli, to move physical objects with the mind.

telepathy — Evolved human power exhibited by Matt Parkman and, later, Peter Petrelli, to hear others' thoughts.

teleporting/teleportation — Evolved human power exhibited by Hiro Nakamura, which allows him to move through space and time.

"Texas" Tina (Deirdre Quinn) — *Heroes* character: Niki Sanders' confidante and occasionally Micah's babysitter.

Thayer, Agent Eliza (Stacy Haiduk) — *Heroes* character: FBI special agent, Agent Hanson's humorless, by-the-book supervisor.

Thompson (Eric Roberts) — *Heroes* character: Bennet's sinister Company boss. Shot in the head by Bennet in "Landslide."

Times Square — Iconic New York locale to which Hiro transports himself at the end of "Genesis."

Tishler, Adair (Molly Walker) — *Heroes* actress.

Tokyo — The Japanese hometown of the Nakamuras, Ando Masahashi, and Yamagato Industries.

T-Rex — An Isaac Mendez painting shows Hiro brandishing Takezo Kenzei's sword in a face off with a Tyrannosaurus Rex, a misleading rendering of a moment (in "Godsend") in the Museum of Natural History in which Hiro assumes this posture in front of a skeleton of the prehistoric predator.

U

Uluru the Invincible — Rock monster that appears in several of Isaac's paintings and comic books, and the screensavers of both Hiro and Micah, who chastised Isaac in a vision in the graphic novel "Isaac's First Time."

"Unexpected" — The sixteenth episode of season 1.

Union Wells High School —The Odessa, Texas, high school attended by Claire Bennet, Zach, Brody Mitchum, and Jackie Wilcox; Jackie is murdered there by Sylar during homecoming festivities.

University of Madras — Institution where geneticists Chandra Suresh and his son Mohinder teach.

Utah — Western state that serves as a locale for several *Heroes* events: D.L. Hawkins (who did time in prison in the state) and Micah go there when they flee from Jessica; Hiro passes through (and boards a Greyhound); Niki turns herself in to the police.

V

Ventimiglia, Milo (Peter Petrelli) — *Heroes* actor. Best known aside from *Heroes* for playing Luke's nephew on *Gilmore Girls* and Rocky's son in *Rocky Balboa*.

W

Walker, Molly (Adair Tishler) — *Heroes* character: a young evolved human able to pinpoint the precise location of anybody on earth, a power she shares with the late Shanti Suresh. The FBI, assisted by Matt Parkman, saves her twice from Sylar ("Don't Look Back," "One Giant Leap").

Wilcox, Jackie (Danielle Savre) — *Heroes* character: Claire Bennet's former friend and fellow cheerleader. Murdered by Sylar, who mistakes her for Claire.

Wilmer, Candice (Missy Peregrym) — *Heroes* character: an "illusionist" in the employ of The Company, able to assume the appearance of others (Sandra Bennet, Claire Bennet, Niki Sanders, etc.). Brutally beaten, perhaps killed, by Jessica/Niki in "How to Stop an Exploding Man." In the possible future of "Five Years Gone" she has been killed by Sylar.

Witherson, Dr. (Paula Winsome) — *Heroes* character: a psychiatrist who tries to help Niki and is savagely beaten by Jessica.

Y

Yamagato Industries — The Japanese corporation run by Hiro's father Kaito Nakamura and the employer of both Hiro and Ando. The official Web site is yamagatofellowship.org.

Z

Zach (Thomas Dekker) — *Heroes* character: Claire's once and future friend and accomplice, whose sexual orientation remains ambiguous.

Zatta, Christopher — *Heroes* writer ("Parasite"). *Heroes* gave him his first ever writing assignment. Also wrote a *Heroes* graphic novel.

Zehetner, Nora (Eden McCain) — *Heroes* actress.

Season 1 Episode Guide

"GENESIS" (1.1: 9/25/2006), written by Tim Kring and directed by David Semel, opens on the eye of Peter Petrelli and his dream of flight. We meet most of season 1's major players: Mohinder Suresh as he lectures on the cockroach and the threshold of true human potential at the University of Madras in India; Niki Sanders as she strips for her Web site; her son Micah rebuilding a computer's memory; Claire Bennet taking a dive; Nathan Petrelli candidating in his campaign office; Hiro Nakamura furrowing his brow and stopping the clock in Japan; Isaac Mendez riding through the desert on a horse with no name and painting the future; Peter Petrelli hospicing Charles Deveaux; Angela Petrelli, caught shoplifting (is this the same Angela Lansbury–in–*Manchurian Candidate* of later in the season?); and HRG, Mr. Bennet (as we learn at the end of the episode), who is snooping around Mohinder's father's apartment. In this busy initial outing, Claire rescues a fireman from a burning train car; Mohinder finds his father's eponymous files; several of the above see a total eclipse that does not have Tim Kring's name on it; Jessica steps out of the mirror to kill some vermin who need killing; Hiro teleports into the women's restroom at sidekick Ando's request and then makes a much bigger leap to New York City; Peter reprises his dream and tries to fly and is caught by Nathan, who flies up to meet him.

"DON'T LOOK BACK" (1.2: 10/2/2006), written by Tim Kring and directed by Allan Arkush, finds Peter waking up in a hospital, told by the lying Nathan (who denies flying — we won't trust him again until the season finale) that he tried to kill himself and ended up on a fire escape; Mohinder finds a pretend plumber in his father's apartment and needs neighbor Eden McCain's help in fending him off; Hiro loves New York and finds Isaac's *9th Wonders* comic book about *his* adventures; Claire flirts like a cheerleader — with the quarterback who will later "kill" her; Niki begins to realize she is killing people in her spare time (and other personality); Jackie Wilcox proves to be a fame-hungry bitch, taking credit for Claire's heroism; Mrs. Petrelli tells Peter his dad offed himself; Isaac has lost his head, as Hiro discovers (and gets himself arrested); Matt Parkman becomes Molly Walker's hero; we meet Sylar on Chandra Suresh's answering machine; Peter confronts Nathan on a rooftop and finds himself hovering in mid-air (confirming Nathan's "lying sack of . . ." status). At episode's end, five weeks (and twenty-one episodes) into the future; Hiro teleports away as a thermonuclear blast levels Manhattan.

In **"ONE GIANT LEAP"** (1.3: 10/9/2006), written by Jeph Loeb and directed by Greg Beeman, Ando is watching Niki on his office computer when Hiro returns, shows him Isaac's comic book, and tells him about the blast; Peter practices flying (unsuccessfully) on a playground; Parkman reads Audrey Hanson's mind; Simone Deveaux pleads with Isaac to go into rehab, who wants instead to stop the cataclysm his paintings foretell; re-enacting a scene from his comic books, Hiro turns Ando into a true believer; Parkman and Hanson have a run-in with Sylar, who is still stalking Molly; Hiro and Ando fly to America — in a plane!; Mohinder and Eden practice breaking and entering at Sylar's place, where they find another map and clear serial killer signatures; we meet Matt Parkman's wife and understand why their marriage is boring; on a first-date-from-hell, Claire, struggling to escape from Brody's sexual assault, falls and embeds a tree branch into her skull, awakening in a morgue on the autopsy table with her chest cavity cut open (she hates it when she does that).

"COLLISION" (1.4: 10/16/2006), written by Bryan Fuller and directed by Ernest Dickerson, finds a captive Matt undergoing tests supervised by Bennet, and the Haitian "goes deep" for the first time; Hiro and Ando and (separately) Niki arrive in Las Vegas; Claire gets herself together and arises from the autopsy table; Simone and Peter get it on; Hiro uses his powers at the roulette wheel; Peter begins to understand his spongeworthiness; Isaac reveals that he has been prophetically stalking Simone and Peter; Niki (and then Jessica) entrap Nathan in a schizo–ménage a trois; Isaac shoots up and paints Sylar's attack on the cheerleader; Hiro and Ando go *Rain Man* in new suits but are thrown out of the casino; Claire avenges herself on Brody (and his car); Bennet and the Haitian abduct Nathan; a barely recognizable bad-ass Future Hiro stops time on a subway car in order to bring a "different without the scar" Peter a message.

Future Hiro, in the appropriately titled **"HIROS"** (1.5: 10/23/2006), written by Michael Green and directed by Paul Shapiro, tells Peter to go to Isaac for help and instructs him to embrace the catchphrase for season 1's first arc; Nathan escapes from Bennet and the Haitian by flying away; Mohinder doesn't believe Peter's account of Future Hiro's visit; Hiro and Ando witness the landing of "Flying Man" at a desert diner; Matt plans a special day for Janice, which she finds more endearing than we do; Peter sees Isaac's painting of the catchphrase; Bennet has the Haitian "hollow out" the quarterback and "take everything" (including his knowledge of the Union Wells High football playbook); Peter takes up painting and goes all white-eyeball too; the police pursue D.L., Niki's husband, and he later materializes (literally) at her house; Nathan embraces corruption at the hands of the still mysterious Linderman and seeks a bigger bribe; Matt and Janice make love and the earth does not move (for us); Hiro reaches Peter by phone and is informed he "has a message" for him.

Peter passes on the catchphrase to Hiro and tells him he will have a sword in **"BETTER HALVES"** (1.6: 10/30/2006), written by Natalie Chaidez and directed by Greg Beeman; D.L. reveals himself to Niki and insists he was set up; Niki and D.L. argue, and she agrees he can stay the night; Micah reunites with his dad, and they share some quality comic book time; Claire meets with her (pretend) birth parents; Eve is revealed to be in the employ of Bennet; Hiro feels guilt over his failure, but Ando reassures him on the nature of the hero's path; Claire learns there was some problem with her "chromosomes" when she was little, and we learn that Bennet faked the meeting with her "bios"; in a battle with Jessica, we learn that D.L. can phase through matter, plunging his hand into her chest and then fleeing; Eden shows up at Isaac's.

In the least eventful episode to date, **"NOTHING TO HIDE"** (1.7: 11/6/2006), written by Jesse Alexander and directed by Donna Deitch, Peter talks to Charles Deveaux and tells him, and shows him, he can fly (in what appears to be a dream); Deveaux dies; Niki awakes to find D.L. and Micah have vanished; Matt tries, and fails, to confess his power to Janice; Simone tells Peter about her father's dreams about people banding together to save the world and reveals that a man named Linderman in Las Vegas has been buying Isaac's paintings; Hanson seeks Parkman's help; we hear for the first time about the radioactive Ted Sprague; Hiro, D.L., and Micah combine to save a car crash victim and discuss comic books, but the latter pair flees when the police arrive; Peter lies for his lying brother to extricate him from scandal; Parkman and Hanson find Sprague in a hospital with his comatose, dying wife, whose thoughts Matt reads, preventing his "explosion"; Micah "heals" a phone and contacts his mother.

"SEVEN MINUTES TO MIDNIGHT" (1.8: 11/13/2006), written by Tim Kring and directed by Paul Edwards, finds Mohinder, back in India, scattering his father's ashes into the ocean and being consoled by his mother; Eve nurses Isaac during rehab at an undisclosed location (actually Primatech Paper); at the Burnt Toast Diner in Midland, Texas, the terminally cute (literally) Charlie Andrews demonstrates amazing memory and waits on Hiro and Ando (in Japanese) — Sylar sits, noirish and still unidentified, at a nearby table; Matt reads Sprague's mind and discovers they had similar experiences with The Company (and a similar mark on their neck); Mohinder finds a key in his father's notebook and, guided by Sanjob Iyer, has lucid dreams; while Hiro uses the john, Sylar kills Charlie in the back room; Mohinder and his mother talk of his sister, who died young; Bennet seeks Isaac's help in saving his daughter; Mohinder sees Sylar murder his father in a dream; a guilty Hiro teleports back in time in the hope of preventing Charlie's death; Janice admits to having had an affair (!); a photo on the Burnt Toast bulletin board of Charlie's birthday party, shows a very worried Hiro.

"HOMECOMING" (1.9: 11/20/2006), written by Kay Foster and Adam Armus and directed by Greg Beeman, begins with announcement of the queen of the title, and it's . . . Claire (thanks to the loser vote); in Utah, D.L. and Micah commit to becoming "Batman and Robin," but then Micah disappears; Bennet grounds Claire to prevent her from going to homecoming; Sanjog tells Mohinder he already has the answer he seeks; Peter meets Ando and, despite being warned he will die, leaves to save the cheerleader; Mohinder suddenly realizes that the password to his father's computer must be "Shanti" (the name of his dead older sister), which reveals "the list" of evolved humans; Claire runs into Peter (literally) at Union Wells High School, but he does not realize she is the one he seeks; Sylar brutally kills Jackie and tosses Claire aside but, as Bennet comes to the rescue, realizes Claire is the one he wants; protecting Claire, Peter pulls Sylar over the side of the stadium, plummeting to the ground below, where he regenerates from his injuries and Sylar flees; Sylar encounters Eden and the Haitian, who control him and put him down; the police arrest a covered-with-blood Peter; Jessica shoots D.L.; Hiro appears six months before at the Burnt Toast just before Charlie's birthday party commences and announces his desire to save her life.

"SIX MONTHS AGO" (1.10: 11/27/2006), written by Aron Eli Coleite and directed by Allan Arkush, takes place, shockingly, six month ago, as Hiro introduces himself to Charlie and declares his intentions; "Gabriel Gray" (Sylar) meticulously fixes a watch and is visited by Suresh; Matt pulls over Eden for a traffic violation and is persuaded to leave her alone (and go eat doughnuts), but when she tries to leave, her path is blocked by the Haitian; Claire makes the cheerleading squad, thereby making possible a certain series catchphrase; Niki is reunited with her abusive father; Suresh runs tests on Sylar, who talks of his dreams of being important; Nathan and Heidi are run off the road by Linderman's henchmen, but Flying Man exits at the last second before the driverless car crashes, leaving his wife crippled (Peter dreams it all); Hiro folds a thousand cranes (with his mind); Sylar steals some of the names on Suresh Sr.'s list; Charlie confesses to having Ali McGraw Disease[1], and just as they are about to kiss, Hiro loses his powers and ends up back in Japan just in time for calisthenics; Brian Davis (who has telekinetic powers) comes to visit "Sylar" (a name he gets off the watch he has been working on for seven years), who murders him and ingests his power; Sylar demonstrates his new power for Suresh; Hiro returns to the Burnt Toast in the present, having failed to save Charlie: "I loved her," he confesses to Ando.

In **"FALLOUT"** (1.11: 12/4/2006), written by Joe Pokaski and directed by John Badham, Bennet and Claire have the big father-daughter talk — about super powers; Peter has a prophetic dream in which Nathan turns into Sylar; the actual Sylar threatens Claire; a fleeing D.L. and Micah hide in a cabin in the woods; Eden decides to go "off the reservation"; Peter is "totally" Claire's hero; an injured Micah reunites Jessica and Niki; at a meeting with Isaac in Texas, Hiro asks the title of the season finale; Niki turns Jessica over to the police; Claire discovers that mom, bro, and Zach have been erased; Isaac sees/paints Hiro battling a T-Rex; Eden's plan to talk Sylar into suicide backfires when she kills herself instead; Peter has his first exploding man dream (Mohinder, Matt, Claire, Nathan, Simone, Hiro and Ando are all there, but no Cowardly Lion, or Tin Man or . . .).

"GODSEND" (1.12: 1/22/2007), written by Tim Kring and directed by Paul Shapiro, finds Peter, two weeks later, still dreaming of the explosion (this time with just a touch of Claude); the FBI raids Primatech and finds nothing; Hiro and Ando find Hiro's sword (actually Takezo Kensei's) at the Museum of Natural History in New York City; Matt accosts Bennet and makes an idle threat to figure him out; Niki/Jessica goes for the insanity defense; Hiro semi-stops time and steals a fake sword, having an encounter with a T-Rex (skeleton) on the way out; Nathan sees Isaac's exploding man painting; Hiro tells Nathan of the explosion and has trouble with his *v*'s; Sprague passes the time in the Nevada desert practicing fireballs; Claire déjà vu's all over again her "Genesis" jump for Zach's camcorder; Bennet leaves Mohinder his business card; Matt finally confesses his power to Janice; Hiro denies being quite so round-faced; Peter sees an invisible man.

As **"THE FIX"** (1.13: 1/29/2007), written by Natalie Chaidez and directed by Terrence O'Hara, opens, Peter pursues "the invisible man . . . Claude Rains," who recognizes him to be "one of those"; Mohinder tells Nathan about the list (of thirty-six individuals) and about Peter's spongeworthiness; Hiro shows "how we roll," but he and Ando are taken captive by mysterious men; Micah and D.L. fight over his parenting; Claire has a heart-to-heart with the Haitian; reading minds at his hearing, Matt settles for being a "liar and not a nut case" and is suspended for six months; Hiro wins two first class airline tickets to Tokyo from a man who knows a guy who has "real power"; Claude begins to train Peter; Janice is in a family way; D.L. breaks into Niki's cell; Micah begins his life of crime; manatees are thoroughly researched; Micah reveals his secret (and a lot of green) to his dad; Hiro and Ando meet the aforementioned man with "real power": Hiro's dad, Sulu; Claire finds her birth mom; Bennet finds a not-dead Sylar.

Claude teaches Peter the fine art of invisible shoplifting and promises to "housebreak" him in **"DISTRACTIONS"** (1.14: 2/5/2007), written by Michael Green and directed by Jeannot Szwarc; Jessica wails on her shrink; Sylar imprisons Bennet, conveniently (for the needs of the narrative) leaving him alive, and goes to kill Claire; Claire and Zach head for Kermit; the Nakamuras argue about family succession and Ando lusts after Hiro's sis; Claire ponders her greeting to real bio-mom: "Hi, I'm your daughter and I can regrow my kidney"; Sylar breaks into the Bennet home; Mrs. Bennet comes dangerously close to revealing her husband's real name; in a touching mother and child reunion, Claire slices her arm with a butcher knife, and mom responds by demonstrating her pyrokinesis; Sylar menaces Mrs. Bennet until Bennet, with gun blazing, and the Haitian storm into the house; Niki/Jessica is/are released at Linderman's bidding; Claude shoves Peter off a rooftop to test his progress (he gets an F in flying; an A+ in regeneration); when Peter begins to explode, Claude decks him; we learn who's her [Claire's] daddy: Nathan.

At the outset of **"RUN!"** (1.15: 2/12/2007), written by Adam Armus and Kay Foster and directed by Roxann Dawson, Nathan offers Melissa Gordon $100,000 in love-child hush money; Parkman finds another job he sucks at: private security guard; Hiro and Ando return to Vegas and become involved in a misguided, better forgotten subplot (we will speak no more of it); Sylar arrives at Zane Taylor's first and pretends to be Mohinder; Nathan's mother scolds him about Meredith and his child, affectionately telling him, "You're a glorified sperm donor," and cautioning him not to "be a sap"; Bennet grounds Claire — again; Jessica kills Malsky (at Linderman's bidding) and throws Parkman out a window; Zane Taylor (a.k.a. Sylar) liquefies a toaster for Mohinder and offers to accompany him on visits to evolved humans; Claire watches bio-dad's visit to bio-mom from afar and throws a rock; Parkman acquires some diamonds; Claire returns home to find her mother unhinged, terrified by Mr. Muggles, unable to recognize her precious dog or daughter; Jessica gets another contract: Nathan.

"UNEXPECTED" (1.16: 2/19/2007), written by Jeph Loeb and directed by Greg Beeman, begins in a cabin in the Nevada desert as Hana Gittelman sends e-mails to Sprague's offline computer and then walks in the door, announcing herself as an evolved human; Mohinder and Sylar visit Dale Smither, a female Bozeman, Montana, auto mechanic with superhearing (Sylar later kills her and steals her power); Claude trains Peter, who finds himself able to use the telekinesis he acquired from Sylar; Mohinder and Sylar talk about controlling special powers and his murder of Suresh, Sr.; on the Deveaux roof Claude talks of pigeons, Darwin, and maximum potential; when Bennet and the Haitian attack, Peter deflects the bullets, grabs Claude, and flies away; furious at Peter for having shown Bennet where he is, Claude flees; Claire accuses her father of his crimes and will not accept his excuse ("I was only protecting my family"); Hiro parts company with Ando (after telling him, "Life is not a comic book") and boards a Greyhound bus (driven by Stan Lee); Matt and Sprague take the Bennets captive; Isaac pulls his gun and fires wildly at a now-invisible Peter, shooting, instead, Simone.

In **"COMPANY MAN"** (1.17: 2/26/2007), written by Bryan Fuller and directed by Allan Arkush, the Parkman/Sprague occupation of Chez Bennet continues; Sprague suggests Bennet not upset him; **fifteen years ago**: Thompson hires Bennet, asking him about his interest in paper and warning him that some of what he will do will be "morally gray" ("I'm comfortable with morally gray," Bennet responds) and introducing an incredulous HRG to a just-become-visible Claude; **in the present**: Parkman learns the Haitian didn't erase all of Claire's memory; **fourteen years ago**: Claude and Bennet meet with Kaito on the Deveaux roof, and (while little Hiro looks on) Kaito gives Bennet Claire, until she starts "manifesting"; **in the present**: Bennet blocks Matt's telepathy by thinking in Japanese and tries to get his hands on a hidden gun, but Sprague beats him to it and is ready to shoot Mrs. Bennet until, at Bennet and Claire's telepathic request, Parkman (who hears Sprague pull the trigger in his mind) shoots Claire; Parkman insists they must go to Primatech to learn the truth; **fourteen years ago**: Bennet tells Thompson his wife has become suspicious, subserviently acknowledging he is ready to do as he is told, and is informed about The Company's new evolved human, a Haitian boy who can erase memory; **in the present**: at Primatech, Bennet secures some powerful tranquilizers and a hypodermic; Bennet accosts the Haitian and learns that he was following higher instructions in sparing Claire's memory; **seven years ago**: in a car, Bennet tells Claude they are investigating a security breach, but Claude, who had been eavesdropping when Bennet was ordered to kill him for harboring an evolved human, goes invisible when Bennet shoots him on a bridge and disappears; **in the present**: Claire tries to get Lyle and her mother out of the house, but Sprague discovers she faked her death; grabbing Claire, Sprague burns fingerprints into her neck (which immediately heal) and ties up Claire and her mother; Bennet and Parkman return, ready to reveal the truth; Thompson enters and shoots Sprague, setting him off, which ignites the interior of the house; Claire returns inside and takes the tranquilizer from her father and while Matt takes Bennet out of the house, walks through the flames toward Sprague; after the house is rocked by a blast, an extra-crispy Claire walks out alive, as Thompson looks on, aware now that Claire has manifested; Bennet meets Candice Wilmer, brought in, according to Thompson, to clean up Bennet's mess, and he promises to bring in Claire immediately; **three years ago**: Claire helps her father pick out his horn rimmed glasses; **in the present**: on the same bridge where Claude was shot, the Haitian (as planned) wounds Bennet, who then tells him to "go deep" to wipe out any trace of their plan to enable "Claire bear" to go free.

"PARASITE" (1.18: 3/5/2007), written by Christopher Zatta and directed by Kevin Bray, begins with confirmation of Simone's deadness; Isaac shoots at Peter; Bennet tells Thompson he remembers nothing; Mohinder and Sylar inspect the list, and Sylar offers to go see Isaac, but Mohinder has put something in his chai to knock him out; the police come to visit Isaac about the death of Simone but leave after Simone (in reality, Wilmer) appears; Mohinder tortures Sylar and they debate which of them is the worst parasite; Jessica slaughters the feds investigating Linderman; Sylar escapes; Hiro gets the sword and teleports (with Ando) to New York (the Deveaux roof) *after* the blast; Linderman talks about the choice between a life of happiness and a life of meaning — and refuses to give Nathan any of his pot pie; Peter shows up at Mohinder's and Sylar pins him against the wall, announcing "You're like me; I'd like to see how that works," and then begins to cut open Peter's skull (his forelock falls to the floor).

The Company, with the help of Candice Wilmer, is trying, unsuccessfully, to trick Bennet into revealing Claire's whereabouts at the beginning of **".07%"** (1.19: 4/23/07), written by Chuck Kim and directed by Adam Kane; Linderman explains himself to Nathan, insisting he is a "humanitarian," and revealing his power (as a healer); Bennet uses Parkman and Sprague to escape from Primatech; Linderman explains the episode title to Nathan (the New York City blast will only slaughter .07 percent of the world's population); the people of the world "need hope," Linderman is convinced, "but they trust fear," and Nathan will be the leader who rallies humanity — as President of the United States; in a repeat of the final scene of "Parasite," Peter is attacked by Sylar, but customary skull-slicing doesn't work because of Peter's healing ability; Mohinder falls from the ceiling, and Peter goes invisible; Sylar gathers shards of glass and propels them toward Peter, leaving him dead, but Sylar doesn't get to consume him because Mohinder rams him from behind with something (a large painter's frame?) handy; Angela explains her grandmotherly wisdom to Claire; Isaac gives a courier the last of the *9th Wonders* comics to deliver and his sketch book to keep; Mohinder brings Peter's corpse to his mother's and is asked to leave; Linderman meets Jessica and asks a small favor: to borrow Micah (Jessica refuses); given her moment with Peter, Claire brings him back to life by removing a shard of glass from his skull; Bennet, Sprague, and Matt talk in a café, and Bennet explains why they need to take out the "Walker tracking system" in New York, but he does not know (and learns from Matt) that Linderman is in charge of Primatech ("You're middle management," Matt realizes, laughing); Jessica (actually Wilmer) turns Micah over to Linderman; Sylar comes to kill Isaac, but he shows no fear, despite being crucified to the floor, instead becoming philosophical: "I've wasted my life, destroyed everything good that came to me, but at least I have done one good thing before I died. I stopped the bomb. I finally get to be a hero"; Sylar then kills him and paints with his newfound skill; Hiro and Ando look out at a decimated New York, Hiro realizes that something must have gone wrong and he must fix it; arriving at Isaac's apartment they find a strange timeline hung from the ceiling and, waiting for them, Future Hiro, also with a sword; "You!" Future Hiro exclaims. "Me?" Hiro answers.

Five years in the future, **"FIVE YEARS GONE"** (1.20: 4/30/07), written by Joe Pokaski and directed by Paul Edwards, Hiro and Future Hiro meet; Future Hiro explains the timeline, learns that Peter did save the cheerleader but did not prevent the exploding man, and informs Hiro he must go back to kill Sylar with his sword; Homeland Security bursts in (led by Matt) and takes Hiro captive (Ando and Future Hiro escape); Future Hiro explains that only Peter Petrelli has the requisite power to stage a rescue, and they leave for Las Vegas to find him; Ando and Future Hiro find Jessica stripping and get a clue about where Bennet is (but not Peter, who is there but invisible, and with a prominent scar) — the one Future Hiro inquired about before (in "Hiros"); Matt calls President Petrelli, who is suspicious about Hiro's appearance on the anniversary of the destruction of New York; Nathan wants the evolved humans exterminated (even though he *is* one); Bennet and Gittelman help a newly discovered evolved human go underground; Bennet rejects a request for help until Ando tells him that Hiro helped save his daughter; Claire works as a waitress at the Burnt Toast, watches Nathan on TV ("He's old enough to be my father"), flirts with fiancé Andy, and waits on Bennet (who tells her she must flee); Matt and Homeland Security burst in and taser Future Hiro; Peter bursts in, freezes time, and liberates Future Hiro and Ando; Parkman betrays Bennet, finds out where Claire is by reading his mind, and then kills him, later showing up at the Burnt Toast to take Claire captive; Nathan explains his plan to blame the death of the evolved humans on Mohinder; Nathan reveals himself to be Sylar and slices open Claire's skull; Peter, Ando, and Future Hiro come to save Hiro; Parkman shoots Future Hiro and calls Nathan, who flies away (to the crowd's shock) from his anniversary speech; Nathan reveals himself to be Sylar, and he and Peter square off; Hiro teleports Ando back to the Deveaux roof, where they look out at a not-yet-destroyed New York City and he announces, "Now the hard part."

Written by Aron Eli Coleite and directed by John Badham, **"THE HARD PART"** (1.21: 5/7/07) begins with Hiro and Ando back in present-day New York (Hiro shouts to New York that he will save it); Peter (who is drawing comics) and Claire talk about their destinies; Sylar paints and, to his shock, realizes for the first time about the exploding man; Thompson makes demands of Mohinder and introduces him to Molly Walker, who needs his antibodies; D.L. and Jessica discover their lives have been Linderman's "science experiment" and learn Micah will die in the New York blast; with Ando and Hiro looking on, Sylar visits his (clearly deranged) mother (bringing a snow globe for her collection), fixes a family heirloom clock, wonders if it might be okay if he does not turn out to be special the way his mother insists, and uses cryokinesis to turn her apartment into a kind of snow globe; Sylar's mother threatens him with a pair of scissors, and she is stabbed in the struggle; Hiro bursts in, stops time, and prepares to kill Sylar, but Sylar breaks free from the time-hold, grabs Hiro's sword and freezes it until it breaks (Ando bursts in and they teleport away); Peter gives Claire a gun to shoot him and prevent his explosion; Sylar tells his mother's corpse that he will be special — that he can even be president; as Bennet, Sprague, and Matt approach, Peter starts to explode.

As **"LANDSLIDE"** (1.22: 5/14/07), written by Jesse Alexander and directed by Greg Beeman, begins, Peter gets his imminent explosion under control (after pleading with Claire to shoot him); Ando gives Hiro a pep talk and finds a sword repairman in the Yellow Pages; Linderman tells Nathan about his "weak" father and cures Heidi Petrelli; Hiro deems Nathan a "villain"; Kaito Nakamura trains Hiro for his final battle; Linderman tells Micah that he needs him to talk to some machines (a.k.a. fix the election); the FBI arrests Sprague; Kaito elicits from Hiro new dedication and resolve to be "strong enough to cut out my heart"; Mohinder treats Molly, whose powers have returned, and asks her help in finding Sylar; Parkman saves Bennet from Thompson's gunfire, and Bennet, in turn, saves him, putting two bullets in his boss's head; Mohinder and Bennet face off over Molly; Sylar pulls a Magneto and stops the truck carrying Sprague, flipping it end over end, and then slicing open Sprague's skull; Hiro completes his training, only to learn that Ando has gone off on his own to save the world; D.L. and Jessica storm into Linderman's office, and he tries to buy off Jessica (offering her $20 million to kill D.L. and walk away); Niki overcomes Jessica and rejects the offer, which causes Linderman to shoot D.L., who, before he collapses, punches his fist into Linderman's skull; Nathan begins to give his acceptance speech, which is intercut with a montage of all the other characters as they prepare for the big showdown, including Sylar on a rooftop looking at the Empire State Building, setting off fire bombs in his hands and announcing "Boom."

Written by Tim Kring and directed by Alan Arkush, **"HOW TO STOP AN EXPLODING MAN"** (1.23: 5/21/07), the season finale, begins with Mohinder asking all the big questions (again) over a montage of some of the season's big events; Linderman shoots D.L. (again), and D.L. kills Linderman (again); Jessica and D.L. escape as he manages to phase them through a wall; Molly's adorableness puts an end to the Mohinder/Bennet standoff; Hiro acknowledges to his dad "the wind at the back of history" and goes off to save Ando; a white-eyed Sylar sees/paints the final showdown — with Peter; Nathan and his mom reaffirm their vows; Bennet tells Peter he must stop Sylar and orders him to protect Claire no matter what while they find Sylar using the "tracking system" (a.k.a. Molly); Claire flees when Peter involves an untrusted Nathan; Peter almost explodes but conveniently passes out; Molly tells us about the man who is worse than Sylar; Parkman goes off in search of Sylar; Peter dreams a conversation with Charles Deveaux; Sylar nearly slices off Ando's head, but Hiro teleports in and whisks him away — to Japan; a distraught Niki finds "Jessica" (actually Candice) and a prostrate Micah; Claire castigates Angela and Nathan over their plan to let New York be destroyed — not believing their insistence that events are beyond her child's understanding, Claire declares her allegiance to her other family by leaping out the window, quickly recovering from her fall; Jessica whomps Candice and finds Micah; Ando sings a "bad ass" Hiro's praises; Deveaux (who knows "about everything") tells Peter the truth: that he has had the power all along, that he is the one who is "good," that love is all that matters; Bennet reveals his real name: Noah; Sylar (after flicking Bennet aside) faces off in Kirby Plaza with Peter and telekinetically paralyzes him; freezing Parkman's bullets and projecting them back into him, Sylar prepares to whack Peter with a parking meter, but Jessica intercepts and hits Sylar with it; Peter pummels an injured Sylar but begins to go nuclear (Sylar caustically insists Peter is now the villain and he's the hero); Hiro teleports in and guts Sylar with his sword; Peter pleads with Hiro to kill him, but with his last strength Sylar expels Hiro from the scene (he teleports away before hitting a building); Sylar expires, images of each of his victims (last of all himself) flashing before his eye as he dies; Claire arrives, takes her injured father's gun, and prepares to shoot him, when Nathan flies in, exchanges expressions of love with his brother, Peter, and confides, "You saved the cheerleader, so we could save the world," grabbing Peter and flying away (they explode high above); Molly begs Matt not to die; Mohinder speaks of "our shared experience of the fantastic and the mundane," and "End of Volume One" appears over an open manhole cover (a trail of [Sylar's?] blood leads to the hole), from which a cockroach emerges; as eagles soars over a verdant landscape on which the title "Chapter Two: Generations" appears, Hiro falls into the frame and finds himself caught in a 1671 face-off "outside Kyoto Japan" between samurai on horseback and Takezo Kensei, flying the Helix banner. A total eclipse blots out the sun.

EPISODE TITLE LOCATOR

EPISODE	LOCATION OF ONSCREEN TITLE
Genesis (1.1)	Superimposed on the Manhattan rooftop from which Peter Petrelli is about to leap in the series' opening scene.
Don't Look Back (1.2)	Same as in the pilot.
One Giant Leap (1.3)	On the door of Niki's red Cadillac.
Collision (1.4)	On Claire's "corpse" just before the coroner cuts her open.
Hiros (1.5)	On the frozen-in-time subway car just before Future Hiro appears to Peter.
Better Halves (1.6)	On Isaac's painting of the destruction of New York on the floor of his studio.

EPISODE	LOCATION OF ONSCREEN TITLE
Nothing to Hide (1.7)	Imposed on the Hudson River in New York.
Seven Minutes to Midnight (1.8)	On the sands on a beach in India as Mohinder scatters his father's ashes.
Homecoming (1.9)	On the plaza at Union Wells High School.
Six Months Ago (1.10)	On the door of Gabriel Gray's watch repair shop.
Fallout (1.11)	On the wall of Peter Petrelli's cell in Odessa, Texas.
Godsend (1.12)	On Niki's prison cell.
The Fix (1.13)	On the floor of Niki's padded cell.
Distractions (1.14)	On the metronome that Dr. Witherson is using in her treatment of Niki.
Run! (1.15)	On the floor of Nathan Petrelli's office.
Unexpected (1.16)	On Matt Parkman's sock drawer (where the diamonds are hidden).
Company Man (1.17)	In the sky over the Bennet house.
Parasite (1.18)	Again on Isaac's painting of the destruction of New York on the floor of his studio — and the smoking gun with which he has shot Simone.
.07% (1.19)	On the roof of the cell at Primatech containing Mr. Bennet.
Five Years Gone (1.20)	Spread out over a devastated New York skyline.

EPISODE	LOCATION OF ONSCREEN TITLE
The Hard Part (1.21)	Spread out over an intact New York skyline.
Landslide (1.22)	Yet again on Isaac's painting of the destruction of New York on the floor of his studio — and Hiro's broken sword.
How to Stop an Exploding Man (1.23)	On Sylar's color palette as he paints in Isaac's studio.

THE POWERS OF HEROES

CHARACTER	POWER/ABILITY
Andrews, Charlie	Enhanced memory
Bennet, Claire	Instant cell regeneration
Claude	Invisibility
Davis, Brian	Telekinesis
Deveaux, Charles	Unknown but suspected
Gittelman, Hana	Cyberpathy
Gordon, Meredith	Pyrokinesis
Haitian, the	Mind manipulation and memory erasure
Hawkins, D.L.	Phasing through matter

CHARACTER	POWER/ABILITY
Iyer, Sanjob	Dream manipulation
Jessica	Superhuman strength
Linderman, Mr.	Healing
McCain, Eden	Persuasion
Mendez, Isaac	Precognition
Nakamura, Hiro	Manipulation of space and time
Nakamura, Kaito	Unknown but suspected
Parkman, Matt	Telepathy
Petrelli, Angela	Unknown but suspected
Petrelli, Mr.	Unknown but suspected
Petrelli, Nathan	Flight
Petrelli, Peter (now and in the future)	Empathic mimicry, flight, instant cell regeneration, invisibility, precognition, telekinesis, telepathy, thermonuclear energy
Sanders, Micah	Technopathy
Sanders, Niki	See *Jessica*
Smither, Dale	Superhearing
Sprague, Ted	Thermonuclear energy
Suresh, Mohinder	Unknown but suspected
Suresh, Shanti	Unknown but suspected to be similar to Molly Walker's

CHARACTER	POWER/ABILITY
Sylar	Violent mimicry, cryokinesis, enhanced memory, liquefaction, persuasion, precognition, super-hearing, telekinesis, thermonuclear energy
Sylar (Future)	Previous powers plus flight, instant cell regeneration, phasing through matter, illusion
Taylor, Zane	Liquefaction
Walker, Molly	Able to pinpoint the precise location of anybody on Earth
Wilmer, Candice	Illusion

BODY COUNT:
UNNATURAL DEATHS IN HEROES

VICTIM	KILLER	EPISODE DEATH OCCURS OR IS REVEALED	LOCATION OF MURDER	NOTES
Agents Alonzo and Quesada	Jessica	"Parasite"	The Corinthian Hotel in Las Vegas	Slaughter commissioned by Linderman.
Andrews, Charlie	Sylar	"Seven Minutes to Midnight"	In the back room at the Burnt Toast	Evolved human power stolen.
Bennet, Claire	Sylar	"Five Years Gone"	The Petrelli mansion	Takes place in one possible future.
Bennet, Claire	Brody Mitchum	"One Giant Leap"	Football field	Claire regenerates.

VICTIM	KILLER	EPISODE DEATH OCCURS OR IS REVEALED	LOCATION OF MURDER	NOTES
Bennet, Mr.	Matt Parkman	"Five Years Gone"	Homeland Security, New York	Takes place in one possible future.
Company Doctor	Sylar	"Distractions"	At Primatech	
Davis, Brian	Sylar	"Six Months Ago"	At his home in New York	Evolved human power stolen.
Deveaux, Simone	Isaac Mendez	"Unexpected"	Isaac's studio in New York.	Takes a bullet intended for Peter Petrelli.
Future Hiro	Matt Parkman	"Five Years Gone"	Homeland Security holding cell in New York	Takes place in one possible future.
Gray, Virginia	Sylar	"The Hard Part"	Her apartment in New York	Stabbed accidentally in a struggle with her son over a pair of scissors.
Hawkins, D.L.	Sylar	"Five Years Gone"	Unknown	Presumed to have taken place in one possible future since Sylar later possesses D.L.'s special power.
Linderman, Mr.	D.L. Hawkins	"Landslide"	In his office at Kirby Plaza in New York	Death not certain at season's end.

VICTIM	KILLER	EPISODE DEATH OCCURS OR IS REVEALED	LOCATION OF MURDER	NOTES
Linderman's thugs	Jessica	"Genesis"	In Niki Sanders' home in Las Vegas	
Malsky, Aaron	Jessica	"Run!"	In the diamond district of Los Angeles	His killing was commissioned by Linderman.
Masahashi, Ando	Exploding Man	"Five Years Gone"	New York	Takes place in one possible future.
McCain, Eden	Sylar	"Fallout"	At Primatech	Forced to commit suicide when her powers are turned back on herself.
Mendez, Isaac	Sylar	".07%"	Isaac's studio in New York	Evolved human power stolen.
Petrelli, Nathan	Sylar	"Five Years Gone"	Unknown	Presumed to have taken place in one possible future since Sylar later possesses Nathan's special power.
Petrelli, Nathan	An exploding Peter Petrelli	"How to Stop an Exploding Man"	In the sky over New York	Death not certain at season's end.

VICTIM	KILLER	EPISODE DEATH OCCURS OR IS REVEALED	LOCATION OF MURDER	NOTES
Petrelli, Peter	Sylar	".07%"	Isaac's studio in New York	Peter regenerates after Claire removes a shard of glass from his skull.
Petrelli, Peter	An exploding Peter Petrelli	"How to Stop an Exploding Man"	In the sky over New York	Death not certain at season's end.
Sanders, Micah	Exploding Man	"Five Years Gone"	New York	Presumed to have taken place in one possible future.
Smither, Dale	Sylar	"Unexpected"	Bozeman, Montana	Evolved human power stolen.
Sprague, Karen	Ted Sprague	"Nothing to Hide"	A hospital in Los Angeles.	Killed accidentally by exposure to her husband's radiation.
Sprague, Ted	Sylar	"Landslide"	Street in New York	Evolved human power stolen.
Suresh, Chandra	Sylar	"Six Months Ago"	In a taxi in New York	Death not certain at season's end.
Sylar	Hiro Nakamura	"How to Stop an Exploding Man"	Kirby Plaza in New York	Evolved human power stolen.
Taylor, Zane	Sylar	"Run!"	In his home in New York	Shot twice in the head.

VICTIM	KILLER	EPISODE DEATH OCCURS OR IS REVEALED	LOCATION OF MURDER	NOTES
Thompson	Mr. Bennet	"Landslide"	Kirby Plaza	
Walker family	Sylar	"Don't Look Back"	Walker house in Los Angeles	The real target, Molly Walker, escapes.
Wilcox, Jackie	Sylar	"Homecoming"	Union Wells High School	The real target, Claire Bennet, escapes.
Wilmer, Candice	Sylar	"Five Years Gone"	Unknown	Presumed to have taken place in one possible future because Sylar later possesses Candice's power.

APPEARANCES OF THE HELIX

Like *Lost*'s mysterious numbers, *Heroes*' Helix shows up in unexpected places but much more often. Although the Helix also appears throughout *Heroes 360* and the graphic novels, the following table illustrates some of its many occurrences within episodes. Notice that whereas several occurrences seem consciously made (such as the image on a front door), others (such as the doodle on Claire's geometry book or the swirl in a plate of pasta) seem to come subconsciously from people who may not "see" the shape, much less understand what it means. The Helix not only unifies people affected by The Company but it may become a subconscious product of their thoughts.

WHERE THE HELIX CAN BE FOUND	EPISODE
Chandra Suresh's computer program, created for tracking evolved humans	"Don't Look Back"
Chandra Suresh's map	"Don't Look Back"
On Peter's "flying" picture	"Don't Look Back"
Paintings by Isaac Mendez	"Don't Look Back"
Swimming pool at the Walker home	"Don't Look Back"
Cover of *9th Wonders* comics	"Don't Look Back"
Photos on the map in Sylar's apartment	"One Giant Leap"
Activating Evolution cover	"One Giant Leap"
Haitian's necklace	"One Giant Leap"
Claire Bennet's geometry book	"One Giant Leap"
Lizard's tank in Chandra Suresh's New York apartment	"Godsend"
Dish of pasta	"Godsend"
Hilt of Future Hiro's sword	"Godsend"; "Hiros"
Tattoo on Jessica's shoulder	"Collision"; "Hiros"; "Fallout"
Greyhound bus station in Utah	"Homecoming"
Broken glass in the Bennet home (after Sylar attacks Sandra)	"Distractions"

WHERE THE HELIX CAN BE FOUND	EPISODE
Door of the Bennet house as Ted Sprague begins to explode	"Company Man"
Thompson's office	"Company Man"
Formed by stones on a museum curator's table	"Parasite"
As part of a display in Linderman's office (next to information about Niki and D.L.)	"The Hard Part"
Jittetsu Arms banner and their Yellow Pages advertisement	"Landslide"
Samurai banner (in 1761 Japan)	"How to Stop an Exploding Man"

HEROES GRAPHIC NOVELS

TITLE	#	MAIN CHARACTER	AUTHOR (S)
Aftermath	5	Claire Bennet	Joe Pokaski
Bully	19	Micah Sanders	Chuck Kim
Control	7	Matt Parkman	Oliver Grigsby
Crane, The	2	Hiro Nakamura	Aron Eli Coleite
Death of Hana Gittelman 1, The	33	Hana Gittelman	Aron Eli Colcite
Death of Hana Gittelman 2, The	34	Hana Gittelman	Aron Eli Coleite
Exploding Man 1	17	Ted Sprague	Jesse Alexander & Aron Eli Coleite
Exploding Man 2	18	Ted Sprague	Jesse Alexander & Aron Eli Colcite

TITLE	#	MAIN CHARACTER	AUTHOR (S)
Family Man	23	Mr. Bennet	Jesse Alexander
Fathers and Daughters	11	Mr. Bennet & Eden McCain	Andrew Chambliss
Hell's Angel	22	Mr. Bennet, Claude, & Claire Bennet	Jesse Alexander
Isaac's First Time	8	Isaac Mendez	Aron Eli Coleite
It Takes a Village	35	The Haitian	Joe Kelly
Life Before Eden	9	Eden McCain	Pierluigi Cothran
Monsters	1	Mohinder Suresh	Aron Eli Coleite
Path of the Righteous	21	Hana Gittelman	Aron Eli Coleite
Road Kill	20	Sylar	Joe Pokaski
Snapshots	4	D.L. Hawkins	Joe Pokaski
Stolen Time	6	Niki Sanders	Joe Pokaski
String Theory	30	Future Hiro	Joe Pokaski
Super Heroics	12	Peter Petrelli	Harrison Wilcox
Trial by Fire	3	Nathan Petrelli	Chuck Kim
Turning Point	10	Audrey & Sylar	Christopher Zatta
Walls 1	31	Future Peter	Joe Pokaski
Walls 2	32	Future Peter	Joe Pokaski
War Buddies 1: The Lonestar Files	24	Hana Gittelman	Mark Warshaw
War Buddies 2: Unknown Soldiers	25	Mr. Petrelli, Linderman	Andrew Chambliss & Pierluigi Cothran

TITLE	#	MAIN CHARACTER	AUTHOR (S)
War Buddies 3: Unknown Soldiers	26	Mr. Petrelli, Linderman	D.J. Doyle
War Buddies 4: No Turning Back	27	Mr. Petrelli, Linderman	Timm Keppler
War Buddies 5: Introductions	28	Mr. Petrelli, Linderman	Harrison Wilcox & Oliver Grigsby
War Buddies 6: Call to Arms	29	Hana Gittelman	Mark Warshaw
Wireless 1	13	Hana Gittelman & Bennet	Aron Eli Coleite
Wireless 2	14	Hana Gittelman & Bennet	Aron Eli Coleite & Joe Pokaski
Wireless 3	15	Hana Gittelman	Aron Eli Coleite & Joe Pokaski
Wireless 4	16	Hana Gittelman	Aron Eli Coleite & Joe Pokaski

HEROES AROUND THE WEB

O *Heroes the Series* — www.heroestheseries.com: The first fansite for *Heroes*, constantly updated with *Heroes* information and news. The best maintained fansite on the Web, a must-visit for all fans.

O *The HeroesWiki* — www.heroeswiki.com: When it comes to all things *Heroes*, the *Heroes* wiki offers thousands of articles that provide fans with answers about their favorite series.

O *The OWI (Organization Without Initials)* — www.the-owi.com: The *OWI* is a fan haven with links to other *Heroes* fansites, interactive quizzes, contests, fan art, fiction, and other creative projects.

O *Got Heroes?* — www.got-heroes.com: This forum has spoilers, galleries, links to other top sites, and discussion — a veritable *Heroes* feast. The discussion function is active and lively, and offers an extensive theories section.

O *Superhiro* — www.superhiro.org: This unofficial NBC message board hosts an environment for fans to discuss the show, post their theories, or present their art for examination.

O *The Heroes Chronicles* — www.theheroeschronicles.com: This blog posts updates and discussion about the show, and keeps fans apprised of updates to the graphic novels and the *Inside Heroes* episode series.

O *Heroes Info* — heroesinfo.com: This feed site categorizes what other people are saying — from episode reviews to theories — about the series and provides helpful links that are perfect for whiling away an afternoon with *Heroes.*

O *Heroes TV* — www.heroes-tv.com: This site easily provides the most fan-written fiction on the Web, with a thriving message board community continually posting new story content.

O *Heroes Media* — www.heroesmedia.com: This site is user-updated to provide current media news about *Heroes,* bringing articles, links to stories, or other *Heroes* sites to keep fans well informed.

O *Heroes Links* — www.sirlinksalot.net/heroes.html: Not sure where to go? Go to *Heroes Links* and find a neatly organized list of new news content about the series and the most updated fansites.

ENDNOTES

INTRODUCTION

1 *Heroes* also received eight Emmy nominations, including Best Drama and Best Supporting Actor (Masi Oka).

2 To make an even stranger connection between *Star Trek* and *Heroes*, the latter's Sylar (actor Zachary Quinto) would like to play the former's young Spock in J.J. Abrams' upcoming *Star Trek* prequel to classic *Trek* (GustavoLeao, "Zachary Quinto Wants to Play Young Spock in *Star Trek XI*.")

ARE THESE *HEROES LOST?*

1 In addition to ratings reports issued by NBC or reported in entertainment news, *Heroes'* fan sites, such as HeroesTV.com, publish weekly updates about ratings and allow fans to see just how well their favorite series is faring in the ever-important commercial market. HeroesTV.com provides archives of ratings records at its site: www.heroestv.com.

2 The series' loyal fans quickly began a campaign to bring back the

series, and indeed the creators already had planned a second season's episodes. The fan Web site www.nutsonline.com/jericho became the rallying point, achieving a victory when *Jericho* was picked up for at least seven episodes. Nuclear holocaust, it seems, is a fan-approved plot point.

3 Kring learned about the significance of a major character's demise from fan reaction to Isaac Mendez's death, one long foreseen in the story but disliked by some fans. "There's a whole new season with a whole new concept coming, and Isaac was in the way." Kring was "surprised that fans would not expect there to be major death on his NBC hit series."

THE CREATION OF *HEROES*

1 The role of the walk in the creative process has a long history. See Rebecca Solnit's wonderful book *Wanderlust*.

2 Looking back over season 1, and thinking of the excessively prolific and obsessive single author of shows like *Ally McBeal* and *Boston Legal*, Kring would tell Josh Weiland that "a show like this couldn't be done like a David E. Kelley show, . . . where you write every episode yourself. It's logistically not that kind of show" ("*Heroes* Post-Game").

3 Picked up by NBC in May 2006, *Heroes* went on the air on September 25, 2006.

4 Loeb goes on to reveal more — much more — about the fantastic secrets of the *Heroes* room, of course, but it's just possible he is not being completely honest with interviewer Craig Byrne when he regales him with Jesse Alexander's power to teleport into the future in order to ascertain future developments of the show; Natalie Chaidez's "mojo," allowing her to enter Alexander's "mind and pluck . . . out the scenes we need"; and the "classified" evolved human powers — "super speed, . . . multiplexing . . . heat vision" — exhibited by other members of staff. "Damn you, Craig!" Loeb concludes, "I probably have said too much." (Byrne, "*Heroes*' Finest: An Interview with Jeph Loeb"). Indeed.

5 The account of writing practice on *Heroes* I have patched together here from interviews with Kring and Loeb is confirmed by one of the actors, Masi Oka (Hiro). See Furey.

6 Fearing cancelation out of the gate, Whedon and company began the practice, continued throughout its run, of making each year's finale both a season and (potentially) a series ender. See David Lavery, "Apocalyptic Apocalypses" for more on *Buffy* narrative strategies.

7 See David Lavery's "Climate Change."

8 Cast and crew admit to more than one mistake in Jensen's "The Bomb Squad," including having Hiro lose his powers in mid-season and not knowing precisely how to handle the complexities of Niki/Jessica.

COMIC BOOK *HEROES*

1 These wonderful words are from cartoonist Art Spiegelman's blurb on Jones's book (Spiegelman won a special Pulitzer Prize for *Maus* [1973–91], his comic retelling of the story of the Holocaust). In case you aren't up on your Yiddish words, a "goniff" is a thief or swindler; a "shmendrick" is a nincompoop — an inept individual; and a "shlemiel" is, of course, an habitual failure or dolt.

2 A glance at a definition of the term shows it to be ripe with metaphoric possibilities for a show such as *Heroes*: "The process of analyzing an existing system to identify its components and their interrelationships and create representations of the system in another form or at a higher level of abstraction. Reverse engineering is usually undertaken in order to redesign the system for better maintainability or to produce a copy of a system without access to the design from which it was originally produced. (*Reverse engineering* in *The Free On-line Dictionary of Computing*).

3 In an interview with Comic Book Resources, Kring reveals how this technique came about largely by accident in the editing room. See Weiland, "1-on-1."

4 Issues of *9th Wonders* show up often: for example, we see the covers of #5 ("flying man" Nathan in a costume and mask), #9 (bearing the image, perhaps, of Jessica), #13 (the "I Fought Uluru" cover), and #14 (Hiro's "I did it" on the cover).

GROWING PAINS

1 Of course, Superman sometimes "dies" within the course of a comic (or movie). Harlan Ellison once added up all of the times Superman had "died" in a story and came up with roughly two deaths per year. He then suggested that the Doomsday story stands out as *the* "Superman death story" only because of the hype that surrounded it.

2 Often the mentor is actually Athena disguised in order to better steer Odysseus's son, Telemachus, in the right direction. One couldn't ask for a better guide through perilous times than the goddess of wisdom and war.

THE MAKING OF A HIRO

1 Campbell, as do most writers of myths and legends, emphasizes male heroes. Although women are now recognized for their heroic deeds and are often the stars of the action in film, television, and literature, the majority of classical heroes are male; the use of "he" in a summary of Campbell's work and *Heroes'* narration is consistent with a traditional analysis of epic heroes.

2 Several popular Web sites and books base their specific twelve-step self-help programs on Campbell's *Hero*. A psychoanalytical approach involving twelve steps for self-help and recovery, which has been paraphrased for Hiro's twelve steps to becoming a hero, can be found at www.am-psychotherapists-new-york-city.com /Joseph-Campbell.html. Campbell's description of the hero's journey has been summarized in many ways, although the basic concept remains the same: the hero's leaving home to accept a quest or other call to adventure, gathering new experiences and knowledge, being tested, completing the quest, and returning home to share what he's gained (anything from wealth to the beautiful princess as his bride to new information to benefit his people). This framework has been used to help people through any self-help journey. See, for example, Carnes's *A Gentle Path Through the Twelve Steps*.

3 In fact, Lucas decided to create a modern myth after he read Campbell's writings about disparate myths across cultures. Lucas was concerned "[t]here was no modern mythology to give kids a sense of values, to give them a strong mythological fantasy life." *Star Wars* fit the bill and has become recognized as a myth for the twentieth century ("American Masters: George Lucas").

4 Rhonda Wilcox's *Why Buffy Matters: The Art of Buffy the Vampire Slayer* explains this depth of character development. See, for example, the chapters "Pain as Bright as Steel: Mythic Striving and Light as Pain" and "I Think I Can Name Myself: Naming and Identity in *Buffy the Vampire Slayer*."

5 Several excellent Web sites provide information about the Bushido Code: "Bushido: The Way of the Warrior"; Matrasko, "Bushido, Warrior Code of Conduct"; and Friday, "The Historical Foundations of Bushido" provide more detail and discuss conflicting viewpoints about the origins and credo of the samurai.

6 The "Helix," or godsend character, pops up frequently throughout the first season. See the Enhancement titled "Appearances of the Helix."

7 "Hope" creates yet another *Star Wars* association; the original *Star Wars* movie, always considered the fourth installment in the linear story, has been renamed *Star Wars IV: A New Hope*.

THE *HEROES* KALEIDOSCOPE

1 At least two chapters of the graphic novel show the word *soma* in graffiti — "Aftermath" (#4) and "Control" (#7). Soma is the drug that keeps the masses content and subservient in *Brave New World*.
2 By coincidence, at the beginning of the third season of *Buffy the Vampire Slayer*, Buffy assumes a new identity, works as a waitress, and calls herself Anne.

FINALE FACE-OFF

1 The closing words of *Television without Pity*'s recaplet of *Lost*'s "Through the Looking Glass."
2 See David Lavery's "The Crying Game."

EPISODE GUIDE

1 Roger Ebert's term (inspired by the movie *Love Story* [1970]) for the cinema-specific ailment that afflicts dying, beautiful women in the movies, leaving them perpetually attractive while wasting away.

BIBLIOGRAPHY

"ABC Details 'Lost's' Final Years." *CNN.com*, May 7, 2007. www.cnn.com/2007/SHOWBIZ/TV/05/07/television.lost.reut/index. html.

"American Masters: George Lucas." PBS. www.pbs.org/wnet/american-masters/database/lucas_g.html.

Andreeva, Nellie. "New Characters on Tap for 'Heroes,' 'Prison Break.'" Reuters. May 24, 2007. www.reuters.com/article/ televisionNews/idUSN2428733120070524.

Beeman, Greg. Blog. "Episode 20: Five Years Gone." April 30, 2007. gregbeeman.blogspot.com/2007/episode-20-five-years-gone.html.

Bernstein, Abbie. "We Could Be Heroes," *Dreamwatch*, 25, December 2006, 41.

—. "With Great Power . . ." *Dreamwatch*, 23, September 2006, 32–5.

Brioux, Bill. "Everyday 'Heroes' Saving the World." *Toronto Sun*, September 2, 2006. jam.canoe.ca/Television/TV_Shows/ H/Heroes/2006/09/25/1893708.html.

"Bushido: The Way of the Warrior." mcel.pacificu.edu/as/ students/bushido/bindex.html.

"The Buzz: *Heroes* Ratings Are In." September 26, 2006. www.heroes-tv.com/modules/news/article.php?storyid=91.

Byrne, C. "*Heroes'* Finest: An Interview with Jeph Loeb." www.9thwonders.com/interviews/jeph.php.

—. "Joining the Bee-Team: An Interview with Greg Beeman." www.9thwonders.com/interviews/beeman.php.

Campbell, Joseph. *The Hero with a Thousand Faces*, Princeton, NJ: Princeton University Press, 1949.

Carnes, Patrick. *A Gentle Path Through the Twelve Steps: A Classic Guide for All People in the Process of Recovery*. Center City, MN: Hazelden, 1994.

"CGC-Certified Action Comics #1 4.0 Sells." *Scoop*, May 19, 2006. scoop.diamondgalleries.com.

"Cliff-Hanger Countdown." *Heroes. TV Guide*, May 21, 2007, 30–1.

Coleite, Eli Aron, story. Gunnell, Micah, art. Heroes Novel 2 — Hiro. Aspen Comics Production. NBC. *Heroes*. www.nbc.com/Heroes/novels/downloads/Heroes_novel_002.pdf.

Comic-Con International. "2006 Comic-Con International Copy Points." 2006 *Comic-Con.Com* June 1, 2007. www.comic-con.org/cci/cci_pr_0611.shtml.

Comic-Con International. "There Shall Be Heroes." *Comic-Con International San Diego 2007 Update #2*. San Diego, CA: Comic-Con, June 2007, 3–5.

Davis, Jason. "Using His Powers For Good: Tim Kring Makes *Heroes* of Us All." *Creative Screenwriting*, May/June 2007, 59–62.

Douglas, Edward. "Exclusive: *Heroes* Creator Tim Kring!" August 2006. www.superherohype.com/news/heroesnews.php?id=4685.

—. "Exclusive: *Heroes'* Jeph Loeb." www.superherohype.com/news/heroesnews.php?id=4638.

Elfman, Douglas. "Fiery End to a Way-Cool Season." *Chicago Sun-Times*. May 22, 2007. www.suntimes.com/ entertainment/elfman/395821,CST-FTR-heroes22.article.

Eliot, T.S. *The Sacred Wood*. London: Methune, 1920.

Elliot, Sean. "Exclusive Interview: *Heroes* Creator Tim Kring on Swords, Death, Dinosaurs, and Yes, Even Toys." *iF*. January 19, 2007. www.ifmagazine.com/feature.asp? article=1857.

Extended Interview with Tim Kring. Comic-Con 2007. www.comic-con.org/cci/cci07prog_kring.shtml.

Fraser, James G. *The Golden Bough: The Roots of Religion and Folklore.* 1890. New York: Random House, 1981.

Friday, Karl. "The Historical Foundations of Bushido." www.koryu.com/library/kfriday2.

Frye, Northrop. *The Anatomy of Criticism: Four Essays.* 1957. Princeton, NJ: Princeton University Press, 1971.

Furey, Emmett. "*Heroes* Panel at Paley Festival — Full Report Comic Book Resources. www.comicbookresources.com/news/newsitem.cgi?id=9952.

Gilbert, Matthew. "Superpowers Can't Save 'Heroes' Finale." *Boston Globe,* May 22, 2007. www.boston.com/.news/globe/living/articles/2007/05/22/superpowers_can146t_save_145heroes146_finale/.

GustavoLeao. "Zachary Quinto Wants to Play Young Spock in *Star Trek XI.*" TrekWeb, May 29, 2007. trekweb.com./articles/2007/05/29/Zachary-Quinto-Wants-to-Play-Young.shtml.

Hawthorne, Nathaniel. *The Complete Short Stories of Nathaniel Hawthorne.* Garden City, NY: Doubleday, 1959.

"Hero Worship." Questions and answers. *SciFi,* April 2007, 42–8.

"Heroes 360." www.nbc.com/Heroes/360/.

Heroes Poll. Heroes the Series Web site. April 4, 2007. www.heroestheseries.com.

"*Heroes* Spinoff Among New Series for Fall." *The Toronto Star.* May 15, 2007. www.thestar.com/artsentertainment/ article/213796.

HeroesTV.com. www.heroestv.com/.

Hibberd, James. "Networks Going for Fantastic Dramas." *Television Week,* April 2, 2007, 10–11.

Hinman, Michael. "CBS Gets Personal Nut Delivery, Campaign at 7 Tons: Fans Spend More than $20,000 to Support *Jericho.*" *SyFyPortal.* May 20, 2007. www.syfyportal.com/ news423689.html.

—. "Death Should Always Be Expected on 'Heroes,' Creator Says." *SyFy Portal.* www.syfyportal.com/news423563.html.

Holland, Lila. "2006 Upfronts." May 10, 2007 TV.Com. www.tv.com/story/4475.html retrieved May 30, 2007.

Huddleston, Kathie. "TV in Focus: *Heroes.*" *SciFi,* April 2007, 12.

Huxley, Aldous. *Brave New World*. Reprint. New York: Harper, 1998.

Jensen, Jeff. "The Bomb Squad," *Entertainment Weekly*, May 11, 2007, 32–5.

—. "The Powers That Be." *Entertainment Weekly*, November 10, 2006.

Jones, Gerard. *Men of Tomorrow: Geeks, Gangsters, and the Birth of the Comic Book*. New York: Basic Books, 2004.

"Joseph Campbell's 12 Stages in the Hero's Journey." www.am-psy-chotherapists-new-york-city.com/Joseph-Campbell.html.

Keveney, Bill. "'Heroes' Finale Delivers Big Resolution, Smaller Cliffhangers." *USA Today*, April 22, 2007. www.usatoday.com/life/television/ news/2007-04-22-heroes-main_N.htm?POE=click-refer.

Kring, Tim and Hayden Panettiere. "Thank You and Goodnight." May 21, 2007. blog.nbc.com/heroes/.

Kushner, David. "The Creator," *Wired*, May 2007, 130–3. Available online as "Behind the Scenes with *Heroes* Creator Tim Kring and 'Hiro,' Masi Oka." *Wired*, April 24, 2007. www.wired.com/print/entertainment/hollywood/news/ 2007/04/magkring.

Larry King Live. Interview with the Cast of 'Heroes.' CNN, April 27, 2007.

Lavery, David. "Apocalyptic Apocalypses: The Narrative Eschatology of *Buffy the Vampire Slayer*." *Slayage: The Online International Journal of Buffy Studies*, Number 9 (2003). www.slayageonline.com/essays/slayage9/Lavery.htm.

—. "Climate Change: Television Books, The Series." "Aerial View: Debating Television." Special Issue of *Critical Studies in Television: Scholarly Studies on Small Screen Fictions* 1.1 (Spring 2006), 97–103.

—. "The Crying Game: Why Television Brings Us to Tears." Flow 5.9 (March 9, 2007) jot.communication.utexas.edu/ flow/?jot=view&id=2085.

Lee, Patrick. "*Heroes* Creators Look at Year Two." SciFi Wire. March 20, 2007. www.scifi.com/scifiwire/index.php? category=1&id=40619.

Lindelof, Damon. "Heroic Origins: An Interview with Tim Kring." *9th Wonders*. www.9thwonders.com/interviews/tim.php.

Lindskold, Jane. *Child of a Rainless Year*. New York: Tor, 2005.

Live with Regis & Kelly. Interview with Sendhil Ramamurthy. NBC, May 21, 2007.

Loeb, Jeph. "Citizen Kane." *Fray.* Joss Whedon, Karl Moline, and Andy Owens. Milwaukie, OR: Darkhorse Comics, 2003.

Logan, Michael. "Sci-Fi Preview: *Buffy.*" *TV Guide,* December 4–10, 2006, 31.

—. "Sci-Fi Preview: *Heroes.*" *TV Guide,* December 4–10, 2006, 30.

Matrasko, Cheryl. "Bushido, Warrior Code of Conduct." *Aikido World Journal.* www.aikido-world.com/articles/Bushido-Code%20of%20 the%20Warrior-Origins%20of%20Bushido.htm.

Mitovich, Matt Webb, with Michael Logan. "*Heroes* Creator Solves Finale's Biggest Mystery." *TV Guide News Report.* community.tvguide.com/blog-entry/TVGuide-Editors-Blog/Tv-Guide-News/Heroes-Creator-Solves/800015727.

Moore, Alan and Dave Gibbons. *Watchmen.* DC Comics, 1986–87.

"NBC Ratings Results for the Week of February 26–March 4." The Futon Critic. www.thefutoncritic.com/news.aspx?id= 20070306nbc01.

"The Numbers. May 21–27, 2007." *TV Guide,* June 11, 2007, 15.

Nuts Online Web site. www.nutsonline.com/jericho.

Oatts, Joanne. "U.K. Premiere of *Heroes* Highest to Date." February 20, 2007. *Digital Spy.* www.tv.com/tracking/viewer.html?sls_id=9159& ref_type=101&ref_id=17552&tag= updates;title.

"One of the Heroes Will Die!" *TV Guide,* January 29, 2007, 24–7.

"Overnight Ratings." Broadcast Newsroom. May 22, 2007. panasonic.broadcastnewsroom.com/articles/viewarticle.jsp?id=143134.

Parrish, R. "Interview with Tim Kring." September 2006. www.infuzemag.com/interviews/archives/2006/09/tim_kring.html

Personal interview with James Kyson Lee. FX Lite. Orlando, FL, April 28, 2007.

Personal interview with Noah Gray-Cabey. FX Lite, Orlando, FL, April 28, 2007.

Phegley, K. "'Heroes' Worship: Tim Sale." July 2006. www.wizarduni-verse.com/television/tvother/000987736.cfm.

Plato. *Republic.* Trans. G.M.A. Grube, rev. C.D.C. Reeve. In *Plato: The Complete Works.* Ed., John M. Cooper. Indianapolis: Hackett, 1997.

Poniewozik, James. "Blame It on Bauer." *Time,* March 26, 2007, 74.

"Reverse engineering." The Free On-line Dictionary of Computing.

Denis Howe. May 30, 2007. Dictionary.com. dictionary.reference.com/browse/reverse engineering.

Roush, Matt. "Cult Curiosity." *TV Guide*, October 2–8, 2007, 21.

Shen, M. "Comic Hiro — How TV's Coolest Show Jumped off the Page." November 2006. www.nypost.com/seven/11262006/tv/ comic_ hiro_tv_ maxine_shen.htm?page=0.

Sherri. "NBC Kicks Up Online *Heroes* Promotions." November 6, 2006. TeevBlogger. www.teevblogger.com/2006/11/nbc-kicks-up-online-heroes-promotions.html.

Smith, Z. "Talking *Heroes* and Comics with Tim Sale." November 2006. forum.newsarama.com/showthread.php?t=91047.

Solnit, Rebecca. *Wanderlust: A History of Walking*. New York: Penguin, 2000.

Stepakoff, Jeffrey. *Billion-Dollar Kiss: The Story of a Television Writer in the Hollywood Gold Rush*. New York: Gotham Books, 2007.

"*Supernatural: Origins*." *TV Guide*, April 30–May 6, 2007, 32.

Taylor, Robert. "Reflections: Talking with Tim Sale." December 2006. www.comicbookresources.com/news/newsitem.cgi?id=9054.

Thacker, Joe. "Comic Con or Bust." home.comcast.net/~joe.thacker/ cctrip.htm.

Topel, Fred. "Network Hero." *Starburst*, 350, June 2007, 28–32.

Tulloch, John, and Manuel Alvarado. *Doctor Who: The Unfolding Text*. London: Macmillan Press, 1983.

"The TVaddict.com Interview: Tim Kring HEROES Creator." thetvaddict.com/2006/10/12/exclusivei-interview-tim-kring-hero.

TV Land Awards. April 22, 2007. www.tvland.com/video/ index.jhtml?bcpid=192874560&bclid=792434631&bctid= 792434604.

Ursa. "Comic-Con 2006 News Recap and Pictures!" July 6, 2006. *Heroes the Series*. May 10, 2007. www.heroestheseries.com/2006-comic-con-heroes-recap-and-pictures/.

Weiland, Josh. "1-on-1: Talking with "Heroes" creator Tim Kring." September 2006. www.comicbookresources.com/news/ newsitem.cgi?id=8428.

—. "*Heroes* Post-Game Report with Tim Kring, Part One." Comic Book Resources. http:www.comicbookresources.com/news/ newsitem.cgi?id=10657.

White, Cindy. "*Heroes*' Sylar Will Surprise." SciFi Wire. January 29, 2007. www.scifi.com/scifiwire/index.php?category=1&id=39809.

Wilcox, Rhonda. *Why Buffy Matters: The Art of Buffy the Vampire Slayer*. London: Tauris, 2005.

Wright, Bradford W. *Comic Book Nation: The Transformation of Youth Culture in America*. Baltimore: Johns Hopkins University Press, 2001.

Zigler, Vivi. "Exclusive Web Series On NBC.com Goes Behind The Scenes at "HEROES." May 10, 2007 "Details from NBC on 'Heroes' Summer Content, Inside Heroes, Graphic Novels, Character Profiles." 9th Wonders.com. www.9thwonders.com/boards/index.php?showtopic=55475.

Zimmerman, Paul. "Battle to Be a Network Star: *Heroes*' Greg Grunberg Weathers the Downpour of Success." *Geek*, May 2007, 34–9.

FILMOGRAPHY

24. Fox. Joel Surnow and Robert Cochran. 2001–.

Alias. ABC. J.J. Abrams. 2001–06.

Angel. WB. Joss Whedon and David Greenwalt. 1999–2004.

Batman Begins. Dir. Christopher Nolan. Warner Brothers. 2005.

Buffy the Vampire Slayer. WB and UPN. Joss Whedon. 1997–2003.

Crossing Jordan. NBC. Tim Kring. 2001–2007.

The Dead Zone. USA. Michael Piller and Sean Piller. 2002–.

Desperate Housewives. ABC. Marc Cherry. 2004.

Eternal Sunshine of the Spotless Mind. Dir. Michel Gondry. Focus Features. 2004.

Groundhog Day. Dir. Harold Ramis. Columbia. 1993.

Heroes. NBC. Tim Kring. 2006–.

The Incredibles. Dir. Brad Bird. Buena Vista. 2004.

It's a Wonderful Life. Dir. Frank Capra. RKO. 1946.

The Jacket. Dir. John Maybury. Warner Brothers, 2005.

Jericho. CBS. Rob Thomas. 2006–.

Kill Bill, Volume 2. Dir. Quentin Tarantino. Miramax. 2003.

Lost. ABC. J. J. Abrams. 2004–.

Medium. NBC. Glenn Gordon Caron. 2005–.

Next. Dir. Lee Tamahori. Paramount. 2007.

Premonition. Dir. Mennan Yapo. Sony Pictures. 2007.

Saturday Night Fever. Dir. John Badham. Paramount. 1976.

Smallville. WB/CW. Alfred Gough and Miles Millar. 2001–.

Spider-Man 2. Dir. Sam Raimi. Columbia TriStar. 2004.

Spider-Man 3. Dir. Sam Raimi. Columbia TriStar. 2007.

Star Trek. NBC. Gene Roddenberry. 1966–99.

Star Wars. Dir. George Lucas. Twentieth Century Fox. 1977.

Superman. Dir. Richard Donner. Warner Brothers. 1978.

Superman Returns. Dir. Bryan Singer. Warner Brothers. 2006.

Traveler. ABC. Dave Diglio. 2007–.

Tru Calling. Fox. Jon Harmon Feldman. 2003–05.

Twin Peaks. ABC. David Lynch. 1990–91.

Ugly Betty. ABC. Salma Hayak. 2006–.

Wise Guy. CBS. Stephen J. Cannell and Frank Lupo. 1987–90.

The X-Files. Fox. Chris Carter. 1993–2002.

About the Authors

SEAN HOCKETT recently graduated with honors in film and television at Brunel University in the U.K. He co-authored "Comic Book *Heroes.*"

DAVID LAVERY is chair in film and television at Brunel University in London. The author of numerous essays and reviews, and the author/co-author/editor/co-editor of more than a dozen books on such television series as *Twin Peaks, The X-Files, Buffy the Vampire Slayer, The Sopranos, Seinfeld, Deadwood, Lost,* and *My So-Called Life.* He co-edits *Slayage: The Online International Journal of Buffy Studies* and is one of the founding editors of *Critical Studies in Television.* He has lectured around the world on the subject of television.

MARY ALICE MONEY is a professor emeritus of English at Gordon College in Barnesville, Georgia. She has published articles on

Buffy the Vampire Slayer, Firefly, and Native Americans in westerns, and has presented papers on *The X-Files,* British mysteries, and science fiction. She contributed "The *Heroes* Kaleidoscope" in this volume.

STEVEN PEACOCK is a senior lecturer in film at the University of Hertfordshire in the U.K. He is the co-editor with Sarah Cardwell of "Good Television?" for the *Journal of British Cinema and Television* (Edinburgh University Press), editor of *Reading 24: TV Against the Clock* (I.B. Tauris), and *Colour: Cinema Aesthetics* (Manchester University Press). He wrote "Going Dark in *Heroes.*"

LYNNETTE PORTER had been invested in the idea of heroes long before *Heroes* debuted and immediately became a fan of the series. She occasionally teaches an honors course about heroes in literature, film, and television at Embry-Riddle Aeronautical University, Daytona Beach, Florida, where she is an associate professor. She frequently collaborates with David Lavery and Hillary Robson to create books about other TV series, including *Lost* and *Battlestar Galactica.* She has also published numerous papers, essays, chapters, and a book about J.R. Tolkien's *The Lord of the Rings* and currently is working on additional *LotR*-themed book projects.

HILLARY ROBSON is a recent graduate from Middle Tennessee State University with a masters degree in English. Her major areas of interest include fandom, popular culture, and television studies. She is the author of a chapter in the just-published *Investigating Alias: Secrets and Spies* and co-author (with Lynnette Porter and David Lavery) of *Lost's Buried Treasures: The Unofficial Guide to Everything Lost Fans Need to Know* (forthcoming). Future projects include a contribution to a composition textbook and co-editing a collection on *Grey's Anatomy.*

NIKKI STAFFORD has written a series of guides to popular television shows including *Bite Me: An Unofficial Guide to the World of Buffy the Vampire Slayer, Finding Lost: The Unofficial Guide, Once Bitten: An Unofficial Guide to the World of Angel,* and *Uncovering Alias: An Unofficial Guide* — all published by ECW Press. She blogs at Nik at Nite (nikkistafford.blogspot.com) and lives in Toronto, Ontario. She contributed to the "Finale Face-off."

BEN STRICKLAND divides his time between literature and art. He has spoken on topics ranging from the virtues (and vices) of treating freshman composition classrooms as if they were art studios to fundamental similarities between popular culture and the Western canon. He's been a comic book fan for most of his life and has even tried his hand at writing and drawing a few of his own. His contribution to this book is "Growing Pains: *Heroes* and the Quest for Identity."

INDEX

NOTE: the following does not index the *Heroes* Encyclopedia.